Critical
Issues
in
History

War and Totalitarianism, 1870 to the Present

Critical Issues in History

UNDER THE EDITORIAL DIRECTION OF *RICHARD E. SULLIVAN*

SIX-VOLUME EDITION

1 **The Ancient World to A.D. 400**
   THOMAS W. AFRICA, *University of Southern California*

2 **The Middle Ages, 400-1250**
   RICHARD E. SULLIVAN, *Michigan State University*

3 **The Eve of the Modern World, 1250-1648**
   J. K. SOWARDS, *Wichita State University*

4 **The Early Modern Era, 1648-1770**
   JOHN C. RULE, *Ohio State University*

5 **The Age of Revolution, 1770-1870**
   DAVID L. DOWD, *University of Kentucky*

6 **War and Totalitarianism, 1870 to the Present**
   JOHN L. SNELL, *University of Pennsylvania*

TWO-VOLUME EDITION

VOLUME I   **Ancient Times to 1648**

VOLUME II   **1648 to the Present**

Critical Issues in History

War & Totalitarianism

1870 TO THE PRESENT

EDITED WITH INTRODUCTIONS BY

JOHN L. SNELL

University of Pennsylvania

D. C. HEATH *and Company, Boston*

ILLUSTRATION CREDITS

Cover and page 1: Proposed "harbor" block for replanning
Philadelphia, Lewis Kahn, architect; Ian McCallum, *Architecture
U. S. A.,* New York 1959.

Library of Congress Catalog Card Number: 67-13486
Copyright © 1967 by D. C. Heath and Company
No part of the material covered by this copyright
may be reproduced in any form without written permission
of the publisher.
Printed in the United States of America.

Printed December 1966

Boston
Englewood
Indianapolis
Dallas
San Francisco
Atlanta

PREFACE

This volume, one of a six-volume set, is intended to engage students in *problem-resolving situations* as a technique for enriching their study of European history. The editors who collaborated in preparing these six volumes are convinced that this approach has great value in stimulating interest, encouraging critical thinking, and enhancing historical-mindedness, especially when it is used to supplement the more conventional techniques employed in teaching the general introductory course in European history.

The volume opens with an interpretive essay aimed at placing the five "problems" which follow in the perspective of the period. While all of the problems follow the same structure, the topics they treat are highly diverse: in one, a single man's role in history is debated, while the next examines an ideological issue; in one problem causes are sought, while the next weighs effects.

Each of the five problems is introduced by a short statement defining the issue and directing the student to the crucial questions involved. For the most part selections have been taken from the works of modern historians, with occasional use of the observations of contemporary witnesses. In choosing the selections, the editor has tried to avoid generating conflict for conflict's sake. Rather, he has sought to show how honest divergencies emerge among historians as a result of the complexities of history, varying initial assumptions, different approaches to evidence, and all the other factors that enter into interpretation of the past. The student's efforts to understand how differing interpretations arise and to resolve these differences should increase his ability to manipulate historical data and concepts and deepen his understanding of the historian's craft.

CONTENTS

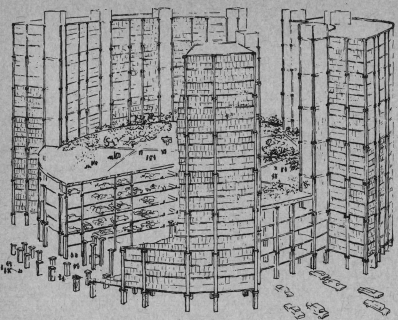

INTRODUCTION

Change is the subject matter of history, but a French saying contends that the more things change the more they remain the same. Does it follow, then, that the student of history is simply studying the same thing over and over again?

There is, indeed, a large element of continuity running through the history of the Western world. In their attempt to strike the right balance between liberty and order, Europeans have developed varied philosophies and constitutions, from the age of Athenian "democracy" to the Magna Carta to the "peoples democracies" of the present, but the theme itself remains a constant one. The desire to make peace permanent is recurrent throughout European history, but willingness to resort to war to preserve rights or avenge real or imagined wrongs has been just as eternal. The creative longing for beauty among Europeans has yielded a rich variety of styles of architecture, sculpture, painting, literature, and music, but the longing itself is endlessly manifested. Similarly, efforts for justice, economic improvement, scientific progress, and religious truth have everlastingly occupied the attention of Europeans from antiquity to the present.

Because these basic aspirations appear throughout European history and because

War and Totalitarianism   659

there are certain common manifestations of these aspirations, we speak of "European Civilization" as if it were a single entity. But the changes from era to era are no less real, and it would be more accurate to speak in the plural of "European Civilizations." The "European Civilization" of 1250 to 1648 is not that of 400 to 1250, and there are substantial differences between the "European Civilization" of 1648–1770 and that of 1770–1870.

The century since 1870 in several aspects represents a continuation of the preceding century. Liberalism and nationalism may not be the movements of the future, as they were in the period 1770–1870, but they remain important. Another of the developments of 1770–1870—industrialization and its consequence, urbanization—goes on apace. And yet the "European Civilization" of 1870 to the present differs markedly from that of 1770–1870. Indeed, there are great differences even within the period from 1870 to the present. In the 1870's it was still somewhat visionary of Jules Verne to contemplate travels by Western Europeans around the world in 80 days. The reality of astronauts from the fringes of European Civilization—the United States and Soviet Russia—circling the globe in little more than 80 minutes marks the present decade. Obviously many changes separate such decades in European Civilization, even if they do fall within the span of a single century.

The developments in the period since 1870 that have been most formative in shaping the present appear to have occurred since 1914. For most Europeans it was "great to be alive" in the period between 1870 and 1914. This was, even for the underprivileged, an Optimistic Era, an era in which Europeans had greater faith in themselves and in their future than Europeans of any previous age. To be sure, an exceptional pessimist like the Russian novelist-philosopher Dostoevski could speak during this period of "our unhappy nineteenth century," but few contemporaries felt this way. Scarcely suspecting that their faith in material progress through secular means might be an illusion, most Europeans viewed the time in which they lived as one of transition toward an era of freedom, peace, and social improvement.

Little happened before 1914 to dispel the confidence of the rank and file. Though the German Empire and the Kingdom of Italy had emerged as newly united nations in 1870–71, their greater grandeur did not prevent the continued rise in power and prosperity of Great Britain, the Third French Republic, and Imperial Russia. The Germans and Magyars of Austria-Hungary had increasing cause to worry about the Slavic minorities of the Habsburg Empire, but they remained dominant in internal affairs, and the Dual Monarchy continued to function in international politics as a Great Power.

We can see in retrospect that the development of Japan and the United States was creating challenges to Europe for the future, but—thanks to the successes of European imperialism after 1870—Europeans in 1914 were more nearly masters of the world than their predecessors had ever been. Indeed, it was in the period 1870–

1914 that "European Civilization" became in significant degree a world civilization. Railroads and steamships had created technical possibilities for this that went far beyond those provided by Roman roads, and the bourgeois "Pax Europa" covered far greater reaches of the earth than had the "Pax Romana" of the Caesars.

Within Europe, the dominance of aristocrats and the bourgeoisie was increasingly challenged by the industrial workers after 1870 as socialism was translated for the first time from an esoteric philosophy of the few into a tangible movement of the many. But the bourgeoisie remained dominant in Western Europe. Both bourgeois and socialist Europeans met with increasing success in their efforts to achieve democratic and constitutional governments and to create "welfare states" in which material security would be guaranteed to all. In 1913 it seemed only a matter of time before aristocratic and semiauthoritarian rule in the empires of Central and Eastern Europe would give way to parliamentary democracy and greater measures of liberty and equality.

The period since 1914 has not fulfilled all the expectations. Since 1914 war and the fear of war have been almost constant companions of Europeans, and the two great conflicts have changed the map of Europe. The Dual Monarchy did not survive the year 1918, Germany lost its unity in 1945, and most of the Great Powers of 1870–1914 have been on the defensive since 1918—victors and vanquished alike. European overseas mastery was challenged even during World War I, and no sensible European since World War II has been able to think of Europe as master of the world. Within Europe the bourgeoisie remains influential in the countries that lie west of the Soviet-oriented states; but even in Western Europe socialism and the industrial workers have won great power, and Communism holds sway in Russia and Central Eastern Europe.

Parliamentary democracy and political freedom—on the ascendancy before 1914—were on the defensive after about 1920. The most enduring totalitarian challenge has been that of Communism, but it is impossible to understand the power Communists have achieved without considering the totalitarian challenge of Nazism in the period 1933–1945. War and totalitarianism have influenced the art and thought of Europe, which even today reflect the uncertainties and fears of an age of conflicting ideologies and violence. The very "spirit" of Europe has changed. Since 1945 many Europeans—in sharp contrast to those of 1870–1914—have even wondered whether European Civilization has a future.

The readings on European Civilization since 1870 that are presented here are grouped around the five problems that seem most essential to treat. Though all five problems fall in the twentieth century, they bring together a number of tendencies that were present in the period 1870–1914. The first four sets of readings treat the two world wars and the two major totalitarian challenges to parliamentary democracy. These subjects have been chosen because they appear to have been most formative in altering European Civilization into its present condition. If one understands World War I, Communism, Nazism, and World War II, one will understand pretty well how the Europe of the 1870's was transformed into the Europe of the present. Indeed, these four developments do much to explain the *world* of the present. The fifth set of readings reflects the contemporary consequences of the two world wars and the continuing challenges of totalitarianism.

Much of the study of history is preoccupied with the questions: *Who? What? When? Where?* A student's first task in reading this section is to obtain factual answers to these four questions. This is a relatively easy task. The fifth question is more difficult to answer: *How?*

The sixth question is at once the most difficult to answer and the most interesting to ask: *Why?* It is also the most important to try to answer, for the most important thing to know about history is *why* things have happened, *why* changes have occurred. And even if definitive answers cannot be found, *why?* is the most important question for historians to ask and for students of history to be asked. This questions puts minds to work in a way that the other questions do not. More than the others, this question forces one to test theories against evidence. It shows the student that historians who know a common body of facts draw different meanings from them. It brings the student up against conflicting interpretations of events and divergent theories of history. It establishes the commonality of purpose between the study of history and the other liberal arts and sciences, that of cultivating empiricism and the habit and power of exercising human reason.

In each of the five groups of readings that follow, the central question confronting a student is that of causation. *Why* did the First World War begin in 1914? *Why* did Communist totalitarianism gain control in Russia in the last year of that war? *Why* did Nazi totalitarianism come to power in Germany in 1933? *Why* was European Civilization, still not fully healed from the wounds of World War I, thrown into an even greater and more disastrous conflict in 1939? *Why* does (or does not) European Civilization have a promising future as well as a rich past?

You should not expect to formulate definitive answers, for these are enduring questions. You will remember them when you have forgotten many of the specific facts about men and movements in Europe's history from 1870 to the present. Probably you will go on looking for answers to these questions in the reading that you do throughout a lifetime. It is certain that historians will.

1

WORLD WAR I: WHICH GOVERNMENTS WERE MOST RESPONSIBLE?

A perceptive young German soldier wrote—using the future tense—early in 1915, "one will have to say: This war stamped its whole character on the period which it began. A surging age is being born, breaking forth here in wars, there in revolutions, here in social transformations, there again in songs and books . . ." So far he has been correct. The failure of diplomacy in 1914 marked the end of an era, not merely the end of peace for four years. Historians are still searching for the causes of the failure.

The readings that follow treat the immediate crisis of 1914. That crisis was the climax of a growth of tension over a period of several decades. Germany's unification in 1870–71 and her subsequent growth in population and industrial production made her the greatest power in Europe.

Bismarck sought even greater security through the Dual Alliance, signed with Austria-Hungary in 1879 and renewed periodically. Alliances with Italy and lesser states followed. Attempts were made to maintain an alliance with Russia as well as the Dual Monarchy, but because of the conflicting interests of the two states in the Balkans, Germany dropped the Russian alliance in 1890. This facilitated the development of a counter-alliance system. France and Russia in 1892 entered into a binding military alliance that remained in effect in 1914.

Meanwhile France and Britain in the 1870's and 1880's had sought to enhance their positions in the European balance of power (and to increase their profits) by expanding their overseas possessions. Germany, Italy, and Russia also joined in the "New Imperialism" of 1870–1914. Thus, instead of bringing increased security to the European powers the New Imperialism increased tensions and friction among them. All the Great Powers created large standing armies and built large peacetime navies. German colonial expansion and the building of a German Navy particularly antagonized the British.

Concerned about their isolation, British leaders in 1904 entered into an "understanding" ("Entente Cordiale") with France. The Entente Cordiale was strengthened in the Moroccan crises of 1905 and 1911. Meanwhile, the extension of German political and economic influence in Turkey challenged both Russia and Britain. These powers had been sharp rivals in the Middle East for a century, but they drew together in 1907. The powers of the Triple Alliance now faced a Triple Entente of France, Britain, and Russia.

German leaders complained of "encirclement." Preservation of the alliance with Austria-Hungary seemed more important to them than ever, and many German leaders wanted to strengthen the alliance by encouraging the expansion of Austrian influence in the Balkans. Russia, as determined as ever to prevent this, gave moral support to the rise of nationalism among the Slavs within the Dual Monarchy and more tangible diplomatic support to Serbia, which blocked Austrian expansion and which hoped to unite the South Slavs (Yogoslavs) as Prussia and Piedmont earlier had united Germany and Italy.

Serbia hoped eventually to add the South Slavs of Bosnia, Herzegovina, and other provinces to its own territory. Since 1878 Austria-Hungary had militarily occupied Bosnia and Herzegovina and in 1908 it formally annexed these former Turkish territories. The assassination of the heir to the Habsburg throne by South Slav patriots on June 28 in Sarajevo, the provincial capital of Bosnia, touched off the crisis of 1914.

Despite the growth of friction from the 1870's to 1914, war between the Great Powers had been avoided, but in 1914 diplomacy failed. Could the war have been prevented? What steps could have avoided it? What steps made war between Austria and Serbia inevitable? What circumstances and actions broadened that conflict into a general war? Larger questions bring your concern about the immediate crisis of 1914 into touch with the major theories of history. To what extent did the leaders of the European nations in 1914 decide their own fates? To the extent that they did, were their false moves made deliberately or by mistake? Were they simply stumbling along, their direction guided by vast, impersonal forces over which they had little or no control? If so, what was the nature of these forces? Metaphysical? Geographical? Economic? Or those of national character, whether determined by race or by the long unwinding of history?

The most important facts upon which historians must base their interpretations of responsibility for the outbreak of the First World War are to be found in the following four readings. These selections offer divergent interpretations of responsibility. Which one do you find the more convincing? Why?

COMMISSION ON WAR GUILT

RESPONSIBILITY AS DEFINED BY THE VICTORS

Most Germans in 1914 were convinced that they were fighting a defensive war. The peoples of the Entente nations were just as certain that war had been forced upon them by the "Central Powers." The Entente version of historical causation was written into the Treaty of Versailles in 1919 in the so-called "war guilt clause,"

Article 231, which held Germany and her allies exclusively responsible for the outbreak of war in 1914.

Article 231 was designed in part to justify the collection of large sums of "reparations" from the defeated Central Powers. Behind it lay a quick exercise in historical research by the victorious makers of the peace. The Peace Conference in January 1919 created a "Commission on the Responsibility of the Authors of the War and on Enforcement of Penalties." This Commission consisted of representatives of France, Great Britain, Italy, Japan, the United States, Belgium, Greece, Poland, Rumania, and Serbia. The Commission's source material was drawn largely from highly selective collections of diplomatic documents that the belligerents had published during the war. Each had chosen documents to justify its own position in the conflict. These were published in what came to be called the "color books" because of the different colors of the bindings. Thus, for example, the French documents were known as the "Yellow Book," Serbian documents as the "Blue-Book," and Russian documents as the "Orange Book."

The reading that follows is the first chapter of the report presented to the Peace Conference in March 1919 by the Commission mentioned above. Though some reservations were expressed by representatives of the United States and Japan, the report was unanimously adopted by the Peace Conference on May 6, 1919.

The report as history raises several questions. How complete was the information available in 1919? Could official representatives of the victors possibly arrive at a sound historical conclusion? What additional evidence later became available? (Look for the additional facts in the three readings that follow this one.) Were the facts that were emphasized in 1919 those that should be emphasized in a balanced historical account? Later, when you have studied all the readings on the subject, reread this selection and ask yourself whether the judgment of 1919 must be modified and, if so, in what ways.

On the question of the responsibility of the authors of the war, the Commission, after having examined a number of official documents relating to the origin of the World War, and to the violations of neutrality and of frontiers which accompanied its inception, has determined that the responsibility for it lies wholly upon the Powers which declared war in pursuance of a policy of aggression, the concealment of which gives to the origin of this war the character of a dark conspiracy against the peace of Europe.

The responsibility rests first on Germany and Austria, secondly on Turkey and Bulgaria. The responsibility is made all the graver by reason of the viola-tion by Germany and Austria of the neutrality of Belgium and Luxemburg, which they themselves had guaranteed. It is increased, with regard to both France and Serbia, by the violation of their frontiers before the declaration of war.

Many months before the crisis of 1914 the German Emperor had ceased to pose as the champion of peace. Naturally believing in the overwhelming superiority of his Army, he openly showed his enmity towards France. General von Moltke[1] said to the King of the Belgians: "This time the matter must

[1] Chief of the German General Staff, 1906–1914. [Editor's note.]

From the *German White Book Concerning the Responsibility of the Authors of the War* (New York, 1924), pp. 15–21. Used with the permission of the Carnegie Endowment for International Peace.

be settled." In vain the King protested. The Emperor and his Chief of Staff remained no less fixed in their attitude.

On the 28th of June, 1914, occurred the assassination at Serajevo of the heir-apparent of Austria. "It is the act of a little group of madmen," said Francis Joseph.[2] The act, committed as it was by a subject of Austria-Hungary on Austro-Hungarian territory, could in no wise compromise Serbia, which very correctly expressed its condolences and stopped public rejoicings in Belgrade. If the Government of Vienna thought that there was any Serbian complicity, Serbia was ready to seek out the guilty parties. But this attitude failed to satisfy Austria and still less Germany, who, after their first atonishment had passed, saw in this royal and national misfortune a pretext to initiate war.

At Potsdam a "decisive consultation" took place on the 5th of July, 1914. Vienna and Berlin decided upon this plan: "Vienna will send to Belgrade a very emphatic ultimatum with a very short limit of time." . . .

Austria (on July 23) suddenly sent Serbia an ultimatum that she had carefully prepared in such a way as to make it impossible to accept. Nobody could be deceived; "the whole world understands that this ultimatum means war." According to Mr. Sazonoff,[3] "Austria-Hungary wanted to devour Serbia."

Mr. Sazonoff asked Vienna for an extension of the short time-limit of forty-eight hours given by Austria to Serbia for the most serious decision in its history. Vienna refused the demand. On the 24th and 25th of July, England and France multiplied their efforts to persuade Serbia to satisfy the Austro-Hungarian demands. Russia threw in her weight on the side of conciliation.

Contrary to the expectation of Austria-Hungary and Germany, Serbia yielded. She agreed to all the requirements of the ultimatum, subject to the single reservation that, in the judicial inquiry which she would commence for the purpose of seeking out the guilty parties, the participation of Austrian officials would be kept within the limits assigned by international law. "If the Austro-Hungarian Government is not satisfied with this," Serbia declared she was ready "to submit to the decision of the Hague Tribunal."

"A quarter of an hour before the expiration of the time limit," at 5:45 on the 25th, Mr. Pashitch, the Serbian Minister for Foreign Affairs, delivered this reply to Baron Giesl, the Austro-Hungarian Minister.

On Mr. Pashitch's return to his own office he found awaiting him a letter from Baron Giesl saying that he was not satisfied with the reply. . . . At mid-day on the 28th Austria declared war on Serbia. On the 29th the Austrian army commenced the bombardment of Belgrade, and made its dispositions to cross the frontier.

The reiterated suggestions of the Entente Powers with a view to finding a peaceful solution of the dispute only produced evasive replies on the part of Berlin or promises of intervention with the Government of Vienna without any effectual steps being taken.

On the 24th of July Russia and England asked that the Powers should be granted a reasonable delay in which to work in concert for the maintenance of peace. Germany did not join in this request.

On the 25th of July Sir Edward Grey[4] proposed mediation by four Powers (England, France, Italy and Germany). France and Italy immediately gave their concurrence. Germany refused, alleging that it was not a question of mediation but of arbitration, as the conference of the four Powers was called to make proposals, not to decide.

On the 26th of July Russia proposed to negotiate directly with Austria. Austria refused.

On the 27th of July England proposed a European conference. Germany refused.

On the 29th of July Sir Edward Grey asked the Wilhelmstrasse[5] to be good enough to "suggest any method by which the influence of the four Powers could be used together to prevent a war between Austra and Russia." She was asked herself to say what she desired. Her reply was evasive.

---

[2] Emperor of Austria and King of Hungary. [Editor's note.]

[3] Russian Minister for Foreign Affairs. [Editor's note.]

[4] British Secretary of State for Foreign Affairs. [Editor's note.]

[5] Location in Berlin of the German Foreign Ministry. [Editor's note.]

On the same day, the 29th of July, the Czar dispatched to the Emperor William II a telegram suggesting that the Austro-Serbian problem should be submitted to the Hague Tribunal. This suggestion received no reply. This important telegram does not appear in the German White Book. It was made public by the Petrograd *Official Gazette* (January, 1915). . . .

As early as the 21st of July German mobilization had commenced by the recall of a certain number of classes of the reserve, then of German officers in Switzerland, and finally of the Metz garrison on the 25th of July. On the 26th of July the German Fleet was called back from Norway.

The Entente did not relax its conciliatory efforts, but the German Government systematically brought all its attempts to nought. When Austria consented for the first time on the 31st of July to discuss the contents of the Serbian note with the Russian Government and the Austro-Hungarian Ambassador received orders to "converse" with the Russian Minister of Foreign Affairs, Germany made any negotiation impossible by sending her ultimatum to Russia. . . .

On the 1st of August the German Emperor addressed a telegram to the King of England containing the following sentence: "The troops on my frontier are, at this moment, being kept back by telegraphic and telephonic orders from crossing the French frontier." Now, war was not declared till two days after that date, and as the German mobilization orders were issued on that same day, the 1st of August, it follows that, as a matter of fact, the German Army had been mobilized and concentrated in pursuance of previous orders.

The attitude of the Entente nevertheless remained still to the very end so conciliatory that, at the very time at which the German fleet was bombarding Libau, Nicholas II gave his word of honor to William II that Russia would not undertake any aggressive action during the *pourparlers,* and that when the German troops commenced their march across the French frontier Mr. Viviani telegraphed to all the French Ambassadors "we must not stop working for accommodation."

On the 3d of August Mr. von Schoen[6] went to the Quai d'Orsay with the declaration of war against France. Lacking a real cause of complaint, Germany alleged, in her declaration of war, that bombs had been dropped by French aeroplanes in various districts in Germany. This statement was entirely false. Moreover, it was either later admitted to be so or no particulars were ever furnished by the German Government.

Moreover, in order to be manifestly above reproach, France was careful to withdraw her troops ten kilometers from the German frontier. Notwithstanding this precaution, numerous officially established violations of French territory preceded the declaration of war.

The provocation was so flagrant that Italy, herself a member of the Triple Alliance, did not hesitate to declare that in view of the aggressive character of the war the *casus foederis* ceased to apply.

CONCLUSIONS

1. *The war was premeditated by the Central Powers together with their Allies, Turkey and Bulgaria, and was the result of acts deliberately committed in order to make it unavoidable.*

2. *Germany, in agreement with Austria-Hungary, deliberately worked to defeat all the many conciliatory proposals made by the Entente Powers and their repeated efforts to avoid war.*

[6] German Ambassador to France. [Editor's note.]

HARRY ELMER BARNES

AN EXTREME REVISIONIST VIEW

Each year during the decade after 1919 saw the publication of new volumes of documents from the prewar records of the foreign ministries of most of the European powers that were involved in the crisis of 1914. The volumes of documents that appeared after 1919 were far more complete and more scrupulously edited than were the wartime "color books."

Over a period of several years some 40 volumes of documents were published on German foreign policy for the whole period 1871–1914. The new Communist rulers of Russia felt no desire to make the tsarist regime appear in a favorable light, and indeed they wanted to make the "capitalist" policies of Russia's prewar allies, France and Britain, appear imperialistic. Immediately after seizing power in November 1917 they began publishing copiously from the foreign ministry archives of Imperial Russia. Prewar British, Austrian, Serbian, and Belgian documents also were released in the 1920's and, more slowly, France in 1929 began to publish documents on its prewar diplomacy. Only Italy among the Great Powers held back publication of its relevant documents on the origins of World War I until after World War II.

German scholars—like other Germans—were eager to refute the "war guilt" thesis that had been used to justify the punitive terms of the Versailles Treaty. It was to be expected that they would avidly study the new documents and publicize those that softened the responsibility of Germany for the conflict. In the United States, too, interest ran high in the new documents. Scholars who had made up their minds during the conflict that the Central Powers were at fault found new evidence to support their positions. Other scholars, variously motivated, found evidence to revise the almost unanimous wartime opinion in this country that Germany and Austria were exclusively responsible. A "revisionist" school of historians made its weight felt in the early 1920's. In an isolationist America, "revisionism" became quite popular.

The boldest American case for revisionism—though not the best—was made by Harry Elmer Barnes while he served as professor of sociology and history at Smith College, 1923–1930. Barnes was quick to draw conclusions from the new documents, quick to take a revisionist position in print, and not content to publish only in scholarly journals. By 1924 he was waging a lively polemical battle in the press against historians who upheld the "orthodox" interpretation of war guilt. Two years later Barnes published a book-length account of the "genesis" of the war, though the documents were still appearing.

The ways in which Barnes used historical evidence were justifiably subjected to severe criticism by many scholars, but the Barnes book became the most popular treatise among the extreme revisionists. It had practical political results, providing ammunition for Germans and others who wanted to put an end to Germany's payment of reparations and otherwise revise the Treaty of Versailles.

After 1945 Barnes would devote himself—with much less success—to a campaign to relieve Germany of responsibility for the outbreak of the Second World War. The reading that follows is taken from his volume of 1926. Note that Barnes reached conclusions diametrically opposite from those of the Commission on War Guilt. What facts does he ignore or play down? Is doing so sound historianship? How reliable are the conclusions that Barnes reached?

We may here briefly summarize the general situation in what may be regarded as a brief statement of the revisionist point of view as it appears to the present writer. The general European system after 1870, based as it was upon nationalism, militarism, secret alliances, and imperialistic aims, naturally inclined Europe toward war. The system does not, however, explain why war came in 1914, as the same general European situation had been prevailing for many years prior to that time, though certain problems had become more acute in the years immediately preceding the World War, particularly in the Near East and Morocco.

The Franco-Russian Alliance concluded by 1894 was transformed into an offensive organization following 1912 through the cooperation of Izvolski[1] and Poincaré.[2] Both recognized that the chief objects of Russian and French foreign policy, the seizure of the Straits and the return of Alsace-Lorraine, could be realized only through a general European war. From 1912–14 their joint plans involved a manipulation of the Balkan situation in such a fashion as to be able to take advantage of any crisis likely to provoke a European war, an arrangement to get England so involved that she would be bound to come in on the side of France and Russia, and a great increase in military preparations in France and Russia.

It was decided that Serbia would be the most favorable area in which to create the desired incident in the Balkans. In the early spring of 1914 prominent officers in the Serbian General Staff laid a plot for the assassination of the Archduke, Franz Ferdinand. The Serbian civil government was aware of the plot for at least a month before its execution, but made no adequate effort to stop the plot or to warn Austria. Prominent Russians were also aware of the plot, but the degree of the complicity of Russia is as yet uncertain.

When the assassination came, the French and Russians recognized that the impending clash between Austria and Serbia would constitute a highly appropriate episode over which to bring about the desired conflict. The year 1914 was a particularly desirable year for the Entente because there was imminent danger that England might develop more happy relations with Germany, and that the French Radicals might be able to secure the repeal of the French Army Bill. Poincare went to St. Petersburg, and, before knowing the terms of the Austrian ultimatum, renewed his pledge of two years earlier to support Russia in a war over the Balkans, and indicated that the probable Austro-Serbian conflict would meet the conditions demanded by the French in supporting Russia in intervention in the Balkans.

The Franco-Russian procedure in 1914 was to indicate a show of conciliation and concessions on the part of Serbia, and apparent Franco-Russian willingness to settle the dispute through diplomacy, while secret Franco-Russian military preparations were to be carried on which would ultimately make a diplomatic settlement quite impossible. Hence, Russia urged Serbia not to declare war on Austria, and, to insure a sufficiently conciliatory Serbian reply to

[1] Russian Ambassador to France, 1910–1917. [Editor's note.]

[2] President of France in 1914. [Editor's note.]

An Extreme Revisionist View

Austria the Serbian response to the Austrian ultimatum was drafted in outline in the French Foreign Office. Russia did not desire to have Serbia precipitate matters prematurely by a declaration of war on Austria, because this would have affected European opinion, particularly English opinion, unfavorably and would also have brought about military activities altogether too rapidly for Russia, whose mobilization over a vast area would necessarily be slow as compared with that of Austria and Germany.

On the 24th of July, the moment Russia and France learned of the terms of the Austrian ultimatum to Serbia, they began that dual program of a diplomatic barrage combined with secret military preparations which had made a European war inevitable by the afternoon of July 30th. Russia sent a diplomatic message to Serbia counselling moderation, but at the same time decided upon the mobilization of the four great military districts of Central and Southern Russia as well as of the Russian fleets. Russian money in Germany and Austria was also called in.

On the same day Viviani telegraphed to the French Foreign Office that the Austro-Serbian situation was likely to develop serious European complications, and the French troops in Morocco were ordered home. Both countries began systematic military preparations for war on the 26th of July. By the 29th the time had come when Russian military preparations had gone far enough to warrant a general mobilization, and the Tsar was persuaded to consent to this order. A telegram from the Kaiser, however, induced him to revoke the order, but the next day Sazonoff and the army officials once more extracted from the Tsar his reluctant consent to the order for general mobilization. The French and the Russians had understood for a generation that once Russian general mobilization was ordered there would be no way of preventing a general European war. General Dobrorolski[3] has told us with great candor that the Russian authorities in 1914 fully realized that a European war was *on* as soon as the mobilization order had been sent out of the general telegraph office in St. Petersburg late in the afternoon of July 30th.

The French authorities had been thoroughly informed as to the nature and progress of the Russian military preparations, but they made no effort to restrain them, though the French well knew that

[3] Chief of the Mobilization Section of the Russian General Staff in 1914. [Editor's note.]

these military activities were bound to render a European war inevitable. They actually urged the Russians to speed up their military preparations, but to be more secretive about them, so as not to alienate England or provoke Germany to countermobilization. On the night of July 31st the French government went still further and finally decided for war, handing this information to Izvolski about midnight of the 31st. France was, thus, the first country to declare itself for war in the European crisis of 1914.

The Austrian statesmen in 1914 decided that the time had come when it would be necessary to control the Serbian menace, and they consciously planned an ultimatum to Serbia of such severity that it would be practically impossible for Serbia to concede all of these demands. The plan, then, was to make a show of diplomacy but to move toward certain war. This program was much like that of France and Russia, save for the fact that *Austria desired to provoke nothing but a local punitive war while the plans of France and Russia envisaged a general European conflict.* This is the most important point to be borne in mind when estimating the relative war guilt of Austria as against that of France and Russia.

Germany, formerly friendly to Serbia, was alarmed by the assassination of the Archduke and the resulting menace to her chief ally. Germany therefore agreed to stand behind Austria in the plan of the latter to execute her program of punishing Serbia. The answer of the Serbians to the Austrian ultimatum, however, impressed the Kaiser as satisfactory, and from that time on he was opposed to further military activity on the part of Austria against Serbia.

In cooperation with Sir Edward Grey, Germany began on the 27th of July to urge upon Austria direct negotiations with Russia and the mediation of her dispute with Serbia. Austria at first refused to listen to this advice and declared war upon Serbia on the 28th. Germany then became alarmed at the rumored Russian military preparations and vigorously pressed Austria for a diplomatic settlement of the dispute. Austria did not give way and consent to this until the 31st of July, which was too late to avert a general European war because the Russian mobilization was then in full swing. Germany endeavored without success to secure the suspension of military activities by Russia, and then, after unexpected hesitation and deliberation, declared war upon Russia.

The Russian general mobilization, undertaken with full connivance of the French, was ordered at a time when diplomatic negotiations were moving rapidly toward a satisfactory settlement of the major problems in the crisis. Hence, the Russian general mobilization not only initiated military hostilities, but was also the sole reason for the failure of diplomatic efforts.

England was for peace provided France was not drawn into the conflict, but was determined to come into the War in case France was involved. As France decided from the beginning to stand with Russia for war, and as England refused to attempt to restrain either France or Russia, England was inevitably drawn away from her encouragement of the German efforts towards a diplomatic settlement of the crisis and into the support of the military aggression of France and Russia. She made her decision to enter the War after Germany had proposed to keep out of Belgium and to refrain from attacking France if England would remain neutral. In fact, Germany even suggested that she might guarantee the integrity of France and the French colonies in the event of war if England would promise neutrality. The Belgian issue in England was a pure subterfuge, exploited by Sir Edward Grey to inflame British opinion against Germany and to secure British support of his war policy.

The United States entered the War in part because the British blockade of the ports of the Central Powers led us to have our chief financial stake in the Entente, and partly because of the pro-British sympathies of Ambassador Page and President Wilson, which made it impossible for them to attempt to hold England strictly to international law on the seas. The English violations of international law in regard to neutral rights provoked the German submarine warfare in retaliation. This submarine warfare furnished the ostensible excuse for the American entry into the conflict. Yet, nearly a year before the resumption of submarine warfare, Mr. Wilson had secretly conveyed to England his intention to enter the war on the side of the Entente if Germany would not accept terms of peace which only a conquered state could have been expected to concede.

In estimating the order of guilt of the various countries we may safely say that the only direct and immediate responsibility for the World War falls upon Serbia, France and Russia, with the guilt about equally distributed. Next in order—far below France and Russia—would come Austria, though she never desired a general European war. Finally, we should place Germany and England as tied for last place, both being opposed to war in the 1914 crisis. Probably the German public was somewhat more favorable to military activities than the English people, but, as we have amply explained above, the Kaiser made much more strenuous efforts to preserve the peace of Europe in 1914 than did Sir Edward Grey.

SIDNEY BRADSHAW FAY

A MORE SCHOLARLY CASE FOR REVISION

While Barnes was on center stage during the mid-1920's, a more systematic and restrained scholar, Sidney B. Fay, rigorously and patiently subjected the documents to critical study. Like Barnes a professor at Smith College when he began his studies, Fay was called in 1929 to Harvard University, where he enjoyed a distinguished career (1929–46). When his two-volume study of the *Origins of the World War* appeared in 1928, it was obvious to fellow-historians that Fay had made a much better case for revisionism than Barnes. His evidence and judgments were sound, and the conclusions he reached differed from those of Barnes as well as from those of the Commission on War Guilt. For decades Fay's work was regarded by many historians in this country and in Europe as the most reliable account of the origins of the war. His fame established by these two volumes, Fay served as president of the American Historical Association in 1946. The following selection is taken from Fay's study of 1928.

What new facts do you gain from Fay's account? What differences in emphasis does he give to facts that appear in the two preceding treatments? When you have finished reading the Fay selection you will do well to draw up a chart showing the governments assigned responsibility by these three readings. Which reading places heaviest responsibility upon Austria? Which upon Germany? Which upon Russia, France, or Serbia? Which governments are assigned secondary or tertiary responsibility by each of the three interpretations? How convincing is the evidence that each account presents to support its interpretation?

None of the Powers wanted a European War. Their governing rulers and ministers, with very few exceptions, all foresaw that it must be a frightful struggle, in which the political results were not absolutely certain, but in which the loss of life, suffering, and economic consequences were bound to be terrible. This is true, in a greater or less degree, of Pashitch, Berchtold,[1] Bethmann,[2] Sazonoff, Poincaré, San Giuliano[3] and Sir Edward Grey. Yet none of them, not even Sir Edward Grey, could have foreseen that the political results were to be so stupendous, and the other consequences so terrible, as was actually the case.

For many of the Powers, to be sure, a European War might seem to hold out the possibility of achieving various desired advantages: for Serbia, the achievement of national unity for all Serbs; for Austria, the revival of her waning prestige as a Great Power, and the checking of nationalistic tendencies which threatened her very existence; for Russia, the accomplishment of her historic mission of controlling Constantinople and the Straits; for Germany, new economic advantages and the restoration of the European balance which had changed with the weakening of the Triple Alliance and the tightening of the Triple Entente; for France, the recovery of Alsace-Lorraine and the ending of the German menace; and for England, the destruction of the German naval danger and of Prussian militarism. All these advantages, and many others, were feverishly striven

[1] Austro-Hungarian Foreign Minister in 1914. [Editor's note.]

[2] German Chancellor, 1909–1917. [Editor's note.]

[3] Italian Minister for Foreign Affairs, 1910–1914. [Editor's note.]

and intrigued for, on all sides, the moment the War actually broke out, but this is no good proof that any of the statesmen mentioned deliberately aimed to bring about a war to secure these advantages. One cannot judge the motives which actuated men before the War, by what they did in an absolutely new situation which arose as soon as they were overtaken by a conflagration they had sought to avert. And in fact, in the case of the two Powers between whom the immediate conflict arose, the postponement or avoidance of a European War would have facilitated the accomplishment of the ultimate advantages aimed at: Pashitch knew that there was a better chance for Serbian national unity after he had consolidated Serbian gains in the Balkan Wars, and after Russia had completed her military and naval armaments as planned for 1917; and Berchtold knew that he had a better chance of crushing the Greater Serbia danger and strengthening Austria, if he could avoid Russian intervention and a general European War. . . .

Nevertheless, a European War broke out. Why? Because in each country political and military leaders did certain things which led to mobilizations and declarations of war, or failed to do certain things which might have prevented them. In this sense, all the European countries, in a greater or less degree, were responsible. One must abandon the dictum of the Versailles Treaty that Germany and her allies were solely responsible. It was a dictum exacted by victors from vanquished, under the influence of the blindness, ignorance, hatred, and the propagandist misconceptions to which war had given rise. It was based on evidence which was incomplete and not always sound. It is generally recognized by the best

War and Totalitarianism

historical scholars in all countries to be no longer tenable or defensible. They are agreed that the responsibility for the War is a divided responsibility. But they still disagree very much as to the relative part of this responsibility that falls on each country and on each individual political or military leader.

Some writers like to fix positively in some precise mathematical fashion the exact responsibility for the war. This was done in one way by the framers of Article 231 of the Treaty of Versailles. It has been done in other ways by those who would fix the responsibility in some relative fashion, as, for instance, Austria first, then Russia, France and Germany and England. But the present writer deprecates such efforts to assess by a precise formula a very complicated question, which is after all more a matter of delicate shading than of definite white and black. Oversimplification, as Napoleon once said in framing his Code, is the enemy of precision. Moreover, even supposing that a general consensus of opinion might be reached as to the relative responsibility of any individual country or man for immediate causes connected with the July crisis of 1914, it is by no means necessarily true that the same relative responsibility would hold for the underlying causes, which for years had been tending toward the creation of a dangerous situation.

One may, however, sum up very briefly the most salient facts in regard to each country.

Serbia felt a natural and justifiable impulse to do what so many other countries had done in the nineteenth century—to bring under one national Government all the discontented Serb people. She had liberated those under Turkish rule; the next step was to liberate those under Hapsburg rule. She looked to Russia for assistance, and had been encouraged to expect that she would receive it. After the assassination, Mr. Pashitch took no steps to discover and bring to justice Serbians in Belgrade who had been implicated in the plot. One of them, Ciganovitch, was even assisted to disappear. Mr. Pashitch waited to see what evidence the Austrian authorities could find. When Austria demanded cooperation of Austrian officials in discovering, though not in trying, implicated Serbians, the Serbian Government made a very conciliatory but negative reply. They expected that the reply would not be regarded as satisfactory, and, even before it was given, ordered the mobilization of the Serbian army. Serbia did not want war, but believed it would be forced upon her.

That Mr. Pashitch was aware of the plot three weeks before it was executed, failed to take effective steps to prevent the assassins from crossing over from Serbia to Bosnia, and then failed to give Austria any warning or information which might have averted the fatal crime, were facts unknown to Austria in July, 1914; they cannot therefore be regarded as in any way justifying Austria's conduct; but they are part of Serbia's responsibility, and a very serious part.

Austria was more responsible for the immediate origin of the war than any other Power. Yet from her own point of view she was acting in self-defence —not against an immediate military attack, but against the corroding Greater Serbia and Jugoslav agitation which her leaders believed threatened her very existence. No State can be expected to sit with folded arms and await dismemberment at the hands of its neighbors. Russia was believed to be intriguing with Serbia and Rumania against the Dual Monarchy. The assassination of the heir to the throne, as a result of a plot prepared in Belgrade, demanded severe retribution; otherwise Austria would be regarded as incapable of action, "wormeaten" as the Serbian Press expressed it, would sink in prestige, and hasten her own downfall. To avert this Berchtold determined to crush Serbia with war. He deliberately framed the ultimatum with the expectation and hope that it would be rejected. He hurriedly declared war against Serbia in order to forestall all efforts at mediation. He refused even to answer his own ally's urgent requests to come to an understanding with Russia, on the basis of a military occupation of Belgrade as a pledge that Serbia would carry out the promises in her reply to the ultimatum. Berchtold gambled on a "local" war with Serbia only, believing that he could rattle the German sword; but rather than abandon his war with Serbia, he was ready to drag the rest of Europe into war.

It is very questionable whether Berchtold's obstinate determination to diminish Serbia and destroy her as a Balkan factor was, after all, the right method, even if he had succeeded in keeping the war "localized" and in temporarily strengthening the Dual Monarchy. Supposing that Russia in 1914, because of military unpreparedness or lack of support, had been ready to tolerate the execution of Berchtold's designs, it is quite certain that she would have aimed within the next two or three years at wiping out this second humiliation, which was so much more damaging to her prestige than that of

1908–09. In two or three years, when her great program of military reform was finally completed, Russia would certainly have found a pretext to reverse the balance in the Balkans in her own favor again. A further consequence of Berchtold's policy, even if successful, would have been the still closer consolidation of the Triple Entente, with the possible addition of Italy. And, finally, a partially dismembered Serbia would have become a still greater source of unrest and danger to the peace of Europe than heretofore. Serbian nationalism, like Polish nationalism, would have been intensified by partition. Austrian power and prestige would not have been so greatly increased as to be able to meet these new dangers. Berchtold's plan was a mere temporary improvement, but could not be a final solution of the Austro-Serbian antagonism. Franz Ferdinand and many others recognized this, and so long as he lived, no step in this fatal direction had been taken. It was the tragic fate of Austria that the only man who might have had the power and ability to develop Austria along sound lines became the innocent victim of the crime which was the occasion of the World War and so of her ultimate disruption.

Germany did not plot a European War, did not want one, and made genuine, though too belated efforts, to avert one. She was the victim of her alliance with Austria and of her own folly. Austria was her only dependable ally, Italy and Rumania having become nothing but allies in name. She could not throw her over, as otherwise she would stand isolated between Russia, where Panslavism and armaments were growing stronger every year, and France, where Alsace-Lorraine, Delcassé's fall, and Agadir were not forgotten. Therefore, Bethmann felt bound to accede to Berchtold's request for support and gave him a free hand to deal with Serbia; he also hoped and expected to "localize" the Austro-Serbian conflict. Germany then gave grounds to the Entente for suspecting the sincerity of her peaceful intentions by her denial of any foreknowledge of the ultimatum, by her support and justification of it when it was published, and by her refusal of Sir Edward Grey's conference proposal. However, Germany by no means had Austria so completely under her thumb as the Entente Powers and many writers have assumed. It is true that Berchtold would hardly have embarked on his gambler's policy unless he had been assured that Germany would fulfil the obligations of the alliance, and to this extent Germany must share the great responsibility of Austria. But when Bethmann realized that Russia was likely to

intervene, that England might not remain neutral, and that there was danger of a world war of which Germany and Austria would appear to be the instigators, he tried to call a halt on Austria, but it was too late. He pressed mediation proposals on Vienna, but Berchtold was insensible to the pressure, and the Entente Powers did not believe in the sincerity of his pressure, especially as they produced no results.

Germany's geographical position between France and Russia, and her inferiority in number of troops, had made necessary the plan of crushing the French army quickly at first and then turning against Russia. This was only possible, in the opinion of her strategists, by marching through Belgium, as it was generally anticipated by military men that she would do in case of a European War. On July 29, after Austria had declared war on Serbia, and after the Tsar had assented to general mobilization in Russia (though this was not known in Berlin and was later postponed for a day owing to the Kaiser's telegram to the Tsar), Bethmann took the precaution of sending to the German Minister in Brussels a sealed envelope. The Minister was not to open it except on further instructions. It contained the later demand for the passage of the German army through Belgium. This does not mean, however, that Germany had decided for war. In fact, Bethmann was one of the last of the statesmen to abandon hope of peace and to consent to the mobilization of his country's army. General mobilization of the continental armies took place in the following order: Serbia, Russia, Austria, France and Germany. General mobilization by a Great Power was commonly interpreted by military men in every country, though perhaps not by Sir Edward Grey, the Tsar, and some civilian officials, as meaning that the country was on the point of making war,—that the military machine had begun to move and would not be stopped. Hence, when Germany learned of the Russian general mobilization, she sent ultimatums to St. Petersburg and Paris, warning that German mobilization would follow unless Russia suspended hers within twelve hours, and asking what would be the attitude of France. The answers being unsatisfactory, Germany then mobilized and declared war. It was the hasty Russian general mobilization, assented to on July 29 and ordered on July 30, while Germany was still trying to bring Austria to accept mediation proposals, which finally rendered the European War inevitable.

Russia was partly responsible for the Austro-Serbian

conflict because of the frequent encouragement which she had given at Belgrade—that Serbian national unity would be ultimately achieved with Russian assistance at Austrian expense. This had led the Belgrade Cabinet to hope for Russian support in case of a war with Austria, and the hope did not prove vain in July, 1914. Before this, to be sure, in the Bosnian Crisis and during the Balkan Wars, Russia had put restraint upon Serbia, because Russia, exhausted by the effects of the Russo-Japanese War, was not yet ready for a European struggle with the Teutonic Powers. But in 1914 her armaments, though not yet completed, had made such progress that the militarists were confident of success, if they had French and British support. In the spring of 1914, the Minister of War, Sukhomlinov, had published an article in a Russian newspaper, though without signing his name, to the effect, "Russia is ready, France must be ready also." Austria was convinced that Russia would ultimately aid Serbia, unless the Serbian danger were dealt with energetically after the Archduke's murder; she knew that Russia was growing stronger every year; but she doubted whether the Tsar's armaments had yet reached the point at which Russia would dare to intervene; she would therefore run less risk of Russian intervention and a European War if she used the Archduke's assassination as an excuse for weakening Serbia, than if she should postpone action until the future.

Russia's responsibility lay also in the secret preparatory military measures which she was making at the same time that she was carrying on diplomatic negotiations. These alarmed Germany and Austria. But it was primarily Russia's general mobilization, made when Germany was trying to bring Austria to a settlement, which precipitated the final catastrophe, causing Germany to mobilize and declare war.

The part of France is less clear than that of the other Great Powers, because she has not yet made a full publication of her documents. To be sure, M. Poincaré, in the fourth volume of his memoirs, has made a skilful and elaborate plea, to prove *La France innocente*. But he is not convincing. It is quite clear that on his visit to Russia he assured the Tsar's Government that France would support her as an ally in preventing Austria from humiliating or crushing Serbia. Paléologue[4] renewed these assurances in a way to encourage Russia to take a strong hand. He did not attempt to restrain Russia from military

[4] French Ambassador to Russia. [Editor's note.]

measures which he knew would call forth German counter-measures and cause war. Nor did he keep his Government promptly and fully informed of the military steps which were being taken at St. Petersburg. President Poincaré, upon his return to France, made efforts for peace, but his great preoccupation was to minimize French and Russian preparatory measures and emphasize those of Germany, in order to secure the certainty of British support in a struggle which he now regarded as inevitable.

Sir Edward Grey made many sincere proposals for preserving peace; they all failed owing partly, but not exclusively, to Germany's attitude. Sir Edward could probably have prevented war if he had done either of two things. If, early in the crisis, he had acceded to the urging of France and Russia and given a strong warning to Germany that, in a European War, England would take the side of the Franco-Russian Alliance, this would probably have led Bethmann to exert an earlier and more effective pressure on Austria; and it would perhaps thereby have prevented the Austrian declaration of war on Serbia, and brought to a successful issue the "direct conversations" between Vienna and St. Petersburg. Or, if Sir Edward Grey had listened to German urging, and warned France and Russia early in the crisis, that if they became involved in war, England would remain neutral, probably Russia would have hesitated with her mobilizations, and France would probably have exerted a restraining influence at St. Petersburg. But Sir Edward Grey could not say that England would take the side of France and Russia, because he had a Cabinet nearly evenly divided, and he was not sure, early in the crisis, that public opinion in England would back him up in war against Germany. He could resign, and he says in his memoirs that he would have resigned, but that would have been no comfort or aid to France, who had come confidently to count upon British support. He was determined to say and do nothing which might encourage her with a hope which he could not fulfil. Therefore, in spite of the pleadings of the French, he refused to give them definite assurances until the probable German determination to go through Belgium made it clear that the Cabinet, and Parliament, and British public opinion would follow his lead in war on Germany. On the other hand, he was unwilling to heed the German pleadings that he exercise restraint at Paris and St. Petersburg, because he did not wish to endanger the Anglo-Russian Entente and the solidarity of the Triple Entente, because he felt a moral obligation to France, growing out of the Anglo-French military and naval conversations of the past years, and because he suspected that Germany was backing Austria up in an unjustifiable course and that Prussian militarists had taken the direction of affairs at Berlin out of the hands of Herr von Bethmann-Hollweg and the civilian authorities.

Italy exerted relatively little influence on the crisis in either direction.

Belgium had done nothing in any way to justify the demand which Germany made upon her. With commendable prudence, at the very first news of the ominous Austrian ultimatum, she had foreseen the danger to which she might be exposed. She had accordingly instructed her representatives abroad as to the statements which they were to make in case Belgium should decide very suddenly to mobilize to protect her neutrality. On July 29, she placed her army upon "a strengthened war footing," but did not order complete mobilization until two days later, when Austria, Russia, and Germany had already done so, and war appeared inevitable. Even after being confronted with the terrible German ultimatum, at 7 P.M. on August 2, she did not at once invite the assistance of English and French troops to aid her in the defense of her soil and her neutrality against a certain German assault; it was not until German troops had actually violated her territory, on August 4, that she appealed for the assistance of the Powers which had guaranteed her neutrality. Belgium was the innocent victim of German strategic necessity. Though the German violation of Belgium was of enormous influence in forming public opinion as to the responsibility for the War after hostilities began, it was not a cause of the War, except in so far as it made it easier for Sir Edward Grey to bring England into it.

In the forty years following the Franco-Prussian War, as we have seen, there developed a system of alliances which divided Europe into two hostile groups. This hostility was accentuated by the increase of armaments, economic rivalry, nationalist ambitions and antagonisms, and newspaper incitement. But it is very doubtful whether all these dangerous tendencies would have actually led to war, had it not been for the assassination of Franz Ferdinand. That was the factor which consolidated the elements of hostility and started the rapid and complicated succession of events which culminated in a World War, and for that factor Serbian nationalism was primarily responsible.

But the verdict of the Versailles Treaty that Germany and her allies were responsible for the War, in view of the evidence now available, is historically unsound. It should therefore be revised. However, because of the popular feeling widespread in some of the Entente countries, it is doubtful whether a formal and legal revision is as yet practicable. There must first come a further revision by historical scholars, and through them of public opinion.

BERNADOTTE E. SCHMITT

THE REVIVAL OF THE "ORTHODOX" INTERPRETATION

Publication of Fay's study in 1928 did not mean that the field had been abandoned to the revisionists by historians who held Germany primarily responsible for the outbreak of war in 1914. In fact the "orthodox" historians were yet to bring up their heaviest artillery.

During the war, as a young history instructor at Western Reserve University, Bernadotte Schmitt had reached the conclusion that Germany must be held chiefly responsible. Carefully studying the postwar documents, Schmitt reaffirmed and refined his interpretations and bolstered them with carefully and massively assembled evidence. His two-volume study, *The Coming of the War, 1914,* was the most scholarly and convincing of all the accounts that blamed the Central Powers for the war. Schmitt, like Fay, found many adherents among American historians. Fay at Harvard and Schmitt at the University of Chicago (1925–46) became the most distinguished American historians of the origins of World War I. In addition to his teaching duties, Schmitt edited the *Journal of Modern History* from 1929 to 1946.

Schmitt's interpretation found additional support after World War II, partly because the United States and Germany had fought another war and partly because new evidence came to light. In 1945 tons of manuscript documents from the German foreign ministry archives of 1871–1914 were captured by Allied troops. As scholars examined these manuscripts, it became apparent that some material damaging to the German case had not been published in the German documentary collection of the 1920's. The material that was omitted from the documents of the 1920's does not significantly alter the major facts about the crisis of 1914, but Schmitt's position was reinforced by the new postwar conditions and by evidence that the German documentation of the 1920's was not quite complete.

Schmitt's interpretation won additional prestige when a German historian, Fritz Fischer, published in 1961 a major new study of German war aims in the period 1914–1918. Fischer emphasized the imperialistic aspirations of leading Germans before 1914 and showed the continuity between their objectives and the war aims that were formulated after the conflict got under way. Using documents available to scholars only since 1945, Fischer showed that as early as September 1914 the German Chancellor, Theobald von Bethmann Hollweg, had set forth sweepingly imperialistic war aims.

In the meantime, Schmitt had several times restated in summary form his interpretations and the chief evidence in support of them. The following selection presents extracts from a lecture he gave on August 1, 1934. Publishing this lecture in 1960, Schmitt wrote: "I find nothing to change."

When you have read all four of these selections, draw up your own tentative conclusions. It would be well to test them against additional reading in books and documents now available. It would also be the better part of wisdom to reserve a really definitive judgment until a few more years have passed. The policies of both Britain and France prohibit the opening of their unpublished archives on foreign affairs to historians until 50 years have passed. Thus, before 1964, historians have had to rely upon the documents on the 1914 crisis that the British and French governments chose to publish. Now that the archives have been opened, new studies will be published. It remains to be seen whether they will provide evidence to support the bold conclusions of Barnes or evidence that definitively refutes his unrestrained judgment of France, Russia, and Britain in 1914.

The Revival of the "Orthodox" Interpretation

The most spectacular fact about the war was the suddenness with which it broke out. On July 23, 1914, when Austria hurled its ultimatum at Serbia, the only exciting circumstance in Europe was the possibility of civil war in Ireland over the question of Home Rule: two weeks later seven nations were at war. Even in Europe this abrupt transformation from peace to war caused a shock. It is true that for some years before 1914 certain men had been crying that a great European conflict was impending, but they were not heeded by the great masses. Four times in a decade—in 1905, 1908–9, 1911, 1912–13—Europe had been brought to the verge of war. But on each occasion the governments had drawn back, and in spite of ancient grudges and traditional rivalries, the idea had begun to spread that war was not only inhuman but also unprofitable. Statesmen and diplomatists in every country professed their devotion to peace and more or less sincerely believed their professions. Yet within a fortnight inhibitions and restraints were swept away as if they had never existed.

The moral of all this for us is clear enough, namely, that the peace of the world lies at the mercy of some untoward incident. The murder at Sarajevo of the heir to the Austro-Hungarian throne was not the cause of the Great War—it merely provided the occasion. So another assassination, or something else equally stupid, may again open the temple of Janus, just, for that matter, as the blowing-up of a bridge in Manchuria in September 1931 precipitated the Chino-Japanese conflict of recent years. Is there no way of escape from such operations of chance? Sir Edward, later Viscount, Grey, the British foreign secretary in July 1914, subsequently expressed the opinion that if the League of Nations had been in existence at that time war might have been avoided. In view of the League's failure to prevent what was actually, though not legally, war between China and Japan, one must be skeptical. But Grey's argument was sound in principle. What he meant to say, I think, was that when war threatens, the danger can best be exorcised by mobilizing the opinion of neutrals which shall demand that the disputants submit to some kind of mediation or conciliation. . . .

Once the shock of war had been met, there began a fervid and passionate investigation of the causes of the tragedy. From a psychological point of view the very fact that the war had broken out suddenly —unlike previous great conflicts, which were long in coming to a head—made plausible the view that it had been deliberately plotted and then sprung at what seemed an auspicious moment. The conduct of German diplomacy in July 1914 seemed to bear out this theory, and ultimately there emerged a story, which first circulated in Germany itself, to the effect that early in July representatives of the Austrian and German governments had met secretly at Potsdam, under the presidency of the German Emperor, and there decided to bring on a European war. For some years this story was almost universally believed in the Allied countries and in the United States, not less so because there was seemingly good evidence to support it. The Germans were never able to fix so specific a plot on their enemies, but all during the years of the war they believed, and many of them still believe, that Russia, France and Great Britain had been sedulously preparing for a war to annihilate Germany and had therefore seized with alacrity the opportunity offered when Austria decided to punish Serbia for the murder at Sarajevo.

Recent historical research has disposed of many of these legends. The collapse of the empires of the Romanovs, Habsburg and Hohenzollerns has made possible the opening of secret achives in their respective countries, and this in turn forced the victorious powers, Great Britain and France, to publish their diplomatic correspondence. At present the number of documents dealing with international relations in the period from 1871 to 1914 which the historian can peruse is not far from 50,000 and may well reach twice that figure before all the material has been made available. Many private letters have also been published in the autobiographies or biographies of the principal personages involved. Anyone who reads this voluminous material will soon disabuse himself of the notion that the governments of pre-war Europe deliberately plotted a European war. That is not to say that individual statesmen did not, at given moments, toy with the idea of war or try to impress their adversaries by threats of war. Bismarck, whose policy after 1871 was generally pacific, did not hesitate on several occasions, to try to terrorize France and Russia, and his most famous successor, Bülow, boasted that during the first Moroccan crisis of 1905, he had let the situation develop almost to the point of war, confident that at the last minute he could wriggle out. The German

From Bernadotte E. Schmitt, *The Fashion and Future of History: Historical Studies and Addresses* (1960), pp. 130–138. Reprinted by permission of Western Reserve University Press.

War and Totalitarianism

Emperor also talked much of war and gave vent to many belligerent sentiments in the marginal notes which he scribbled on the margins of documents submitted to him. Such dangerous tactics contributed powerfully to the widespread distrust of Germany which prevailed for years before 1914, but they do not prove that the German government was pursuing a policy of deliberate war. Likewise French statesmen such as Delcassé, Clemenceau and Poincaré were at times ready to fight; so also the Russian Izvolsky and the Austrian Aehrenthal, and even a British Liberal like Sir Edward Grey and a British Radical like David Lloyd George could and did show their teeth. But it seems well established that responsible governments, however much they prepared for war by creating enormous armies and building huge navies, however much they might bluster and try to bluff, did not desire an armed conflict; one and all they preferred the maintenance of peace and not only were prepared to, but actually did, make concessions for its sake.

Of the military men one can speak with less confidence. Certainly General Conrad von Hötzendorf, the chief of the Austrian general staff, itched for war and from 1906 on did his utmost to bring it about. Germany also had its school which advocated "preventive war," notably Waldersee in the late 'eighties and early 'nineties; it would also seem that in 1914 the chief of the German general staff, the younger Moltke, welcomed war because he preferred to have it then rather than later. The Grand Duke Nicholas, who commanded the Russian armies in 1914, is thought by some to have been eager for war; so perhaps also certain French generals. The famous British admiral Sir John Fisher was keen to "Copenhagen" the German fleet before it became too strong. But down to 1914 these generals and admirals were kept in hand by the civil authorities and had little influence on policy. What these men contributed was not so much a direct push towards war as the spread of suspicion and fear, for their never-ending demands for bigger and better armaments made for nervousness all around, and often embarrassed the diplomatists who strove for peace.

It cannot, then, be said that the war was the result of a fell conspiracy on the part of conscienceless and ambitious men; even those who in 1914 took the decisions and gave the orders that issued in war did so in the conviction that no other course lay open to them in the interests of their respective states. The one exception was Austria, which for several years had been desirous of a military reckoning with Serbia if a plausible excuse could be found—which was provided by the murder at Sarajevo.

Fundamentally the war of 1914 was caused by the fact that the frontiers of states did not correspond to the distribution of peoples. Germany and France were enemies because in 1871 Germany had taken Alsace-Lorraine against the wishes of the population who, whatever their racial origins and past connections, then considered themselves French. The Austro-Hungarian monarchy contained eleven different people, most of whom lived in subordination, both political and economic, to two or three privileged races and were vainly endeavoring to secure some measure of self-government. The Balkans were restless because the Christian populations desired to be emancipated from Turkish rule. Russia also had numerous non-Russian minorities who deeply resented Russian domination. Everywhere minorities were harshly treated by the governments under whom they were forced to live and gradually became more or less disloyal. Not only that, but many minorities had kinsmen across the frontier with whom they wished to be united. The Rumanians lived partly in Austria, partly in Hungary, partly in Rumania. The Yugoslavs were divided between Austria, Hungary, Serbia, Montenegro and, until 1812, Turkey. The Poles had long before been partitioned between Prussia, Russia and Austria. Bulgarians, Greeks and Italians also had failed to achieve national unity. The *Zeitgeist* made it inevitable that these several disunited peoples should strive for unity. They could achieve it only by the destruction of existing governments or existing constitutions and a wholesale remaking of the map of Europe. Since the existing governments were not in the least disposed to permit this, the only means to the end desired was war.

It was this irrepressible conflict which led the European governments to devote so much time, energy and treasure to the fashioning of armies. Germany was convinced that it could hold Alsace-Lorraine only by the sword and therefore maintained an army deemed sufficient for the purpose. Austria and Russia were in the same boat, for they could keep their subject races in submission only by force. France and Italy could hope to liberate their kinsmen under German and Austrian rule only by war. Thus the German system of universal military service had to be and was adopted by all the Continental powers, and once adopted, there was no escape from it.

Every increase in strength, every technical improvement in *matériel* made by one country had to be met all around, and after forty years of competition, the relative strength of all was not greatly altered. The principal result had been an increase of fear and suspicion.

A similar competiton in naval armaments was engendered by rivalries for colonies and concessions abroad. Unlike the conflicts of nationality on the continent of Europe which often involved the traditions of centuries, these overseas rivalries, which were of recent origin, could be and were compromised. If we leave out of account the Russo-Japanese war, the Great Powers of Europe managed to divide Africa, parts of Asia and the islands of the Pacific without war. Similarly, trade competition and commercial wars could be dealt with by means of tariffs, either by raising or by reducing them, and except in the case of Austria and Serbia, where the situation was peculiar, trade rivalry had, in my judgment, comparatively little to do with the war of 1914. But the steady building-up of vast navies contributed powerfully to international ill-feeling, and the primary issue between Great Britain and Germany was assuredly their competition for the mastery of the seas.

Now the most fatal aspect of this enormous expenditure on armies and navies was not the money involved or even the training of millions of men in the ways of war, but the progressive insecurity felt by every nation. Governments and generals invariably asserted that armaments were necessary to secure peace, but actually the greater armaments became, the less secure did any country feel, because it was more and more alarmed by the armaments of its neighbors. In 1912 the chief of the German general staff declared that the position of Germany was more dangerous than at any time since the establishment of the empire forty years before—yet Germany, by general admission, possessed the finest military machine in the world and the second strongest fleet. And Winston Churchill talked in much the same strain, although the British navy was the most formidable aggregation of fighting ships ever known. Thus unstable political frontiers had created a feeling of insecurity, and so recourse was had to armaments which might defend those frontiers. Yet armaments seemed unequal to the task. What then?

Obviously, try to find friends who will help you, on condition that you in turn will help them. Hence the system of alliances, which began with the Austro-German alliance of 1879. When this alliance was expanded in 1882 into a Triple Alliance by the inclusion of Italy, some counter-weight became necessary and was found by the conclusion of a Franco-Russian alliance between 1891 and 1894. Originally both alliances were defensive, being formed to preserve the *status quo,* and for some years they existed side by side, neither really threatening the other. But with the passage of time each alliance was modified, with a view to permitting changes in the *status quo.* In the end this new tendency was bound to become dangerous.

For many years the maintenance of equilibrium between the Triple and Dual Alliances was facilitated by the isolation of Great Britain, which co-operated now with one, now with the other group. But in the early years of this century Great Britain began to find its isolation costly and even dangerous, and it was forced to surrender its casting vote in favor of one group or the other. It tried to make a bargain with Germany—and failed. Thereupon it adhered to the other side, to France and Russia. Great Britain never joined the Dual Alliance, but it became a diplomatic partner, thereby creating the Triple Entente. Also it made certain military and naval arrangements with France which could be put into effect if Great Britain decided to join France in War. By July 1914 the schism of Europe was complete: Triple Alliance stood face to face with Triple Entente. Each side was determined to preserve, if possible, the balance of European power in its favor.

This explains what happened in July 1914. Theoretically the quarrel between Austria and Serbia which was brought to a head by the murder at Sarajevo concerned only those two countries. Actually Serbia occupied, at the moment, the key position in European politics. Were it brought under Austrian control, which would surely result if Serbia accepted the Austrian ultimatum, Austria and Germany would effectually dominate the Balkan peninsula and establish a close connection with Turkey where German influence was already predominant. The Central Powers would, in short, obtain the ascendency of Europe. Therefore Russia in the first line and France in the second resisted the pretensions of Austria, and if they could keep Serbia from the clutches of Austria, they might themselves secure the ascendency of Europe. And Great Britain was drawn into the conflict by the same consideration: it was unwilling to let Germany, with its threat to

British naval supremacy, acquire a dominant position on the continent, because Germany would then be able to make good its challenge on the seas. Thus, in the end, the principle of the balance of power proved no more effective for the maintenance of peace than bloated armaments. Stripped of diplomatic verbiage, this was the issue which lay behind the thousands of telegrams exchanged between July 23 and August 4, 1914.

The Great War, then, was the consequence of the system of alliances and armaments which had grown up since 1871. But while all the Great Powers were involved in this system, it does not follow that all were equally responsible for the crash of 1914. The documents now available leave no doubt in my mind that the primary responsibility rests with the Central Powers, for it was they who put the system to the test. Austria-Hungary decided to seize the opportunity offered by the murder at Sarajevo for the long-desired reckoning with Serbia and formulated a plan of military invasion. The Austrian statesmen were well aware that this would probably provoke intervention by Russia and not unnaturally, before making their final decision, inquired what would be the attitude of Germany. There was the possibility that German support of Austria would deter Russia from action; if it did not, only German assistance would permit Austria to fight Russia as well as Serbia.

The German Emperor and the German government, having had the Austrian plan explained to them, accepted it with alacrity and urged its immediate execution. According to the existing evidence William II and Chancellor Bethmann Hollweg believed, or affected to believe, that Russia would not intervene; why they did so remains to this day a complete puzzle, for both had previously declared, on more than one occasion, that an Austrian invasion of Serbia would cause Russia to interfere. Nevertheless both recognized that Russia might come forward as the defender of Serbia. Therefore, when they sanctioned the Austrian policy, they knew that they were running the risk of a European war. Since they assumed that Great Britain would not take part in a European war arising out of a Balkan question, they may have argued to themselves that Russia, even with the support of France, would back down before the superior military power of Germany and Austria-Hungary. In either case, they put the system to the test. If Germany had said to its ally that Austria must be content with some punishment of

Serbia less severe than military action, Austria would have had to submit to this advice, and in all probability war would not have broken out in July 1914. It may be noted that the German decision was taken by the political authorities, for the military chiefs were not consulted, only being informed of the decision when made. The soldiers were, however, nothing loath, and certainly did nothing to prevent the crisis from developing into war.

The crisis was created by the action of Austria, which refused to recede one jot or tittle from its demands that had been calculated to make war with Serbia unavoidable, and of Germany, who supported the Austrians to the limit. But the crisis was immediately regarded by Russia and France as a test of the balance of power. They would have preferred to fight later, and they offered their opponents numerous opportunities for negotiation and compromise. But because they thought themselves sufficiently well prepared to risk a war, they refused to accept the Austro-German programme in toto. The Russians did their best to make clear to the Central Powers that they would fight if necessary, but Germany either would not take the Russian warning seriously or did not care if war did come. In such circumstances peace had no chance.

But peace might have had a chance if the one country which, more than any other, namely Great Britain, sincerely desired peace, had pursued a different course. As already stated, the German government, when deciding to support Austria to the limit, did so in the expectation that Great Britain would remain neutral—although the German ambassador in London had for eighteen months consistently reported his conviction that Great Britain would assist France if it were attacked by Germany. When, as the crisis developed, it began to appear that Great Britain would probably not remain neutral if war came, the German Emperor and the German government became alarmed: to fight Russia and France was one thing, to add Great Britain to the list of enemies completely altered the situation. In consequence Berlin began, within certain limits, to urge Vienna to make concessions which might possibly prevent war. Unfortunately, these moves were made too late, because Austria had already declared war on Serbia and Russia had begun mobilization; also the German pressure was relaxed at the critical moment, and in the end Austria yielded nothing.

2

WHY COMMUNIST TOTALITARIANISM IN RUSSIA?

In the midst of the First World War two revolutions shook Russia in 1917, and out of them the Communists, or "Bolsheviks" as they were then called, emerged as Russia's new masters. They were led by N. Lenin and claimed to be followers of Karl Marx.

History, according to the theories of Marx, is determined by impersonal economic forces. The history of societies in which the means of production are held by private owners is the story of class struggle. Writing in the nineteenth century, Marx contended that the contemporary class struggle was that of the industrial working class, which he called the "proletariat," against the "bourgeoisie," as he called the capitalists as a class.

Marx wrote history and political theory in universal terms, not in the context of any single state. He argued that a bourgeoisie that cut across national lines would increasingly exploit the proletarians as capitalism developed. The hard-pressed workers of the world would rise above the forces of nationalism that separated them and unite in class solidarity. When driven to desperation by an advanced capitalist system, the workers would overthrow their capitalist masters and establish what Marx called "the dictatorship of the proletariat." Since the proletariat was made up of the workers, and since all would work once the proletariat seized power, in the logic and semantics of Marxist theory "the dictatorship of the proletariat" would be pure democracy, the government of all by all. The "dictatorship of the proletariat" would replace the capitalist system with socialism, common ownership of the means of production. Then there would be no more class struggle. Since states were instruments of class exploitation, the state would eventually "wither away." The human individual would at last be free to develop his full potentialities.

Capitalism was indeed a harsh system as it existed in the middle of the nineteenth century, and the noble dream of Marxism inspired large numbers of idealistic Europeans in the decades that followed. European labor organized in these decades, often under Marxist leaders. But these very developments and the development of political democracy in Europe resulted in alterations in the character of capitalism. As the decades passed, workers in Western and Central Europe went on strikes, voted in increasing numbers, and enjoyed higher living standards instead of suffering intensified misery. By the 1890's a number of socialists in Western and Central Europe were abandoning Marxism or modifying Marx's theories to reflect the new reality. Many ceased to advocate revolution and had no liking for any kind of dictatorship, not even a "dictatorship of the proletariat." These democratic socialists were sometimes called "revisionists."

Other European socialists prided themselves on being better "Marxists" because they continued to advocate revolution, but some of the radicals changed Marx's theories even more drastically than did those they derided as "revisionists" or "reformists." One of the revolutionaries was the man who is known in history by his pen name, N. Lenin. Born in 1870, Lenin began his political career in the 1890's. It is significant that he grew up in Russia. There the harsh features of capitalism were least softened by labor and welfare legislation before 1914.

The most fundamental difference between the theories of Marx and those of Lenin was a difference between two views of history. Marx believed in the "economic determinism" of history. In Marxist theory, economic forces shaped politics. Inherent in Lenin's whole thought and action, in contrast, was the conviction that politics could determine economic systems and thus the course of history.

From this fundamental reversal of Marxist theories, other differences between Lenin and Marx flowed. Marxist theory held that the proletariat would first successfully rebel in an advanced capitalistic country; Lenin preached instead that socialist revolution could be touched off in Russia, where capitalism was still in an early stage of development and the bourgeoisie was a small element in society. Marxist theory had predicted a scientifically inevitable and spontaneous mass rising of desperate workers; Lenin insisted that the Revolution must be deliberately made by a small, tightly organized, and disciplined party under his direction that would think and act for the masses. Marx thought he had found scientific truth about history and society, and he did not like to bend or depart from his doctrine. In comparison Lenin was a practical-minded opportunist. As he wrote on one occasion, "Our teaching is not dogma. . . . Life will show us. . . . We know the direction. . . . But only the experience of millions, as they move to the task, will discover the road."

Another difference between Marx and Lenin would spell totalitarianism for Russia instead of a "withering away of the state" after 1917. Marx had talked about creating a "dictatorship of the proletariat"; Lenin openly admitted many times that he planned, instead, to establish a "dictatorship of the *vanguard* of the proletariat"—in other words, of his own party—which only later and in ways he could never describe would, he said, be transformed into a "dictatorship of the proletariat."

The creation of a "dictatorship of the *vanguard* of the proletariat" has been the goal of the Communist parties of other countries ever since in the period of their striving for power. All have considered themselves alone to be the vanguards of the proletariat in their respective countries, and the totalitarian governments they have created, unlike the state in Marxist theory, have not "withered away." They contend that the withering away cannot be expected until capitalism everywhere is eliminated. In the meantime, they have reshaped "European Civilization" from East Germany to the easternmost reaches of Russia, and have imposed their reshaped European Civilization upon China, North Korea, Cuba, and much of Vietnam.

What was started in Russia in 1917 became a way of life for hundreds of millions of people in every quarter of the globe by the early 1960's. To the Communists it is an emerging world civilization and its ultimate triumph is inevitable.

Lenin created the first Communist Party in history as a wing within the Russian Social Democratic Labor Party (RSDLP), which was started in 1898 by a handful of leaders. Political parties were not legally permitted in Russia, and its operations were clandestine and fragile. For almost two decades two other political parties that were organized illegally at about the same time were much more important. These were the Social Revolutionary Party (SR's) and the Constitutional Democratic Party (Kadets). The SR's spoke for the peasant masses of Russia. They wanted to take the landed estates that remained in the hands of the nobility. Their leaders saw the future of Russia in terms of agricultural socialism. The Kadets were industrialists, merchants, and professional men who were pressing for more rapid development of capitalist industry, increased recognition for the still small middle class, and creation of a parliament under a constitutional monarchy more or less on the British model. Until Lenin split it, the RSDLP included both "soft" (Menshevik) and "hard" (Bolshevik) revolutionaries who took their inspiration from Marxist theory and tried to inspire the emerging but backward and small industrial working class. Many of the leaders of the RSDLP lived in Western Europe as exiles. Because tsarist Russia remained overwhelmingly rural, the SR's were by far the largest of the three movements. But as industry developed, both the Kadets and the RSDLP would grow in size and influence, especially in the industrial centers of Moscow and the pre-1918 capital city of St. Petersburg (called Petrograd during World War I and Leningrad after 1924).

Industry did grow rapidly if belatedly in Russia during the reign of Nicholas II. Coal production was tripled in the 1890's. Railroad mileage was doubled, including that of the Trans-Siberian Railroad that stretched across the wastelands of Siberia out to Vladivostok on the Pacific. As a producer of pig iron Russia moved from seventh place to fourth place among the nations of Europe between 1890 and 1914. Still, iron and steel production lagged far behind that of Germany, France, and Great Britain. Wages were much lower, working conditions were poorer, and hours were longer ($11\frac{1}{2}$ hours per day) in the factories of Russia than in those of Western and Central Europe. Labor unions were organized but grew slowly. Political reformers of all types continued to be restricted by police repression and censorship.

Then in 1904 tsarist Russia found itself fighting an unsuccessful war against Japan, which in February had attacked Russian installations on the Pacific without warning. All those who favored political changes grew bolder as the war went badly for the tasarist regime. Though the industrial workers made up only about 10 per cent of the population of Russia, they were concentrated in a few key cities. Their strikes in St. Petersburg touched off the revolution of 1905. In an attempt to forestall a total revolution, Nicholas II made peace in September on terms favorable to Japan. To undermine the more radical revolutionaries, he promised in October to establish a

National Assembly, or Duma, with some of the powers of a parliament. Some Kadets, satisfied by this moderate reform, were henceforth known as "Octobrists." Other Kadets continued to press in the Duma for more genuine parliamentary government. Leaders of the RSDLP, not satisfied at all, had sought in October 1905 to push the revolution in a socialist direction. To coordinate the rebellion of various labor groups in St. Petersburg, they founded a "Soviet" or "Council" of leaders of industrial workers. But this first Soviet was suppressed by the resurgent tsarist regime in December 1905, and more Russian Marxists went into exile.

Peasant revolts had broken out in 1905, but by 1906 they were brought under control. The government tried between then and 1914 to satisfy the land hunger of the peasants and create a new class of conservative-minded owners of individual farms. But great numbers of peasants continued to live in "mirs," communal villages that made collective decisions. When the First World War began in 1914 about one fourth of the farmland was still held by the nobility, though it was worked by peasants who wanted it for themselves and who looked to the SR's to get it for them.

World War I, like the war with Japan in 1904–05, placed strains on Russia that neither Russian industry nor the Russian military forces were able to bear. The results were horrendous casualties at the front, lack of effective organization in the interior, disruption of agriculture, inadequate clothing, and worsening food shortages. In March 1917 the tsardom was overthrown and a Provisional Government took its place until November (February and October by the calendar Russia then used).

At first the Provisional Government was led by Kadets, but even when SR's rose to positions of leadership the government did not move quickly to give the peasant the lands of the nobility. Rural rebellion got under way. Nor could the Provisional Government cope with the economic and military problems created by the war. Thus it might be argued that it was really German military force that broke first the tsarist regime and then the Provisional Government. In November Lenin and the Bolsheviks seized power.

The readings that follow present diverse interpretations of the reasons for the revolutions of 1917 and their success. The first selection treats only the March Revolution and the fourth treats the November Revolution. The second and third readings discuss both revolutions. As you read each of these, make certain that you grasp the author's central interpretation. What does he believe to have been the principle reason for the success of the revolutions? What chief evidence does he present to support his interpretation? What evidence do you gain from the other readings that might cast doubt on his interpretation or cause you to qualify it or supplement it? Finally, when you have read all four selections and reconsidered each interpretation in the light of the *total* evidence available, decide tentatively upon an interpretation of your own.

Then consider some larger questions in the light of what you have learned about the Russian revolutions of 1917. Do they tend to support Marx's theory of history? The "great man" theory? The theory of history as a series of accidents? Or yet another theory?

In the group of readings on the outbreak of World War I you noted that interpretations changed as new historical sources (evidence) became available. Are new sources about the Russian revolutions of 1917 likely to become available? If so, are they likely to change either the major facts or the interpretations now available? Are historians likely ever to agree on a common synthesis or interpretation about the revolutions of 1917? Would it be more difficult or less difficult to reconcile the divergent interpretations that follow about 1917 than to arrive at a unified interpretation of responsibility for the outbreak of War in 1914? Why?

WILLIAM HENRY CHAMBERLIN

A SPONTANEOUS REVOLT OF WAR-WEARY RUSSIANS

In Marx's view, when the revolt of the workers against capitalism came it would be spontaneous; in Lenin's view it would be deliberately planned and carried out. Which way, in fact, did the March and November revolutions occur? Did they bear out the prophecies of Marx, those of Lenin, or those of neither?

In the selection that follows William H. Chamberlin unambiguously tells you his view of the character of the March Revolution. Born in Brooklyn in 1897, Chamberlin graduated from Haverford College in the year of the Russian revolutions and became a journalist. Five years after the revolutions—in time to interview many participants—Chamberlin went to Russia as correspondent for a distinguished Boston newspaper, the Christian Science Monitor, and remained there in that capacity until 1934. In 1934 he published his third book about Russia, but for historians the best was to come in 1935, a large, two-volume study of The Russian Revolution, 1917–1921. In the opinion of many scholars, this remains the best history of the subject. The reading that follows is taken from the first volume of Chamberlin's study.

Since 1940 Chamberlin has authored several other books while working as an independent writer and lecturer. In 1959 he published an autobiographical account, Evolution of a Conservative. Does the following reading suggest that his political views prejudiced his interpretation of the history of Russia in 1917? You may wish to consult Chamberlin's autobiographical book in an attempt to determine when and why he became a conservative. It may also be pertinent to find out what kind of conservative he became, because there are about as many varieties of both "liberals" and "conservatives" as there are interpretations of history.

The collapse of the Romanov autocracy in March 1917 was one of the most leaderless, spontaneous, anonymous revolutions of all time. While almost every thoughtful observer in Russia in the winter of 1916–1917 foresaw the likelihood of the crash of the existing regime no one, even among the revolutionary leaders, realized that the strikes and bread riots which broke out in Petrograd on March 8 would culminate in the mutiny of the garrison and the overthrow of the government four days later.

The Tsarina was not distinguished by political perspicacity; and it is not surprising that she should write to her husband, who was at the Headquarters of the General Staff in Moghilev, on March 10, when the capital was in the grip of a general strike: "This is a hooligan movement, young people run and shout that there is no bread, simply to create excitement, along with workers who prevent others from working. If the weather were very cold they would all probably stay at home. But all this will pass and become calm, if only the Duma will behave itself."

But it was not only the Tsarina who failed to see the impending storm. The Socialist Revolutionary Zenzinov declared: "The Revolution was a great and joyous surprise for us, revolutionaries, who had worked for it for years and had always expected it." The Menshevik Internationalist Sukhanov observes: "Not one party was prepared for the great overturn." The Bolshevik worker Kaourov, who took an active part in the Revolution, testifies that on March 8 "no one thought of such an imminent possibility of revolution." As for the leaders of the Duma, they might whisper among each other about the possibility of a palace *coup d'état;* but the last thing they desired was an uncontrolled movement from below.

Wartime circumstances alone made any effective guidance of a mass uprising impossible. The men who afterwards distinguished themselves in the Bolshevik Revolution were either living abroad, like Lenin and Trotzky and Zinoviev, or in prison or in Siberian exile, like Stalin, Kamenev and Dzerzhinsky. The more prominent leaders of other revolutionary parties were also absent from Petrograd in the decisive days. The Bolshevik members of the Duma had been exiled to Siberia in the first months of the War, and the Menshevik members of the War Industries Committee were arrested by the zealous Minister of the Interior, Protopopov, early in the year. There was a skeleton underground Bolshevik organization in Russia; but its activities were narrowly circumscribed by lack of experienced professional revolutionaries, lack of funds, and the all-pervading espionage. Indeed most of the members of the Bolshevik Petrograd Party Committee were arrested at a critical moment in the development of the movement, on the morning of March 11.

So the police measures for the protection of the Tsarist regime were almost perfect. At first sight and on paper the military measures seemed equally imposing. Petrograd had a huge garrison of about 160,000 soldiers. To be sure the fighting quality of this garrison, as subsequent events were to prove, was in inverse ratio to its size. The original Guard regiments had been sent to the front (a grave strategic error, from the standpoint of the internal security of the old regime); and the troops quartered in Petrograd consisted mainly of new recruits, untrained, housed in crowded barracks, often poorly fed.

But the Tsarist authorities did not rely primarily on the unwieldy garrison for the suppression of any possible uprising. The Minister of the Interior, Protopopov, proposed to operate against insurgent throngs first with police, then with Cossack cavalry units, bringing troops into operation only in the last resort. An elaborate plan for the suppression of disorder in the capital had been submitted to the Tsar in January. A combined force of 12,000 troops, gendarmes, and police was created for this specific purpose; and a military commander was appointed in each of the six police districts into which the city was divided.

Military preparations, therefore, had not been neglected, even if there were serious omissions, quite consistent with the frequently slipshod character of Tsarist administration, in paying little attention to the morale of the troops in the capital and in selecting as commander of the Petrograd Military District,

A Spontaneous Revolt of War-Weary Russians

General Khabalov, a man of little experience in commanding troops in actual military operations. The unforeseen circumstances that upset all the governmental calculations were the stubbornness of the demonstrators and the ultimate unreliability of the garrison.

The atmosphere of Petrograd was so charged with discontent in this third winter of an unsuccessful war that very slight causes were sufficient to bring about a formidable explosion. There had been intermittent strikes throughout January and February. Although there was not an absolute shortage of bread poor transportation and faulty distribution made it necessary for the workers and their wives, in many cases, to stand in long queues for bread and other products. The poorer classes of the city were not apathetic from actual hunger; but they were angry and annoyed at the growing cost of living and the other deprivations which the War brought with it. Something of a sense of crowd psychology, of a sense of massed power must have developed also, from the noteworthy growth in the number of industrial workers up to approximately 400,000 as a result of the presence of many war industry plants in the capital.

The movement that was to end in the overthrow of the Romanov dynasty started on March 8, which is observed by Socialist parties as Women's Day. After speeches in the factories crowds of women poured out on the streets, especially in the workingclass Viborg section of the city, clamoring for bread. Here and there red flags appeared with inscriptions: "Down with Autocracy." There were occasional clashes with the police; but the day passed off without serious conflicts. Almost ninety thousand workers struck and fifty factories were closed. A circumstance that enhanced the militant mood of the demonstrators was a lockout at the large Putilov metal works. The workers of this plant were proverbially turbulent, with a long record of strikes; and when a wage dispute had come up in one department the management on March 7 declared a general lockout. So a coincidence of three factors—the dissatisfaction with the food situation, the celebration of Women's Day and the Putilov labor dispute, which let loose over twenty thousand workers for active participation in the demonstration—combined to give the first impetus to the Revolution.

The movement gained in scope and intensity on March 9, when the number of strikers was estimated at 197,000. There was a concerted drive by the workers to reach the central part of the city. Although the police guarded the bridges over the Neva, which was to some extent a boundary between the workingclass and the governmental parts of the city, it was relatively easy to cross the river on the ice, and meetings and demonstrations were held in the centre of the capital. An ominous symptom for the government appeared: the Cossacks showed little energy in breaking up the crowds. So a Cossack squadron rode off, amid loud cheers, leaving undisturbed a revolutionary gathering on the Nevsky Prospect, the main boulevard of Petrograd; and the police reports of the day note an incident on Znamenskaya Square, when the Cossacks responded with bows to the applause of a throng which they did not disperse.

Attacks on the police became more common on this second day of the movement, the mobs using as weapons lumps of ice, cobblestones, heavy sticks. However, firearms were not used in suppressing the disorder and there was still no general conviction of an impending crisis. The British Ambassador, Sir George Buchanan, telegraphed to Foreign Minister Balfour: "Some disorders occurred to-day, but nothing serious."

The 10th witnessed to a large extent a repetition of the events of the 9th, but on a larger scale. The strike became general; newspapers ceased to appear; the students in the universities abandoned their studies. The numbers both of the demonstrators and of the forces employed by the government increased; and there was a longer casualty list on both sides. Although there was still no mutiny, insubordination and passivity on the part of the troops, especially of the Cossacks, were more noticeable. On Znamenskaya Square a Cossack even cut down a police lieutenant, Krilov, with his sabre. The instinctive strategy of the crowd adapted itself to the mood of the troops. While there were fierce attacks on the police (by this time the police in the riotous Viborg district no longer ventured to appear on the streets, but were barricaded in their stations) there was an attempt to conciliate the troops and to avoid provoking them.

So far as there was organized leadership in the movement it aimed at winning over the troops, rather than at arming the workers. So the Bolshevik Shlyapnikov, one of the three members of the Bureau of the Central Committee of the Party, tells how he opposed the more hotheaded workers who continually demanded arms, or at least revolvers: "I decisively refused to search for arms at all and demanded that the soldiers should be drawn into the uprising, so as to get arms for all the workers. This was more difficult than to get a few dozen revolvers; but in this was the whole programme of action."

These three days of turmoil naturally affected the national and local legislative bodies, the Duma and the Petrograd City Council; and speeches were made demanding the appointment of a ministry responsible to the Duma. The Laborite deputy and radical lawyer Alexander Kerensky, destined to play a leading part in subsequent months, attacked the government so sharply in the Duma on the 9th that the Tsarina expressed a fervent desire that he should be hanged. These speeches, however, had little effect on the movement, because the War Minister forbade their publication, and after the morning of March 10, newspapers ceased to appear as a result of the general strike.

General Khabalov on March 10 received a peremptory telegram from the Tsar worded as follows: "I command you to suppress from tomorrow all disorders on the streets of the capital, which are impermissible at a time when the fatherland is carrying on a difficult war with Germany." This imperial order caused a sharp change in the tactics of the Petrograd authorities. Hitherto the use of firearms had been avoided. On the night of the 10th Khabalov gave his subordinate officers instructions to fire on crowds which refused to disperse after warning. This was the decisive stake of the old regime. If the troops obeyed, the revolutionary movement would be crushed. If they did not obey . . . But this alternative was apparently not considered very seriously.

As a further sign of resolute action the police on the night of the 10th arrested about a hundred persons suspected of holding seditious views, including five members of the Petrograd Committee of the Bolshevik Party. On the surface the course of events on the 11th, which was a Sunday, represented a victory for the government. There was firing on the crowds in four separate places in the central part of the city; and on Znamenskaya Square the training detachment of the Volinsky regiment used machine-guns as well as rifles, with the result that about forty persons were killed and an equal number were wounded. Toward evening there was an outburst of rebellion in one company of the Pavlovsk regiment;

but it was put down with the aid of other troops, and the ringleaders were imprisoned in the fortress of Peter and Paul. The government, which was headed by Prince Golitzin as Premier, apparently felt in a stronger position, because in the evening it adopted a decision to dissolve the Duma, thereby breaking off the half-hearted negotiations which had hitherto been carried on with the President of the Duma, Rodzianko,[1] about possible coöperation between the Ministry and the Duma.

Rodzianko decided to try the effect of a personal appeal to the Tsar and despatched a telegram containing the following gravely warning phrases: "The situation is serious. There is anarchy in the capital. The government is paralyzed. It is necessary immediately to entrust a person who enjoys the confidence of the country with the formation of the government. Any delay is equivalent to death. I pray God that in this hour responsibility will not fall on the sovereign."

But neither this telegram, nor the still more urgent message which Rodzianko sent on the following morning, when the mutiny of the garrison was an accomplished fact, produced any impression on Nicholas II. Rodzianko's second telegram described the growing revolt and ended: "The situation is growing worse. Measures must be adopted immediately, because tomorrow will be too late. The last hour has come, when the fate of the fatherland and the dynasty is being decided."

After reading this message the Tsar impatiently remarked to his Minister of the Court, Count Fredericks: "This fat Rodzianko has written me some nonsense, to which I will not even reply."

There is a double significance in these last urgent appeals of the President of the Duma to the Tsar and especially in his instinctive employment of the phrase "The situation is growing worse," at a moment when the revolution was moving to victory. Like the great majority of the members of the Duma Rodzianko, who was himself a well-to-do landowner, desired to see the monarchy reformed, but not abolished. All Rodzianko's actions in these turbulent days were motivated by two factors: his hope, up to the last moment, that the Tsar would save himself and the monarchical principle by making necessary

[1] President of the Duma, 1911–16; at this time head of the Committee of the Duma. [Editor's note.]

concessions, and his fear that the revolutionary movement would get out of hand.

The decisive hour of the Revolution struck on the morning of March 12, when the centre of attention shifts from rebellious workers with sticks and stones and bottles to insurgent soldiers with rifles and machine-guns. The firing on the crowds on Sunday, the 11th, was the snapping point in the frail cord of discipline that held the garrison of the capital. The mutiny that was to transform the prolonged street demonstrations into a genuine revolution started in the very unit which had inflicted the heaviest losses on the demonstrating crowds: the training detachment of the Volinsky regiment. During the night the soldiers discussed their impressions of the day's shooting and agreed that they would no longer fire on the crowds. When Captain Lashkevitch appeared in the barracks of the detachment on the morning of the 12th he was greeted with shouts: "We will not shoot." He read the telegram of the Tsar, demanding the suppression of the disorders; but this only aggravated the situation. Ultimately Lashkevitch either was shot by the insurgent soldiers or committed suicide; and the troops poured out into the streets under the command of Sergeant Kirpichnikov, one of the many obscure leaders of this unplanned upheaval. They soon aroused the soldiers of the Preobrazhensky and Litovsky regiments, who were quartered in nearby barracks.

Quickly brushing aside the resistance which some officers of the Moscow Regiment endeavored to offer and gaining new recruits among the soldiers of the Moscow regiment for their ranks, the swollen mass of soldiers made for the Viborg District, where they quickly fraternized with the throngs of workers and joined them in hunting down the police and breaking into arsenals, where the workers quickly secured the desired arms.

Khabalov, a weak and incompetent man at best, was thunderstruck as the news of one mutiny after another poured in on him. He formed a supposedly loyal force of six companies under the command of Colonel Kutepov, but it simply melted away as soon as it came into contact with the revolutionary mobs. This largely psychological process of "melting away" recurred, incidentally, whenever there was an attempt to send "reliable" troops against the revolutionary capital. It explains why a movement without organized leadership was nevertheless invincible. This breakdown of normal military discipline cannot be attributed to any single precise cause. It was a compound of many things: war-weariness, hatred of the hard and often humiliating conditions of Russian army service, responsiveness to the general mood of discontent in the country —all explosive stuff that was ignited by the stubborn demonstrations of the workingclass population of Petrograd.

There are two features of the March Revolution that strike the observer again and again. There is the lack of planned leadership, and there is the action of the soldiers independently of their officers. The latter, with very few exceptions, simply disappeared during the decisive hours of the uprising. This fact inevitably exerted a profound effect on the subsequent morale and psychology of the soldiers, who followed leaders from their own ranks, often sergeants and corporals.

Khabalov, with the rapidly thinning remnant of his loyal troops, took refuge in the Winter Palace, where his forces on the afternoon of the 12th were reduced to "fifteen hundred or two thousand men, with a very small reserve of bullets." At the insistence of the Grand Duke Michael, the Tsar's brother, the Winter Palace was evacuated and the last defenders of the old regime took refuge in the neighboring Admiralty, whence they quietly dispersed on the following morning.

So the city passed completely into the hands of the revolutionaries. The accounts of many eyewitnesses of the upheaval are pervaded with a spirit of chaotic exaltation. The monarchy had fallen; and in the masses of the population there were few who mourned it. Vast throngs gathered to watch the burning of the large District Court building and adjoining prison; and the Tauride Palace, where the Duma held its sessions, was a magnet for endless throngs of soldiers, workers, students and curious spectators of all classes. Red bands and ribbons appeared as if by magic; and trucks filled with soldiers raced through the city, with their guns levelled against non-existent enemies. Except for the police, who were given short shrift when they were discovered hiding in garrets or firing from roofs on the crowds, the Revolution, although tumultuous, was, in the main, good-natured. There were relatively few excesses, surprisingly few, if one considers that common criminals were released indiscriminately with political offenders in the prisons which were stormed by the mobs. Class lines had not begun to assume their subsequent sharpness. An atmosphere of vague, formless good-fellowship was prevalent; and the nationalist speeches of Shulgin[2] or Rodzianko evoked the same hearty "Hurrah" as the exhortations of the revolutionary orators. The great mass of the mutinous soldiers scarcely realized what they were doing and were uncertain whether in the end they would be treated as heroes or as criminals.

The anonymous host of workers in collarless blouses and soldiers in grey uniforms overthrew the Romanov dynasty, with its three centuries of absolute rule behind it.

[2] A leading deputy in the Duma. [Editor's note.]

JOHN MAYNARD

THE PEASANTS MADE THE REVOLUTION

Like Chamberlin, Sir John Maynard had ample opportunity to know Russia at first hand as well as from historical research. Two years before Chamberlin was born Maynard went to Russia, saw the coronation of Emperor Nicholas II, and lived for ten months in his empire (1895–96) while mastering the Russian language.

As a British civil servant in India until 1926, Maynard learned well a society that resembled in many particulars the rural society of prerevolutionary Russia. He steeped himself in Russian literature and thought, developing a rare understanding of Russian traditions. As a Fabian Socialist Maynard brought both sympathetic and critical interest to his study of the Communist attempts to build socialism in Russia. In 1933, 1935, and 1937 he again travelled in the U.S.S.R.

Maynard's scholarly writing about Russia was embodied in two major books that reflected his interest in both the pre-1917 and post-1917 developments. In the book that first bore the title *Russia in Flux* he treated Russian history up to the Bolshevik Revolution. Then in 1942 he published a volume on post-1917 developments, *The Russian Peasant and Other Studies*. Sir Bernard Pares, then England's leading academic expert on Russia, considered this "far and away the best book written in English on the Soviet period." The reading that follows is taken from a second book with the title *Russia in Flux*—actually a combination of the two books mentioned above. It is a remarkably balanced and perceptive volume.

Does Maynard's interpretation supplement or refute Chamberlin's? Which gives more weight to deep-seated social discontent?

The incidents which together constituted the revolution of March, 1917, need only be briefly summarised here. The trouble began with a shortage of food in the capital—at that time named Petrograd—and a reduction of the bread ration: but behind these overt grievances was a long story of incompetence, suffering, and mistrust. The capital was crowded with troops, inactive and restless. The fourth Duma was

Reprinted by permission of the publisher from *Russia in Flux* by John Maynard, pp. 181–196, excerpts. Copyright 1958 by The Macmillan Co.

sitting at the Tavrida Palace. Its President, Prince Lvov, warned the Tsar, then at General Headquarters of the field army, that the capital was in a state of anarchy, and asked him to appoint a minister "possessing the confidence of the country," according to the approved formula of parliamentary government. In reply, he received an order dissolving the Duma. On the same night (March 11–12) a part of the Emperor's own Guard mutinied, and next morning mutinous troops fraternised with workers in attacking police and breaking into arsenals. The arrival of mutineers, accompanied by civilian crowds, at the Tavrida Palace caused the Duma — which had been technically dissolved — to decide to sit again in unofficial session and to appoint a Temporary Committee: which became virtually the revolutionary authority. The Ministers of the old regime were arrested or surrendered. Seventy-three policemen lost their lives in attacks by soldiers and workmen. The rest surrendered or disappeared, and no Police Force — under that hated name — has ever come into existence since. The Army everywhere fraternised with the Revolution.

It remained for events to show what — in positive terms — the Revolution meant. The negative intention, that neither Nicolas II nor Alexandra Feodorovna — the "German woman," as the people called her — should rule, was clear enough. For a generation to come, perhaps for longer, Russia was to search for her intention. For the moment, at least, the intention was definite enough: the land for the working commune, with an end alike of landlords and "separators,"[1] and — peace. But it was soon evident that these apparently simple demands involved the whole structure of the State, and constructive change extending to limits as yet unforeseen. . . .

The demands of the peasantry included safeguards for agricultural labour, the fixing of wages, in some cases also of hours, and cessation of the employment of prisoners of war, whose competition kept wages down. Those who had left the Mir under the operation of the earlier legislation for the creation of separate peasant property in land were, in the Central Agricultural and Middle-Volga zones, which were strongholds of the Mir, as well as storm-centres of agrarian disturbances, often forced to return to it. In the earlier stages the Social Revolutionaries exer-

cised a moderating influence in the villages; but, as the excitement grew, and violence was stimulated by the return of deserters from the armies, this influence was lost. Agrarian crime became immensely worse as soon as the harvest was in, and the Government deferred till too late the preparation of the decree for immediate expropriation. In the meanwhile, as we learn from Monkhouse, the position of employers in industry was increasingly difficult. The men made a practice of placing unpopular managers and foremen in wheel-barrows and wheeling them off the premises. There were more serious cases, of beating, even of murder: but savage violence was noticeably less than in the rural areas.

V. A. Rudnev, economist and philosopher, who worked later in the State Planning Commission, was publishing at the end of May a vigorous and instructed attack on war-profiteering, showing that capital was held back in the hope of still higher prices, that fixed prices were being evaded, that wild speculation by middlemen was going on in coal and metal, that useless factories were being erected at Government expense, and that industrialists were deliberately creating anarchy in production. W. G. Groman, a Menshevik statistician and economist, was pointing out that everywhere, except in Russia, the pressure of war-needs was bringing about the State organisation of economic life and labour. The Social Revolutionary and Menshevik organ was demanding the State monopoly of some, and the State control of other, industries, and the State control of credit institutions to prevent speculation, and was hinting at compulsory labour for all. The Executive Committee of the Petrograd Soviet[2] was urging the acceptance of a scheme of State control of national economy. But the Government shrank from offending property interests. It appointed an Economic Council, but otherwise did nothing except raise wages: which led to a further rise of prices.

An abortive demonstration (July 16–19, 1917) in which the Bolsheviks took part, under the slogan "All Power to the Soviets," gave the Provisional Government one of several opportunities for getting

[1] By "separators" Maynard means those peasants who withdrew from the mirs (village communes) after 1905 and became individual farm-owners. [Editor's note.]

[2] In March 1917 leaders of the workers, rebellious soldiers, and left-wing political parties created a "Soviet" (Council) to coordinate revolutionary action. In other cities Soviets were also created. After March the Provisional Government could do little without the co-operation of the Soviets. It was as a member of the Petrograd Soviet that Alexander Kerensky first gained influence in the Provisional Government. Kerensky, as successor to Prince Lvov, was head of the Provisional Government from July until the Bolsheviks seized power in November. [Editor's note.]

War and Totalitarianism

rid of opponents whom we now know to have been dangerous to it. None of these was grasped. The explanation seems to be that only three or four months ago all the victims of the old régime had been released, and all, including Lenin, warmly welcomed back to their native land, in the glow of exaltation and unity of sentiment which the first days of the Revolution created. In the light of our later knowledge we know that Lenin was dangerous to the Liberal revolution. But we must not suppose that he then seemed very dangerous. The Peasant Congress laughed uproariously when he offered, on behalf of the Bolsheviks, to accept power. He commanded only a tiny minority among the peasants: Bolshevism was not a soldiers' movement, its strength lay in the factories; but the idea that the factories might lead the peasantry was still limited to a few. No doubt a ruthless Government, or even a Government of the old-fashioned police type, would have made sure of Lenin's good behaviour in the old fashioned way. But any statesman or administrator might, at this stage, have underrated the Bolshevik leader's importance. And the men of the Provisional Government were legally minded, and Kerensky himself a lawyer, disposed to wait for a "case" before taking action, and to believe in the effectiveness of conciliation and oratory. . . .

Prince Lvov, who had held the office of Prime Minister since the establishment of the Provisional Government, resigned on July 20, 1917. He was dissatisfied with the projects of agrarian legislation submitted by Chernov,[3] which appeared to him to condone the seizures. It is evident also that he was unwilling to give his support to the measures of "strong" government, which were being forced on the ministry by the July disturbances and the collapse at the front. Kerensky became President of the Council of Ministers, retaining the portfolios of War and Navy. The death penalty, which had been abrogated in March, was restored "for major crimes committed by men on military duty." Military censorship of newspapers and letters was re-established, and power taken to suppress newspapers, prohibit meetings, and arrest by administrative order.

So far as legal authority was concerned, Alexander Kerensky was now at the summit of power, with a Cabinet consisting predominantly of moderate socialists, among whom Chernov was the most radical. If we count out the Socialism which has often

been practised by absolute Governments, it was the first Socialist Government in the world: and it might well have seemed that Kerensky had the ball at his feet. But the great questions still remained to be answered. In July the renewed military offensive in Galicia had met with disaster. It was necessary to decide how to restore a routed army, and how to make war or peace; what to do with the insistent demand for land; how to build up the shattered economic life of the country. The setback which the Bolsheviks had received was not of long duration. Early in August the Petrograd workers were mingling with soldiers of the active army, and learning that conditions at the front were returning to those of the Tsarist régime. A week later the influence of the Bolsheviks in the Petrograd factories was already restored, the party had grown from 80,000 in April to 200,000; and the Social Revolutionaries of the Left were beginning to catch up Bolshevik slogans and ideas.

Kerensky's own words show how he proposed to utilise his virtual dictatorship. The Constituent Assembly set for October was postponed to December, and, having thus delayed the opportunity of definite settlement of outstanding questions, he felt the "need of making an inventory of the nation's political forces, and to give the parties, the Soviets and other organisations, an opportunity of appraising themselves." This was not action of the kind demanded by a pressing emergency. For action, Russia was to choose between a military saviour in whom courage and energy were not united with comprehension of the political situation, and the socialist leader at whom she had laughed a few weeks before.

The story of the successive expedients by which the "persuader-in-chief" attempted to establish a government of mutual goodwill and conciliation without grappling with the inescapable problems; of the ignominious collapse of the plan to restore discipline by a military dictatorship; of the suspicion of betrayal to the interests of the Right which the negotiations brought upon Kerensky; of Lenin's deadly sarcasm that Kerensky was "a Kornilovist[4] who had accidently quarrelled with Kornilov"; of the revival of the Red Guard under the name of the Armed Workers' Militia, has already been told too often

[3] S. R. leader; Minister of Agriculture in the Provisional Government. [Editor's note.]

[4] General Lavr Kornilov was commander of the military forces. When he moved troops toward Petrograd in an apparent attempt to seize power, he was relieved of his command. [Editor's note.]

and too well to need recapitulation here. The Head of the Government, who now combined military with civil authority in his own person, could look for support neither on the Right nor on the Left, and was henceforth hurried, helpless on the stream, towards the approaching roar of the falls.

Meanwhile, the Social Revolutionary Minister of Agriculture, Chernov, had a long struggle over his bill to prohibit sale of land pending settlement of the land question. He succeeded in passing it when the Kadet Ministers resigned in July. Landlords were at this time destroying their own crops to keep them from the peasants, and the Provisional Government had still not put the law into force in September. Chernov then resigned from the Ministry. September showed a great increase in rural crimes of violence, but October beat all records. The disturbances were most intense in the regions of the minority nationalities, where, in some cases, the peasant movement began to merge with the strike movement of the urban workers. We now hear that Churches require special protection by the *Mirs*, that the lines of communication between the surplus-producing provinces and the towns are virtually cut, that stock is disappearing, and famine threatens the towns. Destruction was widespread. Libraries, works of art, bloodstock, conservatories, and experimental stations, were in many cases destroyed, animals hamstrung, houses burned, masters or agents sometimes murdered. It was now far more than a mere seizure of estates and property.

General Verkhovsky issued an order from the War Office on October 24th which declared that "ruin in the rear, destructive riots, burning of grain in transit, violence and atrocities, threaten the Front Line with hunger and cold, supplies of food and accoutrements being held up." The whole territory of the Republic was now divided into military areas, whose commanding officers were to co-operate with the civil Commissars. In his last days of power, Kerensky was ordering the suppression of disobedient Land Committees, exhorting Commissars to use military force, and, at last, preparing a decree for the legal expropriation of the landowners whom he could not protect.

The bread ration, which had been a pound a head per day in March, was reduced to three-quarters in October. The price of bread had been doubled in September, and the Minister of Supplies in the Coalition Government had resigned in consequence.

Three-quarters of a pound is a starvation diet for men to whom bread is the staff of life, as it was, and still is, in Russia. It has been calculated by Chamberlain that real wages in the second half of 1917 were less than two-thirds of what they were in the first half of 1916. The cities were full of queues, shortages, and discontent. In a pamphlet in September Lenin was demanding effective measures to ascertain who was plundering the Public Treasury, a progressive tax properly enforced, and—significantly—the firing squad for profiteers. "It is doubtful whether any revolutionary government can get on without capital punishment applied to exploiters," he wrote.

It was being demonstrated, not for the first time and not for the last time, that, in Chernov's words, "the peasantry is the real autocrat of Russia." For it was the peasantry—working unconsciously through its control of the fuel and food supply, and confronting its rulers with an ill-fed and disordered army and with a hungry mob of city workers—which brought down the Provisional Government.

Certain constitutional changes, including the proclamation of a Republic (which had been delayed till September 16th) and the dissolution of the Fourth Imperial Duma (which had been sitting at the March Revolution and had served as the basis of the Provisional Government), ended with the appointment of a Council of the Republic or Pre-Parliament, and the formation of the last of the coalitions of the Provisional Government. Sir George Buchanan, the British Ambassador, told his Government that the Bolsheviks "alone have a definite political programme and are a compact minority. . . . If the Government are not strong enough to put down the Bolsheviks by force, at the risk of breaking altogether with the Soviet, the only alternative will be a Bolshevik Government." In a few weeks there was a demand for the dissolution of the Pre-parliament and for the convening of a second all-Russian congress of Soviets, whose meeting was fixed for the day on which the Bolshevik revolution took place. The Pre-Parliament survived till its dispersal by soldiers on the fateful day of November 7th.

Early in October Kerensky made another attempt to secure the support of all the Socialist parties, including the Bolsheviks. He held a conference at which he said that he was willing to work for a transition to a new system of government, if they would take the responsibility of dissolving the coalition

War and Totalitarianism

with the propertied classes, represented by the Kadet ministers, and point out a person willing to form a new Provisional Government, "as I personally could not carry out the task conscientiously." But these overtures were not successful.

In the meanwhile the Germans were making their naval advance towards the Gulf of Finland and had occupied the island of Oesel. Since September, the foreign Embassies had been informed of the Government's intention to move from Petrograd to Moscow, which caused rumours of an intended surrender of the capital. Disorders among the troops in Finland had caused the Finns to throw themselves into the arms of Germany. Insurrection had broken out in Turkestan. The Allied Conference on war-aims, for which the Provisional Government had hoped, had been abandoned. Kerensky's attempt to secure his position in the capital by moving troops from the disaffected garrison to the front was abortive. As soon as they had formed for the march, the soldiers dispersed, so thoroughly that some units on arrival at the railway had already lost three-quarters of their effectives. On October 9th, Buchanan, as dean of the diplomatic corps, read to Kerensky and the other ministers a note from the British, French, and Italian ambassadors, warning the Government of the need of measures to restore order both in front and rear. The Soldiers' Committee election in October showed a sharp swing towards the Bolsheviks. Even the Cossack rank and file were moving in that direction. The municipal elections showed similar results, partly because all the garrison, including soldiers merely passing through Petrograd, recorded their votes. Soldiers from the front were declaring that, if peace were not made by a stated date in November, they would leave the trenches and make peace themselves. Officers were being deprived by their men of horses and arms, displaced from their functions, and even murdered. On November 3rd guards were posted by the Government to protect the Embassies in Petrograd.

The November Revolution, enormous in its ultimate significance, was, from the military standpoint, so easily achieved, and was so undramatic in itself, that it is natural to ask why insurrection was necessary. In October Bolshevik majorities were secured both in Moscow and Petrograd, and, on a superficial examination, it might seem that the cause was won, and that it was only necessary for the Soviets of the two capitals, now controlled by the party of Lenin, to carry out the peaceful assumption of power.

For the Western constitutionalist, accustomed to the constitutional game, and assuming that majorities will have their way, the answer may seem difficult. But Lenin was not a Western constitutionalist, and did not expect power to be automatically transferred by a change in the balance of votes in a popular assembly: though he might, and did, value such a change, as one of the indications that the balance of opinion—and therefore of opportunity for power—was changing. He had reasons now for believing that the transfer of power would be forestalled or resisted, unless it were clinched by accomplished facts: and that the moment was favourable for the accomplishing of those facts. But he was, in fact, always bent upon insurrection at the right moment, and the variation of tactics at different times merely meant that the right moment appeared to him nearer or more distant.

The reasons were first put before the Bolshevik Central Committee on September 28th, before majorities had been secured in the Soviets of Petrograd and Moscow. On this occasion, Kamenev moved the rejection of Lenin's proposal for the seizure of power, and succeeded in carrying the negative motion. In October, both the external and the internal situation had changed. The German naval advance had taken place: but mutinies had occurred in the German fleet nearer home, indicating to the sanguine temper of the revolutionaries the early advent of world-revolution. At the same time there were rumours of a peace between the Imperial Powers at the expense of Russia. The Provisional Government's plan to withdraw part of the Petrograd garrison, to make room for other troops less friendly to revolution, had been thwarted by a counter-order of the Petrograd Soviet, which had thus demonstrated the Government's weakness. Beside the electoral successes in the two capitals, the intensification of disturbances in the rural areas seemed to offer an opportunity. The Bolsheviks were politically in a strong position, having a legally permitted organisation and a score of newspapers, and the metropolitan Soviets and a majority of the masses in the capital on their side. An odd jumble of reasons, but the great strategist of revolution saw his chance, and backed it.

Lenin's resolution for armed insurrection within an early period was carried. But some prominent party-men, including—the names are interesting in view of later history—Rykov and Tomsky, were cool towards it, and Zinoviev and Kamenev[5] voted against. The two latter prepared a written protest, arguing that there was no justification for the Party to stake its existence on a rising. They would get one-third or more of the seats in the Constituent Assembly, and the Constituent Assembly, when it met, would be obliged to seek support in the Soviets. Neither the majority of the people of Russia, nor the majority of the international proletariat, was with the Bolsheviks, and the forces of the opposing parties were stronger than they appeared to be. The immediate task, they urged, was to use the Congress of Soviets, summoned for an early date in November, to consolidate the proletarian party and its organisation, and to establish close relations with the railway, post-office, and telegraph workers and with bank employees. In other words, they desired a peaceful and democratic development of the Revolution, and took their stand upon the strictly Marxian ground that insurrection, when the time is not ripe for it, is mere adventurism. This protest of the two dissentients was communicated to the non-party newspapers, which aroused great indignation as a betrayal of plans. They also demanded the convocation of a *plenum* of the Central Committee to review the decision. Lenin described the action of the pair in publishing their protest as "strike-breaking"—an evident appeal to the feeling of working-men against the blackleg—and threatened to move their expulsion from the party. Evidently the Government was now aware of the intention to make an early insurrection, though the date for it was not yet fixed. It could no longer be supposed that the preparations were being made against the possibility of German attack.

It seems that the dissentient pair might have done as they pleased if they had not published their protest. The case is interesting as an illustration of the degree of liberty enjoyed by members of the party, within the party: a matter which subsequently played a part in the controversies between Stalin and Trotsky. Another illustration of this liberty was given by the division in the party over the question of boycotting the Pre-Parliament which was set up by the Democratic Conference of September to give a parliamentary basis of government, pending the convocation of the always deferred Constituent Assembly. Lenin, Trotsky, and Stalin stood for boycott, and the rank and file of the party appear to have been with them. But the advocates of co-operation, including

Kamenev, carried their point in the Central Committee. (October 31, 1917.) The Bolshevik members appeared in the Pre-Parliament, but they withdrew on the fourth day of its sitting.

The Congress of Soviets had been summoned to meet on November 2nd, but it was postponed to November 7th. The plan of the leaders was to confront this assembly with the accomplished fact of the seizure of power.

Another meeting of the Central Committee of the Party appointed a military political center consisting of Sverdlov, Stalin, Bubnov, Uritsky and Dzerzhinsky. The Military Revolutionary Committee of the Petrograd Soviet, which had been created to co-operate in the protection of the capital against the German advance, already included Sverdlov, Uritsky and others of the most active Bolsheviks.[6] It had appointed its own Commissars to each unit of the Petrograd garrison, and to each arsenal and magazine where arms were stored. By November 2nd these Commissars were in control of all arms and ammunition. On November 5th the garrison of the Peter and Paul Fortress undertook to accept orders only from the Military Revolutionary Committee: so the strategic position of that Committee, acting in complete accord with the Bolshevists, was similar to that in which the Bolshevik Party stood before its losses in July. The Peter and Paul Fortress, along with the Kronverksky Arsenal, which was also in Bolshevik hands, occupies a commanding position on the river above the point at which the Great Neva separates from the Lesser. The western end is opposite the Winter Palace, which was the headquarters of the Government and of Kerensky himself. A second Bolshevik stronghold was the workers' district known as Viborg, in the north-eastern part of the city, above the island on which the Fortress of Peter and Paul stands. The Military Revolutionary Committee had its headquarters further up the river, in Smolny, protected by machine-guns and artillery.

All the preparations were conducted in the full light of publicity. A sort of review was held on November 4th: shooting drill was going on. On November 5th the Viborg District Soviet requisitioned cars and first-aid supplies, and the working-women formed Red Cross divisions. It was not till the night of November 5th—6th that the Government decided to take legal proceedings against the Military Revolu-

[5] All these men were eventually purged by Stalin after holding important positions of leadership in the U.S.S.R. [Editor's note.]

[6] Trotsky was the leading figure in the Military Revolutionary Committee. [Editor's note.]

War and Totalitarianism

tionary Committee, to suppress Bolshevik newspapers, and to summon reliable troops: and the news of the decision was at once carried, through the sentries on duty at the official headquarters beside the Winter Palace, to the Bolshevik headquarters. The Government ordered the cruiser *Aurora* to leave the Neva: and the Military Revolutionary Committee countermanded the order; the Government broke up the Bolshevik printing plant and sealed the office: and the Bolsheviks sent troops and restarted the newspaper. The passing along of the news by the sentries on duty, the slipping away of comrades through the November darkness to carry it to Smolny, and the child-like outbursts of Lenin's laughter, when he heard of the restarting of the newspaper, stand out vividly to our imaginations.

On the early morning of November 7th, without resistance, railway stations, telephone exchanges, telegraph and post-offices, lighting-plant, waterworks and other important buildings in Petrograd were seized. The reasons for the Government's long inactivity are made plain by a fact recorded by Buchanan. During the seizure of the buildings, the Cossacks received an order to come out, and disobeyed it. If other evidence of Kerensky's isolation were needed, it is furnished by the fact that his garrison for the Winter Palace, the seat of his government, consisted of military cadets and a shock-company of a Women's Battalion. There were guns but, when the attack came, the gunners could not or would not fire them. Provisions were forgotten. There were plenty of troops cantoned in and about Petrograd—if they had been willing to act: but those of them who were not sympathetic with the Bolsheviks were hostile or indifferent to the Government.

At 10 A.M. on November 7, 1917, the message was broadcast "The Provisional Government is overthrown. The State power has passed into the hands of the Military Revolutionary Committee." Nothing was said about the Soviets in this message: perhaps because the Congress did not meet till that evening. But the insurrection had been called in the name of the Soviets, and the Military Revolutionary Committee was itself a Committee of the Petrograd Soviet.

The members of the Congress of the Soviets were gathering throughout the day, but the session was not begun until nine in the evening, under the name of the Congress of the Soviet Dictatorship. Of the 615 delegates having votes who were present at the opening, 390 were Bolsheviks or Bolshevik sympathizers, presumably Social Revolutionaries of the Left. This Left wing of the Social Revolutionary Party formed a substantial minority of the whole, which had split off from the majority in August over the question of support to the Provisional Government. An eye-witness describes the Congress as consisting largely of young men from the Baltic Fleet and from the front. Most of the peasant delegates were soldiers. Conspicuous by their absence were the middle-aged intellectuals, the old type of peasant with the long beard, and the old Socialist Party leaders. Such was the assembly which assumed the power which the Tsar Of All The Russias had dropped in March 1917.

The Right wing of the Congress protested against the insurrection, and one speaker, Dan, prophesied its collapse and called for a coalition of Socialist parties. Seventy of its members then withdrew and, in conjunction with other moderate Socialists, formed a "Committee for the salvation of the country and the revolution," which became the main organised centre of opposition to the Bolsheviks, with affiliated Committees in the provinces.

Before the dawn of the 8th, news arrived of the capture of the Winter Palace and of the Ministers, except Kerensky, who had left the preceding day. The final capture was an entry, rather than a storm.

How unimpressively, and almost like the finish of a children's game, the great consummation arrived, appears from various anecdotes. The telephone girls, scampering out of the captured telephone exchange—not so much, it appears, from panic as from unwillingness to co-operate with the captors—recall the chorus of Opera Bouffe. On the later afternoon of the 7th, which has passed for ever into the world's calendars as the day of Revolution, the fashionable people were on the Nevsky Prospect as usual, laughing together, and saying that the Bolshevik power would not last more than three days. Rich people in their carriages were scolding the soldiers, and the soldiers "argued feebly, with embarrassed grins."

The news of the capture of the Winter Palace and the Ministers reached the Congress. Resolutions were passed "that the Provisional Government is deposed: that the Congress assumes power: that the Soviet Government proposes immediate peace. It will transfer land to the peasantry, establish control over production, promptly summon a Constituent Assembly; and it guarantees the rights of the nations of Russia to self-determination."

On the evening of the same day, November 8th, it met again; passed, with emotion, the resolution for peace; and then proceeded immediately to agrarian legislation. It voted down a proposal for a coalition, and nominated a purely Bolshevik Council of People's Commissars. The list included Lenin, without portfolio, Rykov for the Interior, Trotsky for foreign affairs, Stalin for nationalities, Lunacharsky for education. It did not include Kamenev or Zinoviev, the two Bolshevik dissentients on the issue of insurrection, nor any of the Social Revolutionaries who had formed part of the Presidium in the Congress of the Soviet Dictatorship: but we shall see that the latter continued for several months to support the Revolutionary Government, and virtually dictated the earliest legislation on agrarian reform.

The Cadets of the Military Schools occupied the Central Telephone Exchange of Petrograd on November 11th: but within a few hours the Bolsheviks were again in possession of the whole city. Kerensky brought a force under General Krasnov to attack the capital. The soldiers melted away, as those of General Ivanov and Krymov had in similar circumstances, and by November 14th, Kerensky was in flight, having narrowly escaped from being delivered up by his Cossacks. In the meanwhile, General Kornilov had escaped from the lenient custody in which he was held by the Provisional Government, and joined Kaledin in the south, where the two laid the foundation of the future civil war. In Moscow there was a fierce struggle for the possession of the Kremlin, ending in the establishment of Bolshevik military control. At General Headquarters at the front, the Commander-in-Chief, General Dukhonin, refused to open negotiations for an armistice, and was murdered by soldiers.

A Revolutionary Government had been established: but none knew better than Lenin that it was easier to establish than to maintain.

COMMUNIST PARTY

THE INFALLIBILITY OF COMMUNIST THEORY AND LEADERSHIP

What view do Soviet Communists take of the revolutions that made Soviet Communist rule possible? The selection that follows is taken from a Soviet history of the Communist Party of the U.S.S.R. It was published in 1936.

To read this selection with the proper understanding you must remember that Communists use history in two ways. In trying to come to power they propagandize a view of history that makes Communist success appear to be an inevitable result of the unfolding of broad, impersonal historical forces. After they come to power they write history to prove that their success was inevitable, to glorify current leaders, to justify current policies, and to win support for future objectives. History—like art, music, and at times even science—is for them simply a means to a political end. It is a pliable instrument of Communist rule rather than an objective view of the past.

What you will read in this selection is an illustration of this fact about Soviet historiography. The book from which the selection was taken was written by

Stalin's handpicked Communist "historians." It was used in indoctrination courses by Communist parties all over the world until Khrushchev called for another rewriting of history after Stalin's death in 1953.

Note with care how the Communist approach to history and the specific circumstances of 1936 distort this interpretation of the revolutions of 1917. Watch particularly for the exaggeration of the part Stalin played in the revolutions and for the treatment here of Leon Trotsky, Lev Kamenev, and Gregory Zinoviev. In the November 1917 revolution, all three served with Lenin — as did Stalin — in the directorate of the Bolshevik Party, the "Politburo." After Lenin died in 1924 all three were rivals with Stalin for leadership of the Party. Trotsky, second only in importance to Lenin in making the revolution in 1917, was the first to be purged by Stalin; by 1928 Trotsky had been forced out of the Communist Party and out of the Soviet Union. Stalin dishonored Kamanev and Zinoviev in 1927 as "Trotskyites" and finally had them executed in 1936. The struggles of the 1920's and 1930's colored the view of 1917 that was presented in 1936 in the Stalinist *History of the Communist Party of the Soviet Union.*

In reading the following selection from that 1936 *History,* watch for ways in which its interpretations differ from those of Chamberlin and Maynard. Which interpretations here agree with those of Chamberlin and Maynard? Try to decide what you can accept as reliable, objective fact and what seems merely suspect interpretation in this reading. (Interpretations are likely to be suspect if they rely on the use of unflattering adjectives and the repetition of emotional generalizations without offering solid factual evidence to support either.) On which revolution does the Communist history seem to offer the sounder interpretation, that of March or that of November?

Read the selection that follows this one and then come back to reexamine this Communist interpretation. Is it possible that the Stalinist history's five reasons for success in November 1917 are sound even though the authors have slanted their narrative account? How well do the five conclusions harmonize with Marx's conception of history?

The war had already been in progress for three years. Millions of people had been killed in the war, or had died of wounds or from epidemics caused by war conditions. The bourgeoisie and landlords were making fortunes out of the war. But the workers and peasants were suffering increasing hardship and privation. The war was undermining the economic life of Russia. Some fourteen million able-bodied men had been torn from economic pursuits and drafted into the army. Mills and factories were coming to a standstill. The crop area had diminished owing to a shortage of labour. The population and the soldiers at the front went hungry, barefoot and naked. The war was eating up the resources of the country.

The tsarist army suffered defeat after defeat. The German artillery deluged the tsarist troops with shells, while the tsarist army lacked guns, shells and

From Central Committee of the C. P. S. U. (B.), *History of the Communist Party of the Soviet Union (Bolsheviks): Short Course,* original edition 1936 (New York, 1939), pp. 173–186, 192–195, 198–210, 212–214. Reprinted by permission of International Publishers Co., Inc. Copyright © 1939, International Publishers.

even rifles. Sometimes three soldiers had to share one rifle. . . .

Dissatisfaction also began to spread to the Russian imperialist bourgeoisie. It was incensed by the fact that rascals like Rasputin, who were obviously working for a separate peace with Germany, lorded it at the tsar's court. . . .

The Mensheviks and Socialist-Revolutionaries tried to direct this incipient revolutionary movement into the channels the liberal bourgeoisie needed. The Mensheviks proposed that a procession of workers to the State Duma be organized on February 14 (February 27), the day of its opening. But the working-class masses followed the Bolsheviks, and went, not to the Duma, but to a demonstration. . . .

The practical work of the Bolshevik Party at that time was directed by the Bureau of the Central Committee of our Party which had its quarters in Petrograd and was headed by Comrade Molotov. On February 26 (March 11) the Bureau of the Central Committee issued a manifesto calling for the continuation of the armed struggle against tsardom and the formation of a Provisional Revolutionary Government.

On February 27 (March 12) the troops in Petrograd refused to fire on the workers and began to line up with the people in revolt. The number of soldiers who had joined the revolt by the morning of February 27 was still no more than 10,000, but by the evening it already exceeded 60,000.

The workers and soldiers who had risen in revolt began to arrest tsarist ministers and generals and to free revolutionaries from jail. The released political prisoners joined the revolutionary struggle.

In the streets, shots were still being exchanged with police and gendarmes posted with machine guns in the attics of houses. But the troops rapidly went over to the side of the workers, and this decided the fate of the tsarist autocracy.

When the news of the victory of the revolution in Petrograd spread to other towns and to the front, the workers and soldiers everywhere began to depose the tsarist officials.

The February bourgeois-democratic revolution had won.[1]. . .

While the Bolsheviks were directly leading the struggle of the masses in the streets, the compromising parties, the Mensheviks and Socialist-Revolutionaries, were seizing the seats in the Soviets, and building up a majority there. This was partly facilitated by the fact that the majority of the leaders of the Bolshevik Party were in prison or exile (Lenin was in exile abroad and Stalin and Sverdlov in banishment in Siberia) while the Mensheviks and Socialist-Revolutionaries were freely promenading the streets of Petrograd. The result was that the Petrograd Soviet and its Executive Committee were headed by representatives of the Compromising parties: Mensheviks and Socialist-Revolutionaries. This was also the case in Moscow and a number of other cities. Only in Ivanovo-Voznesensk, Krasnoyarsk and a few other places did the Bolsheviks have a majority in the Soviets from the very outset.

The armed people—the workers and soldiers—sent their representatives to the Soviet as to an organ of power of the people. They thought and believed that the Soviet of Workers' and Soldiers' Deputies would carry out all the demands of the revolutionary people, and that, in the first place, peace would be concluded.

But the unwarranted trustfulness of the workers and soldiers served them in evil stead. The Socialist-Revolutionaries and Mensheviks had not the slightest intention of terminating the war, of securing peace. They planned to take advantage of the revolution to continue the war. As to the revolution and the revolutionary demands of the people, the Socialist-Revolutionaries and the Mensheviks considered that the revolution was already over, and that the task now was to seal it and to pass to a "normal" constitutional existence side by side with the bourgeoisie. The Socialist-Revolutionary and Menshevik leaders of the Petrograd Soviet therefore did their utmost to shelve the question of terminating the war, to shelve the question of peace, and to hand over the power to the bourgeoisie.

On February 27 (March 12), 1917, the liberal members of the Fourth State Duma, as the result of a backstairs agreement with the Socialist-Revolutionary and Manshevik leaders, set up a Provisional Com-

[1] The revolutions of 1917 occurred in February and October by the old-style calendar then in use in Russia, in March and November by the western calendar, which was introduced in Russia by the Bolsheviks. In Russia the first revolution is called the "February Revolution" and the second the "October Revolution." [Editor's note.]

mittee of the State Duma, headed by Rodzyanko, the President of the Duma, a landlord and a monarchist. And a few days later, the Provisional Committee of the State Duma and the Socialist-Revolutionary and Menshevik leaders of the Executive Committee of the Soviet of Workers' and Soldiers' Deputies, acting secretly from the Bolsheviks, came to an agreement to form a new government of Russia — a bourgeois Provisional Government, headed by Prince Lvov, the man whom, prior to the February Revolution, even Tsar Nicholas II was about to make the Prime Minister of his government. The Provisional Government included Milyukov, the head of the Constitutional-Democrats, Guchkov, the head of the Octobrists, and other prominent representatives of the capitalist class, and, as the representative of the "democracy," the Socialist-Revolutionary Kerensky.

And so it was that the Socialist-Revolutionary and Menshevik leaders of the Executive Committee of the Soviet surrendered the power to the bourgeoisie. Yet when the Soviet of Workers' and Soldiers' Deputies learned of this, its majority formally approved of the action of the Socialist-Revolutionary and Menshevik leaders, despite the protest of the Bolsheviks.

Thus a new state power arose in Russia, consisting, as Lenin said, of representatives of the "bourgeoisie and landlords who had become bourgeois."

But alongside of the bourgeois government there existed another power — the Soviet of Workers' and Soldiers' Deputies. The soldier deputies on the Soviet were mostly peasants who had been mobilized for the war. The Soviet of Workers' and Soldiers' Deputies was an organ of the alliance of workers and peasants against the tsarist regime, and at the same time it was an organ of their power, an organ of the dictatorship of the working class and the peasantry.

The result was a peculiar interlocking of two powers, of two dictatorships: the dictatorship of the bourgeoisie, represented by the Provisional Government, and the dictatorship of the proletariat and peasantry, represented by the Soviet of Workers' and Soldiers' Deputies.

The result was a *dual power.* . . .

The task that confronted the Bolshevik Party was, by patient work of explanation, to open the eyes of the masses to the imperialist character of the Provisional Government, to expose the treachery of the Socialist-Revolutionaries and Mensheviks and to show that peace could not be secured unless the Provisional Government were replaced by a government of Soviets.

And to this work the Bolshevik Party addressed itself with the utmost energy.

It resumed the publication of its legal periodicals. The newspaper *Pravda* appeared in Petrograd five days after the February Revolution, and the *Sotsial—Demokrat* in Moscow a few days later. The Party was assuming leadership of the masses, who were losing their confidence in the liberal bourgeoisie and in the Mensheviks and Socialist-Revolutionaries. It patiently explained to the soldiers and peasants the necessity of acting jointly with the working class. It explained to them that the peasants would secure neither peace nor land unless the revolution were further developed and the bourgeois Provisional Government replaced by a government of Soviets. . . .

After the February Revolution, the organizations of the Bolshevik Party, which had worked illegally under the extremely difficult conditions of tsardom, emerged from underground and began to develop political and organizational work openly. The membership of the Bolshevik organizations at that time did not exceed 40,000 or 45,000. But these were all staunch revolutionaries, steeled in the struggle. The Party Committees were reorganized on the principle of democratic centralism. All Party bodies, from top to bottom, were made elective.

When the Party began its legal existence, differences within its ranks became apparent. Kamenev and several workers of the Moscow organization, for example, Rykov, Bubnov and Nogin, held a semi-Menshevik position of conditionally supporting the Provisional Government and the policy of the partisans of the war. Stalin, who had just returned from exile, Molotov and others, together with the majority of the Party, upheld a policy of no-confidence in the Provisional Government, opposed the partisans of the war, and called for an active struggle for peace, a struggle against the imperialist war. Some of the Party workers vacillated, which was a manifestation of their political backwardness, a consequence of long years of imprisonment or exile.

The absence of the leader of the Party, Lenin, was felt.

On April 3 (16), 1917, after a long period of exile, Lenin returned to Russia.

Lenin's arrival was of tremendous importance to the Party and the revolution.

While still in Switzerland, Lenin, upon receiving the first news of the revolution, had written his "Letters From Afar" to the Party and to the working class of Russia, in which he said:

Workers, you have displayed marvels of proletarian heroism, the heroism of the people, in the civil war against tsardom. You must now display marvels of organization, organization of the proletariat and of the whole people, in order to prepare the way for your victory in the second stage of the revolution. (Lenin, *Selected Works*, Vol. VI, p. 11.)

Lenin arrived in Petrograd on the night of April 3. Thousands of workers, soldiers and sailors assembled at the Finland Railway Station and in the station square to welcome him. Their enthusiasm as Lenin alighted from the train was indescribable. They lifted their leader shoulder high and carried him to the main waiting room of the station. There the Mensheviks Chkheidze and Skobelev launched into speeches of "welcome" on behalf of the Petrograd Soviet, in which they "expressed the hope" that they and Lenin would find a "common language." But Lenin did not stop to listen; sweeping past them, he went out to the masses of workers and soldiers. Mounting an armoured car, he delivered his famous speech in which he called upon the masses to fight for the victory of the Socialist revolution. "Long live the Socialist revolution!" were the words with which Lenin concluded this first speech after long years of exile. . . .

In the political field, Lenin proposed the transition from a parliamentary republic to a republic of Soviets. This was an important step forward in the theory and practice of Marxism. Hitherto, Marxist theoreticians had regarded the parliamentary republic as the best political form of transition to Socialism. Now Lenin proposed to replace the parliamentary republic by a Soviet republic as the most suitable form of political organization of society in the period of transition from capitalism to Socialism. . . .

This meant that Lenin was not calling for a revolt against the Provisional Government, which at that moment enjoyed the confidence of the Soviets, that he was not demanding its overthrow, but that he wanted, by means of explanatory and recruiting work, to win a majority in the Soviets, to change the policy of the Soviets, and through the Soviets to alter the composition and policy of the government. . . .

On June 3 (16), 1917, the First All-Russian Congress of Soviets met. The Bolsheviks were still in the minority in the Soviets; they had a little over 100 delegates at this congress, compared with 700 or 800 Mensheviks, Socialist-Revolutionaries and others.

At the First Congress of Soviets, the Bolsheviks insistently stressed the fatal consequences of compromise with the bourgeoisie and exposed the imperialist character of the war. Lenin made a speech at the congress in which he showed the correctness of the Bolshevik line and declared that only a government of Soviets could give bread to the working people, land to the peasants, secure peace and lead the country out of chaos. . . .

Nevertheless, the Provisional Government received the support of the First Congress of the Soviets and decided to continue the imperialist policy. On that very day, June 18, the Provisional Government, in obedience to the wishes of the British and French imperialists, drove the soldiers at the front to take the offensive. The bourgeoisie regarded this as the only means of putting an end to the revolution. In the event of the success of the offensive, the bourgeoisie hoped to take the whole power into its own hands, to push the Soviets out of the arena, and to crush the Bolsheviks. Again, in the event of its failure, the entire blame could be thrown upon the Bolsheviks by accusing them of disintegrating the army.

There could be no doubt that the offensive would fail. And fail it did. The soldiers were worn out, they did not understand the purpose of the offensive, they had no confidence in their officers who were alien to them, there was a shortage of artillery and shells. All this made the failure of the offensive a foregone conclusion.

The news of the offensive at the front, and then of its collapse, roused the capital. The indignation of the workers and soldiers knew no bounds. It became apparent that when the Provisional Government proclaimed a policy of peace it was hoodwinking the people, and that it wanted to continue the imperialist war. It became apparent that the All-Russian Central Executive Committee of the Soviets and the Petrograd Soviet were unwilling or unable to check the criminal deeds of the Provisional Government and themselves trailed in its wake.

The revolutionary indignation of the Petrograd workers and soldiers boiled over. On July 3 (16) spontaneous demonstrations started in the Vyborg District of Petrograd. They continued all day. The separate demonstrations grew into a huge general armed demonstration demanding the transfer of power to the Soviets. The Bolshevik Party was opposed to armed action at that time, for it considered that the revolutionary crisis had not yet matured, that the army and the provinces were not yet prepared to support an uprising in the capital, and that an isolated and premature rising might only make it easier for the counter-revolutionaries to crush the vanguard of the revolution. But when it became obviously impossible to keep the masses from demonstrating, the Party resolved to participate in the demonstration in order to lend it a peaceful and organized character. This the Bolshevik Party succeeded in doing. Hundreds of thousands of men and women marched to the headquarters of the Petrograd Soviet and the All-Russian Central Executive Committee of Soviets, where they demanded that the Soviets take the power into their own hands, break with the imperialist bourgeoisie, and pursue an active peace policy.

Notwithstanding the pacific character of the demonstration, reactionary units—detachments of officers and cadets—were brought out against it. The streets of Petrograd ran with the blood of workers and soldiers. The most ignorant and counter-revolutionary units of the army were summoned from the front to suppress the workers.

After suppressing the demonstration of workers and soldiers, the Mensheviks and Socialist-Revolutionaries, in alliance with the bourgeoisie and Whiteguard generals, fell upon the Bolshevik Party. The *Pravda* premises were wrecked. *Pravda, Soldatskaya Pravda (Soldiers' Truth)* and a number of other Bolshevik newspapers were suppressed. A worker named Voinov was killed by cadets in the street merely for selling *Listok Pravdy (Pravda Bulletin)*. Disarming of the Red Guards began. Revolutionary units of the Petrograd garrison were withdrawn from the capital and dispatched to the trenches. Arrests were carried out in the rear and at the front. On July 7 a warrant was issued for Lenin's arrest. A number of prominent members of the Bolshevik Party were arrested. The Trud printing plant, where the Bolshevik publications were printed, was wrecked. The Procurator of the Petrograd Court of Sessions announced that Lenin and a number of other Bolsheviks were being charged with "high treason" and the organization of an armed uprising. The charge against Lenin was fabricated at the headquarters of General Denikin, and was based on the testimony of spies and agents-provocateurs.

Thus the coalition Provisional Government—which included such leading representatives of the Mensheviks and Socialist-Revolutionaries as Tsereteli, Skobelev, Kerensky and Chernov—sank to the depths of downright imperialism and counter-revolution. Instead of a policy of peace, it had adopted the policy of continuing war. Instead of protecting the democratic rights of the people, it had adopted the policy of nullifying these rights and suppressing the workers and soldiers by force of arms.

What Guchkov and Milyukov, the representatives of the bourgeoisie, had hesitated to do, was done by the "socialists" Kerensky and Tsereteli, Chernov and Skobelev.

The dual power had come to an end.

It ended in favour of the bourgeoisie, for the whole power had passed into the hands of the Provisional Government, while the Soviets, with their Socialist-Revolutionary and Menshevik leaders, had become an appendage of the Provisional Government.

The peaceful period of the revolution had ended, for now the bayonet had been placed on the agenda.

In view of the changed situation, the Bolshevik Party decided to change its tactics. It went underground, arranged for a safe hiding place for its leader, Lenin, and began to prepare for an uprising with the object of overthrowing the power of the bourgeoisie by force of arms and setting up the power of the Soviets.

The Sixth Congress of the Bolshevik Party met in Petrograd in the midst of a frenzied campaign of Bolshevik-baiting in the bourgeois and petty-bourgeois press. It assembled ten years after the Fifth (London) Congress and five years after the Prague Conference of the Bolsheviks. The congress, which was held secretly, sat from July 26 to August 3, 1917. . . .

The Sixth Congress admitted the *Mezhrayontsi* and their leader, Trotsky, into the Party. They were a small group that had existed in Petrograd since 1913 and consisted of Trotskyite-Mensheviks and a number of former Bolsheviks who had split away from the Party. During the war, the *Mezhrayontsi* were a Centrist organization. They fought the Bolsheviks, but in many respects disagreed with the Mensheviks, thus occupying an intermediate, centrist, vacillating position. During the Sixth Party Congress the *Mezhrayontsi* declared that they were in agreement with the Bolsheviks on all points and requested admission to the Party. The request was granted by the congress in the expectation that they would in time become real Bolsheviks. Some of the *Mezhrayontsi*, Volodarsky and Uritsky, for example, actually did become Bolsheviks. As to Trotsky and some of his close friends, they, as it later became apparent, had joined not to work in the interests of the Party, but to disrupt and destroy it from within.

The decisions of the Sixth Congress were all intended to prepare the proletariat and the poorest peasantry for an armed uprising, for the Socialist revolution. . . .

Having seized all power, the bourgeoisie began preparations to destroy the now weakened Soviets and to set up an open counter-revolutionary dictatorship. The millionaire Ryabushinsky insolently declared that the way out of the situation was "for the gaunt hand of famine, of destitution of the people, to seize the false friends of the people—the democratic Soviets and Committees—by the throat." At the front, courts-martial wreaked savage vengeance on the soldiers, and meted out death sentences wholesale. On August 3, 1917, General Kornilov, the Commander-in-Chief, demanded the introduction of the death penalty behind the lines as well. . . .

The counter-revolutionary General Kornilov bluntly demanded that "the Committees and Soviets be abolished."

Bankers, merchants and manufacturers flocked to Kornilov at General Headquarters, promising him money and support.

Representatives of the "Allies," Britain and France,

also came to General Kornilov, demanding that action against the revolution be not delayed.

General Kornilov's plot against the revolution was coming to a head.

Kornilov made his preparations openly. In order to distract attention, the conspirators started a rumour that the Bolsheviks were preparing an uprising in Petrograd to take place on August 27—the end of the first six months of the revolution. The Provisional Government, headed by Kerensky, furiously attacked the Bolsheviks, and intensified the terror against the proletarian party. At the same time, General Kornilov massed troops in order to move them against Petrograd, abolish the Soviets and set up a military dictatorship.

Kornilov had come to a preliminary agreement with Kerensky regarding his counter-revolutionary action. But no sooner had Kornilov's action begun than Kerensky made an abrupt right-about-face and dissociated himself from his ally. Kerensky feared that the masses who would rise against the Kornilovites and crush them would at the same time sweep away Kerensky's bourgeois government as well, unless it at once dissociated itself from the Kornilov affair.

On August 25 Kornilov moved the Third Mounted Corps under the command of General Krymov against Petrograd, declaring that he intended to "save the fatherland." In face of the Kornilov revolt, the Central Committee of the Bolshevik Party called upon the workers and soldiers to put up active armed resistance to the counter-revolution. The workers hurriedly began to arm and prepared to resist. The Red Guard detachments grew enormously during these days. The trade unions mobilized their members. The revolutionary military units in Petrograd were also held in readiness for battle. Trenches were dug around Petrograd, barbed wire entanglements erected, and the railway tracks leading to the city were torn up. Several thousand armed sailors arrived from Kronstadt to defend the city. Delegates were sent to the "Savage Division" which was advancing on Petrograd; when these delegates explained the purpose of Kornilov's action to the Caucasian mountaineers of whom the "Savage Division" was made up, they refused to advance. Agitators were also dispatched to other Kornilov units. Wherever there was danger, Revolutionary Committees and headquarters were set up to fight Kornilov.

In those days the mortally terrified Socialist-Revolutionary and Menshevik leaders, Kerensky among them, turned for protection to the Bolsheviks, for they were convinced that the Bolsheviks were the only effective force in the capital that was capable of routing Kornilov.

But while mobilizing the masses to crush the Kornilov revolt, the Bolsheviks did not discontinue their struggle against the Kerensky government. They exposed the government of Kerensky, the Mensheviks and the Socialist-Revolutionaries, to the masses, pointing out that their whole policy was in effect assisting Kornilov's counter-revolutionary plot.

The result of these measures was that the Kornilov revolt was crushed. General Krymov committed suicide. Kornilov and his fellow-conspirators, Denikin and Lukomsky, were arrested. (Very soon, however, Kerensky had them released.)

The rout of the Kornilov revolt revealed in a flash the relative strength of the revolution and the counter-revolution. It showed that the whole counter-revolutionary camp was doomed, from the generals and the Constitutional-Democratic Party to the Mensheviks and Socialist-Revolutionaries who had become entangled in the meshes of the bourgeosie. It became obvious that the influence of the Mensheviks and Socialist-Revolutionaries among the masses had been completely undermined by the policy of prolonging the unbearable strain of the war, and by the economic chaos caused by the protracted war.

The defeat of the Kornilov revolt further showed that the Bolshevik Party had grown to be the decisive force of the revolution and was capable of foiling any attempt at counter-revolution. Our Party was not yet the ruling party, but during the Kornilov days it acted as the real ruling power, for its instructions were unhesitatingly carried out by the workers and soldiers.

The months of September and October 1917 witnessed a tremendous increase in the number of seizures of landed estates by the peasants. Unauthorized ploughing of the fields of landlords became widespread. The peasants had taken the road of revolution and neither coaxing nor punitive expeditions could any longer halt them.

The tide of revolution was rising.

There ensued a period of revival of the Soviets, of a change in their composition, their *bolshevization*. Factories, mills and military units held new elections and sent to the Soviets representatives of the Bolshevik Party in place of Mensheviks and Socialist-Revolutionaries. On August 31, the day following the victory over Kornilov, the Petrograd Soviet endorsed the Bolshevik policy. The old Menshevik and Socialist-Revolutionary Presidium of the Petrograd Soviet, headed by Chkheidze, resigned, thus clearing the way for the Bolsheviks.[2] On September 5, the Moscow Soviet of Workers' Deputies went over to the Bolsheviks. The Socialist-Revolutionary and Menshevik Presidium of the Moscow Soviet also resigned and left the way clear for the Bolsheviks.

This meant that the chief conditions for a successful uprising were now ripe.

The slogan "All power to the Soviets!" was again on the order of the day. . . .

At the same time, the Bolsheviks made intensive preparations for the convocation of the Second Congress of Soviets, in which they expected to have a majority. Under the pressure of the Bolshevik Soviets, and notwithstanding the subterfuges of the Mensheviks and Socialist-Revolutionaries on the All-Russian Central Executive Committee, the Second All-Russian Congress of Soviets was called for the second half of October 1917. . . .

The Bolsheviks began intensive preparations for the uprising. Lenin declared that, having secured a majority in the Soviets of Workers' and Soldiers' Deputies in both the capitals—Moscow and Petrograd—the Bolsheviks could and should take the state power into their own hands. Reviewing the path that had been traversed, Lenin stressed the fact that "the majority of the people are *for* us." In his articles and letters to the Central Committee and the Bolshevik organizations, Lenin outlined a detailed plan for the uprising showing how the army units, the navy and the Red Guards should be used, what key positions in Petrograd should be seized in order to ensure the success of the uprising, and so forth.

On October 7, Lenin secretly arrived in Petrograd from Finland. On October 10, 1917, the historic meeting of the Central Committee of the Party took

[2]The account carefully avoids mentioning that Trotsky became Chairman of the Petrograd Soviet at this point. [Editor's note.]

place at which it was decided to launch the armed uprising within the next few days. . . .

Two members of the Central Committee, Kamenev and Zinoviev, spoke and voted against this historic decision. Like the Mensheviks, they dreamed of a bourgeois parliamentary republic, and slandered the working class by asserting that it was not strong enough to carry out a Socialist revolution, that it was not mature enough to take power.

Although at this meeting Trotsky did not vote against the resolution directly,[3] he moved an amendment which would have reduced the chances of the uprising to nought and rendered it abortive. He proposed that the uprising should not be started before the Second Congress of Soviets met, a proposal which meant delaying the uprising, divulging its date, and forewarning the Provisional Government. . . .

On the instructions of the Central Committee of the Party, a *Revolutionary Military Committee* of the Petrograd Soviet was set up.[4] This body became the legally functioning headquarters of the uprising. . . .

On October 16 an enlarged meeting of the Central Committee of the Party was held. This meeting elected a *Party Centre,* headed by Comrade Stalin, to direct the uprising. This Party Centre was the leading core of the Revolutionary Military Committee of the Petrograd Soviet and had practical direction of the whole uprising.

At the meeting of the Central Committee the capitulators Zinoviev and Kamenev again opposed the uprising. Meeting with a rebuff, they came out openly in the press against the uprising, against the Party. On October 18 the Menshevik newspaper, *Novaya Zhizn*, printed a statement by Kamenev and Zinoviev declaring that the Bolsheviks were making preparations for an uprising, and that they (Kamenev and Zinoviev) considered it an adventurous gamble. Kamenev and Zinoviev thus disclosed to the enemy the decision of the Central Committee regarding the uprising, they revealed that an uprising had been

---

[3] He *supported* it. There are so many slantings of facts in this account that no attempt is made to correct all of them. This serves as an example of what to watch for in your own critical reading. [Editor's note].

[4] The account carefully avoids pointing out that Trotsky, as Chairman of the Petrograd Soviet, was also Chairman of this Committee, which functioned as a kind of "general staff" of the Bolshevik Revolution. [Editor's note].

planned to take place within a few days. This was treachery. Lenin wrote in this connection: "Kamenev and Zinoviev have *betrayed* the decision of the Central Committee of their Party on the armed uprising to Rodzyanko and Kerensky." Lenin put before the Central Committee the question of Zinoviev's and Kamenev's expulsion from the Party.

Forewarned by the traitors, the enemies of the revolution at once began to take measures to prevent the uprising and to destroy the directing staff of the revolution—the Bolshevik Party. The Provisional Government called a secret meeting which decided upon measures for combating the Bolsheviks. On October 19 the Provisional Government hastily summoned troops from the front to Petrograd. The streets were heavily patrolled. The counter-revolutionaries succeeded in massing especially large forces in Moscow. The Provisional Government drew up a plan: on the eve of the Second Congress of Soviets, the Smolny—the headquarters of the Bolshevik Central Committee—was to be attacked and occupied and the Bolshevik directing centre destroyed. For this purpose the government summoned to Petrograd troops in whose loyalty it believed.

But the days and even the hours of the Provisional Government were already numbered. Nothing could now halt the victorious march of the Socialist revolution.

On October 21 the Bolsheviks sent commissars of the Revolutionary Military Committee to all revolutionary army units. Throughout the remaining days before the uprising energetic preparations for action were made in the army units and in the mills and factories. Precise instructions were also issued to the warships *Aurora* and *Zarya Svobody*.

At a meeting of the Petrograd Soviet, Trotsky in a fit of boasting blabbed to the enemy the date on which the Bolsheviks had planned to begin the armed uprising. In order not to allow Kerensky's government to frustrate the uprising, the Central Committee of the Party decided to start and carry it through before the appointed time, and set its date for the day before the opening of the Second Congress of Soviets.

Kerensky began his attack on the early morning of October 24 (November 6) by ordering the suppression of the central organ of the Bolshevik Party, *Rabochy Put* (*Workers' Path*), and the dispatch of ar-

War and Totalitarianism

moured cars to its editorial premises and to the printing plant of the Bolsheviks. By 10 a.m., however, on the instructions of Comrade Stalin, Red Guards and revolutionary soldiers pressed back the armoured cars and placed a reinforced guard over the printing plant and the *Rabochy Put* editorial offices. Towards 11 a.m. *Rabochy Put* came out with a call for the *overthrow* of the Provisional Government. Simultaneously, on the instructions of the Party Centre of the uprising, detachments of revolutionary soldiers and Red Guards were rushed to the Smolny.

The uprising had begun.

On the night of October 24 Lenin arrived at the Smolny and assumed personal direction of the uprising. All that night revolutionary units of the army and detachments of the Red Guard kept arriving at the Smolny. The Bolsheviks directed them to the centre of the capital, to surround the Winter Palace, where the Provisional Government had entrenched itself.

On October 25 (November 7), Red Guards and revolutionary troops occupied the railway stations, post office, telegraph office, the Ministries and the State Bank.

The Pre-parliament was dissolved.

The Smolny, the headquarters of the Petrograd Soviet and of the Bolshevik Central Committee, became the headquarters of the revolution, from which all fighting orders emanated.

The Petrograd workers in those days showed what a splendid schooling they had received under the guidance of the Bolshevik Party. The revolutionary units of the army, prepared for the uprising by the work of the Bolsheviks, carried out fighting orders with precision and fought side by side with the Red Guard. The navy did not lag behind the army. Kronstadt was a stronghold of the Bolshevik Party, and had long since refused to recognize the authority of the Provisional Government. The cruiser *Aurora* trained its guns on the Winter Palace, and on October 25 their thunder ushered in a new era, the era of the Great Socialist Revolution.

On October 25 (November 7) the Bolsheviks issued a manifesto "To the Citizens of Russia" announcing that the bourgeois Provisional Government had

been deposed and that state power had passed into the hands of the Soviets.

The Provisional Government had taken refuge in the Winter Palace under the protection of cadets and shock battalions. On the night of October 25 the revolutionary workers, soldiers and sailors took the Winter Palace by storm and arrested the Provisional Government.

The armed uprising in Petrograd had won.

The Second All-Russian Congress of Soviets opened in the Smolny at 10:45 p.m. on October 25 (November 7), 1917, when the uprising in Petrograd was already in full flush of victory and the power in the capital had actually passed into the hands of the Petrograd Soviet.

The Bolsheviks secured an overwhelming majority at the congress.[5] The Mensheviks, Bundists and Right Socialist-Revolutionaries, seeing that their day was done, left the congress, announcing that they refused to take any part in its labours. In a statement which was read at the Congress of Soviets they referred to the October Revolution as a "military plot." The congress condemned the Mensheviks and Socialist-Revolutionaries and, far from regretting their departure, welcomed it, for, it declared, thanks to the withdrawal of the traitors the congress had become a real revolutionary congress of workers' and soldiers' deputies.

The congress proclaimed that all power had passed to the Soviets:

"Backed by the will of the vast majority of the workers, soldiers and peasants, backed by the victorious uprising of the workers and the garrison which had taken place in Petrograd, the Congress takes the power into its own hands"—the proclamation of the Second Congress of Soviets read.

On the night of October 26 (November 8), 1917, the Second Congress of Soviets adopted the *Decree on Peace*. The congress called upon the belligerent countries to conclude an immediate armistice for a period of not less than three months to permit negotiations for peace. While addressing itself to the governments and peoples of all the belligerent countries, the congress at the same time appealed to

[5] Check this sweeping statement against Maynard's account above, pp. 691–98, and that of Fainsod below, pp. 711–14.

"the class-conscious workers of the three most advanced nations of mankind and the largest states participating in the present war, namely, Great Britain, France and Germany." It called upon these workers to help "to bring to a successful conclusion the cause of peace, and at the same time the cause of the emancipation of the toiling and exploited masses of the population from all forms of slavery and all forms of exploitation."

That same night the Second Congress of Soviets adopted the *Decree on Land*, which proclaimed that "landlord ownership of land is abolished forthwith without compensation." The basis adopted for this agrarian law was a Mandate (*Nakaz*) of the peasantry, compiled from 242 mandates of peasants of various localities. In accordance with this Mandate private ownership of land was to be abolished forever and replaced by public, or state ownership of the land. The lands of the landlords, of the tsar's family and of the monasteries were to be turned over to all the toilers for their free use.

By this decree the peasantry received from the October Socialist Revolution over 150,000,000 dessiatins (over 400,000,000 acres) of land that had formerly belonged to the landlords, the bourgeoisie, the tsar's family, the monasteries and the churches.

Moreover, the peasants were released from paying rent to the landlords, which had amounted to about 500,000,000 gold rubles annually.

All mineral resources (oil, coal, ores, etc.), forests and waters became the property of the people.

Lastly, the Second All-Russian Congress of Soviets formed the first Soviet Government—the Council of People's Commissars—which consisted entirely of Bolsheviks. Lenin was elected Chairman of the first Council of People's Commissars.

This ended the labours of the historic Second Congress of Soviets.

The congress delegates dispersed to spread the news of the victory of the Soviets in Petrograd and to ensure the extension of the power of the Soviets to the whole country.

Not everywhere did power pass to the Soviets at once. While in Petrograd the Soviet Government was already in existence, in Moscow fierce and stubborn fighting continued in the streets several days longer. In order to prevent the power from passing into the hands of the Moscow Soviet, the counter-revolutionary Menshevik and Socialist-Revolutionary parties, together with Whiteguards and cadets, started an armed fight against the workers and soldiers. It took several days to rout the rebels and to establish the power of the Soviets in Moscow. . . .

In the interval from October 1917 to February 1918 the Soviet revolution spread throughout the vast territory of the country at such a rapid rate that Lenin referred to it as a "triumphal march" of Soviet power.

The Great October Socialist Revolution had won.

There were several reasons for this comparatively easy victory of the Socialist revolution in Russia. The following chief reasons should be noted:

1) The October Revolution was confronted by an enemy so comparatively weak, so badly organized and so politically inexperienced as the Russian bourgeoisie. Economically still weak, and completely dependent on government contracts, the Russian bourgeoisie lacked sufficient political self-reliance and initiative to find a way out of the situation. It had neither the experience of the French bourgeoisie, for example, in political combination and political chicanery on a broad scale nor the schooling of the British bourgeoisie in broadly conceived crafty compromise. It had but recently sought to reach an understanding with the tsar; yet now that the tsar had been overthrown by the February Revolution, and the bourgeoisie itself had come to power, it was unable to think of anything better than to continue the policy of the detested tsar in all its essentials. Like the tsar, it stood for "war to a victorious finish," although the war was beyond the country's strength and had reduced the people and the army to a state of utter exhaustion. Like the tsar, it stood for the preservation in the main of big landed property, although the peasantry was perishing from lack of land and the weight of the landlord's yoke. As to its labour policy the Russian bourgeoisie outstripped even the tsar in its hatred of the working class, for it not only strove to preserve and strengthen the yoke of the factory owners, but to render it intolerable by wholesale lockouts.

It is not surprising that the people saw no essential difference between the policy of the tsar and the policy of the bourgeoisie, and that they transferred their hatred of the tsar to the Provisional Government of the bourgeoisie.

As long as the compromising Socialist-Revolutionary and Menshevik parties possessed a certain amount of influence among the people, the bourgeoisie could use them as a screen and preserve its power. But after the Mensheviks and Socialist-Revolutionaries had exposed themselves as agents of the imperialist bourgeoisie, thus forfeiting their influence among the people, the bourgeoisie and its Provisional Government were left without support.

2) The October Revolution was headed by so revolutionary a class as the working class of Russia, a class which had been steeled in battle, which had in a short space passed through two revolutions, and which by the eve of the third revolution had won recognition as the leader of the people in the struggle for peace, land, liberty and Socialism. If the revolution had not had a leader like the working class of Russia, a leader that had earned the confidence of the people, there would have been no alliance between the workers and peasants, and without such an alliance the victory of the October Revolution would have been impossible.

3) The working class of Russia had so effective an ally in the revolution as the poor peasantry, which comprised the overwhelming majority of the peasant population. The experience of eight months of revolution—which may unhesitatingly be compared to the experience of several decades of "normal" development—had not been in vain as far as the mass of the labouring peasants were concerned. During this period they had had the opportunity to test all the parties of Russia in practice and convince themselves that neither the Constitutional-Democrats, nor the Socialist-Revolutionaries and Mensheviks would seriously quarrel with the landlords or sacrifice themselves for the interests of the peasants; that there was only one party in Russia—the Bolshevik Party—which was in no way connected with the landlords and which was prepared to crush them in

order to satisfy the needs of the peasants. This served as a solid basis for the alliance of the proletariat and the poor peasantry. The existence of this alliance between the working class and the poor peasantry determined the conduct of the middle peasants, who had long been vacillating and only on the eve of the October uprising wholeheartedly swung over towards the revolution and joined forces with the poor peasants.

It goes without saying that without this alliance the October Revolution could not have been victorious.

4) The working class was headed by a party so tried and tested in political battles as the Bolshevik Party. Only a party like the Bolshevik Party, courageous enough to lead the people in decisive attack, and cautious enough to keep clear of all the submerged rocks in its path to the goal—only such a party could so skilfully merge into one common revolutionary torrent such diverse revolutionary movements as the general democratic movement for peace, the peasant democratic movement for the seizure of the landed estates, the movement of the oppressed nationalities for national liberation and national equality, and the Socialist movement of the proletariat for the overthrow of the bourgeoisie and the establishment of the dictatorship of the proletariat.

Undoubtedly, the merging of these diverse revolutionary streams into one common powerful revolutionary torrent decided the fate of capitalism in Russia.

5) The October Revolution began at a time when the imperialist war was still at its height, when the principal bourgeois states were split into two hostile camps, and when, absorbed in mutual war and undermining each other's strength, they were unable to intervene effectively in "Russian affairs" and actively to oppose the October Revolution.

This undoubtedly did much to facilitate the victory of the October Socialist Revolution.

MERLE FAINSOD

LENIN'S ABILITY AS ORGANIZER AND TACTICIAN

This selection, like the preceding one, was written in the Stalin era. Like the previous reading, this one emphasizes the importance of the Bolshevik Party's organization and strategy in explaining Bolshevik success. But there are major differences between the two accounts. The last selection was written in 1936 by Soviet Communists loyal to Stalin. This one was published in the "cold war" era—in the year Stalin died—by an American student of Soviet government and politics.

The author, Merle Fainsod, is a distinguished professor of government at Harvard University. He has published a number of works on the origin and development of Communist rule in Russia. Note that Fainsod credits Trotsky with quite different and more important contributions to Communist victory in 1917 than one would suspect from reading the Communist "party line" of 1936. In what other facts does Fainsod correct the Stalinist version of history? To what extent does he support, to what extent modify, the Stalinist interpretation and the interpretation of Sir John Maynard?

When you have read all four of the selections in this section reconsider each of them and try to arrive tentatively at a unified interpretation of your own. Why did the two revolutions succeed? Had economic forces and the class struggle made Russia ripe for the first successful proletarian revolution in history? Or did the force of Lenin's personality and the shrewdness of his tactics guarantee success and illustrate the "great man" theory of history? Or was it the war that guaranteed the success of both revolutions? To what extent were the crack-ups of both the tsarist regime and the Provisional Government avoidable accidents, caused by their bad driving in the midst of difficult wartime conditions?

Finally, try to determine how the circumstances of the Bolshevik seizure of power shaped the future of Soviet Russia. Lenin seized power, but his party was only a minority. He did not seize power from tsarist aristocrats or capitalists but from men who spoke for broad segments of Russian society, from SR's and Menshevik Marxists as well as from the Kadets. In view of this fact, what chance was there to build a regime based on the will of the people and offering them freedom and equality of opportunity? What chance was there to build an ideal form of socialism in a single country, especially in one that had not yet been industrialized by capitalism?

Use force as midwife at the birth of socialism and you will mangle the child, some Marxists had warned before 1914. Is it possible, therefore, that the short-run view of Lenin as the genius of success in 1917 should give way in favor of one that emphasizes what came out of the seizure of power? To many socialists the Bolshevik Revolution was not a brilliant success but, because it was premature, a terrible mistake made by a Machiavellian distorter of Marxist doctrine. Certainly it is worth asking, in the light of the experience of 1917 and what followed, whether the end really does justify the means in politics. Or did the means to which Lenin resorted in "speeding up history" make impossible the achievement of the ideal ends that were being sought?

The medium through which the Bolsheviks organized their forces for the final coup was the Military Revolutionary Committee of the Petrograd Soviet. With the Bolsheviks in full control of the Soviet, a resolution to create the committee was carried on October 29, and the committee itself was named on November 2, four days before the insurrection. The staff of the committee was composed only of Bolsheviks and sympathetic Left SR's. Trotsky, the President of the Soviet, also served as chairman of the committee and surrounded himself with a core of reliable Bolsheviks who, in effect, comprised the general staff of the insurrection. Liaison with the Bolshevik Central Committee was maintained through a secret "military revolutionary center," consisting of five members of the committee, Sverdlov, Stalin, Bubnov, Uritsky, and Dzerzhinsky.

The party's role in directing the insurrection was camouflaged behind the façade of the Soviet. This shrewd stratagem provided a measure of pseudo-legality for the organizers of the insurrection. It was of particular value in mobilizing the support of the wavering and hesitant who were ready to respond to an appeal of the Soviet when they would have been unwilling to follow the naked leadership of the Bolsheviks. It was of outstanding importance in dealing with the Petrograd garrison which early in the Revolution had formed the habit of looking to the Soviet as its protector against transfer to the front and refused to take orders not countersigned by that body.

In its preparations for the insurrection, the Military Revolutionary Committee relied heavily on the Bolsheviks' Military Organization, which counted approximately a thousand members in the Petrograd area — among them a number of young officers as well as others with military experience. Through this organization, commissars were assigned "for observation and leadership" to the garrison's combat units, as well as to arsenals, warehouses, and other institutions of military importance. Arrangements were made through the commissars, who were in charge of issuing arms, to prevent the arming of the *Junkers,* or cadets in the military schools, and at the same time to divert rifles and other equipment to the Red Guard. Kernels of resistance developed. The Bolshevik commissar was unable to establish his authority in the important Fortress of Peter and Paul which commanded the Winter Palace. On the afternoon of November 5, this obstacle was overcome when Trotsky appealed to the soldiers of the fortress. With this peaceful surrender went a prize of one hundred thousand rifles, no mean contribution to future success.

On the evening of the fifth, the Provisional Government made a belated attempt to fight back. The decision was made to close the Bolshevik newspapers, *Rabochii Put'* and *Soldat* (Soldier), to initiate criminal proceedings against the members of the Military Revolutionary Committee, to arrest leading Bolsheviks, and to summon reliable military units from the environs of Petrograd. The first tests of strength augured badly for the government. The Bolshevik printing plants were raided by government troops at 5:30 a.m. on November 6 and copies of the newspapers confiscated; by eleven o'clock that morning the newspapers reappeared. The government ordered the cruiser *Aurora,* manned by a Bolshevik crew and moored in the Neva uncomfortably close to the Winter Palace, to put to sea on a training cruise; the order was effectively countermanded by the Military Revolutionary Committee.

On the morning of the sixth, Kerensky appeared before the Pre-Parliament, proclaimed a state of insurrection in Petrograd, and asked for unqualified support in suppressing the Bolsheviks. After prolonged debate, with the Kadets and Cossack delegates in opposition, a resolution drafted by Martov, a Menshevik Internationalist, was adopted by the close vote of 113 to 102, with twenty-six abstentions. The resolution condemned the insurrection,

Reprinted by permission of the publishers from Merle Fainsod, *How Russia Is Ruled* (Cambridge, Mass.: Harvard University Press), pp. 80–86. Copyright 1953, 1962 by The President and Fellows of Harvard College.

Lenin's Ability as Organizer and Tactician

but it pointed the finger of responsibility at Kerensky by calling on him "first of all, to pass immediately a decree transferring the land to the land committees and to take a decisive stand on foreign policy proposing to the Allies that they announce the conditions of peace and begin peace negotiations." The resolution concluded by recommending the creation of "a Committee of Public Safety comprised of representatives of municipal corporations and the organs of the revolutionary democracy, acting in concert with the Provisional Government."

Kerensky at first threatened to resign. A delegation headed by the Menshevik Dan called on the premier to plead for quick action in the spirit of the resolution According to Dan's account,

[We told him] that we had a definite and concrete proposal to make to the Provisional Government: that resolutions on the question of peace, land, and the Constituent Assembly should be passed at once and made known to the population by means of telegraph and by posting bills [in the city]. We insisted that this must be done that very night in order that every soldier and every worker might know of the decisions of the Provisional Government by the next morning. . . .

We pleaded . . . with Kerensky that even from a purely military point of view the struggle against the Bolsheviks would have a chance of success only if the peasant-soldiers knew that they were defending peace and land against the Bolsheviks. . . .

Our conversation did not last very long. Kerensky gave the impression of a man completely enervated and worn out. To every argument he replied with irritation, saying finally with disdain that the government did not need any of our advice, that this was not the time to talk but to act.

Meanwhile, Lenin, still in hiding, had also decided that the moment had come for action. Burning with impatience, he sped a last letter to the comrades of the Central Committee of November 6: "We must not wait! We may lose everything! . . . History will not forgive delay by revolutionists who could be victorious today (and will surely be victorious today), while they risk losing much tomorrow, they risk losing all." Then, addressing himself to those who urged delay until the meeting of the Second All-Russian Congress of Soviets on the evening of the seventh, Lenin continued:

If we seize power today, we seize it not against the Soviets but for them. . . . The government is tottering. We must *deal it the death blow* at any cost. To delay action is the same as death.

On the same day, the Bolshevik Central Committee assembled to make the last dispositions for the uprising. Sverdlov was assigned to keep watch on the Provisional Government, Bubnov was allotted railway communications, Dzerzhinsky posts and telegraphs, and Milyutin the organization of food supplies. Kamenev and Berzin were instructed to negotiate with the Left SR's to insure their support for the insurrection. Lomov and Nogin were dispatched to Moscow to coordinate the activities of the Bolsheviks there. With events rushing toward a denouement, Trotsky took time out on the evening of the sixth to address a meeting of the Petrograd Soviet. In reporting on the measures already taken to checkmate the Provisional Government, he referred to it "as nothing more than a pitiful, helpless, half-government, which waits the motion of a historical broom to sweep it off. . . . But if the government wishes to make use of the hours—24, 48, or 72 —which it still has to live, and comes out against us, then we will meet it with a counterattack, blow for blow, steel for iron."

During the night of the sixth and the early morning of the seventh, the Bolshevik forces moved quickly to seize the strong points of the capital city. Resistance was virtually nominal, and the seizures were accomplished with almost no bloodshed. The military support on which the Provisional Government counted simply melted away. A pathetic effort was made to hold the Winter Palace with the help of the Ural Cossacks, Junkers, officers, and the Women's Battalion who were stationed there. But as the Bolsheviks moved up their forces, the Cossacks and part of the Junkers and officers slipped away, and the Women's Battalion was disarmed after sallying forth in counterattack. Shortly after midnight of the seventh, the attacking forces captured the last stronghold of the Provisional Government and arrested the ministers who remained in the Palace.

The collapse of resistance in Petrograd was complete. The proclamation of the Military Revolutionary Committee summed up the day's happenings:

All railroad stations and telephone, post, and telegraph offices are occupied. The telephones of the Winter Palace and the Staff Headquarters are disconnected. The State

War and Totalitarianism

Bank is in our hands. The Winter Palace and the Staff have surrendered. The shock troops are dispersed, the cadets paralyzed. The armored cars have sided with the Revolutionary Committee. The Cossacks refused to obey the government. The Provisional Government is deposed. Power is in the hands of the Revolutionary Committee of the Petrograd Soviet of Workers' and Soldiers' Deputies.

At eleven o'clock on the evening of November 7, the Second All-Russian Congress of Soviets assembled for its opening session. Of the approximately 650 delegates in attendance, the Bolsheviks claimed 390 and with the help of the Left SR's quickly asserted control over the proceedings. Confronted with a *fait accompli*, the Mensheviks and SR's of the Right and Center abandoned the Congress. Martov, the Menshevik Internationalist whom Trotsky described contemptuously as the "inventive statesman of eternal waverings," attempted to patch up a truce by proposing "to end the crisis in a peaceful manner, by forming a government composed of representatives of all the democratic elements." Trotsky's reply was drenched in vitriol:

What do they offer us? . . . To give up our victory, to compromise, and to negotiate—with whom? With whom shall we negotiate? With those miserable cliques which have left the Congress or with those who still remain? But we saw how strong those cliques were! There is no one left in Russia to follow them. And millions of workers and peasants are asked to negotiate with them on equal terms. No, an agreement will not do now. To those who have left us and to those proposing negotiations we must say: You are a mere handful, miserable, bankrupt; your rôle is finished, and you may go where you belong—to the garbage heap of history.

The Congress concluded it's first day's business by issuing a proclamation announcing its assumption of supreme power, transferring all local authority to the Soviets, and appealing to the country to defeat all efforts of Kerensky and other "Kornilovists" to return to power. With a sure revolutionary instinct for the issues that would attract maximum support for the Bolsheviks, the proclamation promised:

The Soviet authority will at once propose a democratic peace to all nations and an immediate armistice on all fronts. It will safeguard the transfer without compensation of all land . . . to the peasant committees; it will defend the soldiers' rights, introducing a complete democratization of the army, it will establish workers' control over industry, it will insure the convocation of the Constituent Assembly on the date set; it will supply the cities with bread and the villages with articles of first necessity, and it will secure to all nationalities inhabiting Russia the right of self-determination.

The next day Lenin made his first appearance at the Congress and was received with a tumultuous ovation. After the applause had died down, he quickly assumed the reins of leadership with nine fateful words, "We shall now proceed to construct the socialist order." With Lenin presenting the main reports, the Congress approved the important decrees on peace and on land and then concluded its work by entrusting the power of government to the newly created Council of People's Commissars. The Sovnarkom, as it quickly became known, was exclusively Bolshevik in composition; its membership included Lenin as Chairman, Trotsky as Commissar of Foreign Affairs, Rykov as Commissar of the Interior, Lunacharsky as Commissar of Education, and Stalin as Chairman for Nationalities. The hour of triumph had finally come. Lenin rarely indulged in introspection or backward glances, but at that moment he paused in wonder and confided to Trotsky, "You know . . . from persecution and a life underground, to come so suddenly into power . . . *Es schwindelt* [It makes one dizzy]."

If Lenin found victory intoxicating and slightly unbelievable, in the eyes of his opponents the Bolshevik march to power had a nightmarish quality of incredible unreality. In the brief period of eight months, a tiny band of underground revolutionaries, numbering less than 25,000 on the eve of the March Revolution, had catapulted themselves into a governing authority of nearly 150,000,000 people. It is easier to discern in retrospect the significant factors which contributed to the Bolshevik conquest than it was at the time. If the Provisional Government had been able to withdraw from the war and carry through a land settlement satisfactory to the peasantry, it is highly doubtful that the Bolsheviks could have gathered enough support to stage a successful *coup d'état*. Yet to state this alternative, so plausibly reinforced by hindsight, is to miss the tragic imperatives of 1917.

Each of the parties which maneuvered for ascendancy in the months between March and November was the prisoner of its own illusions, its own interests, and its own vision of the future. To a Kadet leader like Milyukov it was inconceivable that Russia could betray her allies and her own national interests by suing for a separate peace; consequently, it was all too easy to attribute his own sense of patriotic exaltation and dedication to soldiers, workers, and peasants who had lost their taste for war. To SR's of the Right like Kerensky, who in a measure shared Milyukov's illusions, the successful prosecution of the war was paramount, with the agenda of economic reforms to be postponed until properly constituted legal bodies could be assembled to deal with them. To SR's of the Center and Left, who were much closer to the aspirations and expectations of the villages, land reform brooked no delay. Frustrated by the procrastinations of the Provisional Government, the Left SR's were thrown into the arms of the Bolsheviks. For Mensheviks of all shades, still loyal to the orthodox Marxian two-stage panorama of capitalist development, the socialist revolution had to be postponed until the bourgeois-democratic revolution was completed. The Mensheviks demonstrated real insight in emphasizing the difficulties of building socialism in a backward country. Their theoretical acumen was less well attuned to the political dynamism and revolutionary *élan* which the downfall of Tsardom released. For the Bolsheviks, economic backwardness was the springboard to power; for the Mensheviks, it pointed a path toward legal opposition in a consolidating bourgeois order. This was hardly a prospect for which the wretched and disinherited could develop more than qualified enthusiasm. As the Revolution deepened, the Mensheviks found themselves out-promised and out-maneuvered, with their strength sharply receding in the urban industrial centers on which they counted heavily.

Until the arrival of Lenin from exile, the Bolsheviks, too, were prisoners of ancient formulas. They oriented their policies on a perspective not very different from that of Menshevism. Lenin reversed this course and set the party on the road to the conquest of power. With an unswerving faith in his goal and a readiness to take any measures whatever to realize it, Lenin, frequently over bitter opposition, managed to transform the party into an obedient instrument of his will. His remarkable talent as a revolutionary strategist was based on an unerring sense for the deeply felt dissatisfactions of the masses and the genius for finding the slogans to catalyze grievances into revolutionary energy. Except for his insistence on striking at the right moment, Lenin had relatively little to do with the actual mechanics of the insurrection. His great contribution was to set the stage for insurrection by identifying Bolshevism with the major forces of mass discontent in Russian society. Lenin did not create the war-weariness which permeated the army and the nation: the material was at hand; his task was to exploit it. With one word—

peace—Lenin and the Bolsheviks fused it into a revolutionary amalgam. The land-hunger of the peasants was an ancient grievance of which all parties were aware. The SR's built their ascendancy in the villages on the promise to satisfy it, but while they temporized, Lenin stole their program from under their noses. When accused of the theft, Lenin replied, "Whether it be according to our ideas or in the direction of the SR program does not matter. The essential point is to give the peasantry a firm conviction that there are no more *pomeshchiks* [landlords] in the villages, and that it is now for the peasants themselves to solve all questions and to build their own life." With one word—land—Lenin insured the neutrality of the villages.

Factory workers constituted the strongest phalanx of Bolshevik support. Lenin bought their support by promising them a government which "takes surplus products from the parasites and gives them to the hungry, that . . . forcibly moves the homeless into the dwellings of the rich, that . . . forces the rich to pay for milk, but does not give them a drop of it until the children of *all* the poor families have received adequate supplies." With two slogans —bread and workers' control—Lenin captured the allegiance of substantial sections of the industrial workers from the Mensheviks.

The Bolshevik Revolution was not a majoritarian movement. The last free elections in Russia, the elections to the Constituent Assembly which took place toward the end of 1917, clearly demonstrated that the Bolshevik voting strength in the country at large was not more than 25 per cent. But, as Lenin subsequently observed, the Bolsheviks did have "an overwhelming preponderance of force at the decisive moment in the decisive points." In the areas and units strategically important to the success of the insurrection—Petrograd, Moscow, the Baltic fleet, and the garrisons around Petrograd—Bolshevik ascendancy turned the scale. The enemies of Bolshevism were numerous, but they were also weak, poorly organized, divided, and apathetic. The strategy of Lenin was calculated to emphasize their divisions, neutralize their opposition, and capitalize on their apathy. In 1902 in *What Is to Be Done?* Lenin had written, "Give us an organization of revolutionaries, and we shall overturn the whole of Russia!" On November 7, 1917, the wish was fulfilled and the deed accomplished.

3

WHY NAZISM IN GERMANY?

In 1922, five years after Lenin's victory placed Russia under a Communist regime, Mussolini became premier of Italy and proceeded to build another type of totalitarian state. While the Communist and Fascist totalitarian systems were evolving in the 1920's Adolf Hitler sought without much success to create a following in Germany for his "National Socialist German Workers Party," or N.S.D.A.P.

As late as 1928 the Nazis could win only 2.6 percent of the votes in national elections. But within four more years the Nazi Party had become the largest in Germany, winning as many as 37 percent of the votes. On January 30, 1933, Hitler was named Chancellor of Germany. He and his fellow Nazis quickly made Germany a totalitarian state that lasted for twelve years. For half of those years, the six years of the Second World War, there seemed a real possibility that Hitler might be able to remodel Europe — including much of the Soviet Union — after the fashion of the totalitarian and racist regime he had established in Germany. The consequences of his twelve-year rule are still being felt in Germany, and they have vitally affected the relationship of the German people with the other nations of Europe. Though Nazism lasted only a tiny fraction of the thousand years that Hitler predicted for his Reich, it will remain an important and disastrous chapter in the history of European Civilization.

How was it possible for the Nazis to gain mastery over the most industrialized and one of the most civilized countries of Europe just fourteen years after that country had cast aside the Hohenzollern monarchy and created a democratic republic?

Some authors have explained the success of Nazism as a reaction against the spread of Communism. The German Communist Party, organized on the first day of 1919, made rapid gains between 1930 and 1933. While it never won more than 17 percent of the votes, even in 1932, it was extremely well organized, highly disciplined, followed orders from Moscow, and commanded much more than 17 percent of the votes in some of the industrial cities of Germany. Germans remembered that the Russian Communists won power in 1917 with no more than 25 percent of the votes of the Russian people. Hitler, playing upon the fear of Communism, identified his party as the most anti-Communist in Germany, and it is quite clear that fear and hatred of the "Reds" brought many converts to Nazism. But many authors believe there were more important reasons for Hitler's climb to power.

Hitler also identified the Nazi Party as the most implacable foe of the Treaty of Versailles, which had been forced upon defeated Germany by the victors in 1919. The Versailles Treaty took away German territory in the east and the west and one million square miles of overseas territory; it left the Rhineland under military occupation until 1930 and restricted the size of Germany's military forces; while taking the best of Germany's mineral resources, it required the new republic to make heavy reparations payments; it outraged the spirits of many Germans by assigning them and their allies exclusive guilt for World War I. Many Germans knew that the Versailles Treaty might have been worse and knew also that their own nation had tried in March 1918 to impose a harsher treaty upon Lenin's Russia. But the spirit of rebellion against the Versailles Treaty was almost unanimous. Hitler promised to undo it and to expand Germany beyond the frontiers of 1914. This won support for the Nazi Party. To a noted French scholar, Maurice Baumont, "the condition of international affairs, exploited to the limit by National-Socialism, explains to a great extent the success of Hitler." Many authors have agreed with Baumont. And yet one may question this interpretation. Resentment against Versailles was present in Germany not only after but before 1928, and in the earlier years the Nazis could win only a small percentage of the votes of the German people. One might do well to ask what happened to change the situation between 1928 and 1933.

To many historians the Great Depression of 1929 offers the chief explanation for the rise of Nazism. By 1932 some six million Germans were unemployed—one tenth of the total population. Desperation became intense, and the moderately conservative governments seemed unable to bring Germany out of the depression. Peasants, workers, industrialists, merchants, intellectuals, and especially the young voters of Germany soured on parliamentary government and looked for a radical solution, for *action*. Hitler promised action, and there is no doubt that the Nazis won many supporters because of the depression. Yet the percentage of unemployed was also high in the western democracies, and they did not succumb to totalitarian regimes; the percentage of unemployed in the United States in 1932 was as high as it was in Germany. Besides, if the depression drove Germany to adopt a new economic system, why did it have to be Nazism? Both the Social Democrats and the Communists favored economic innovations, but neither could gain power in the years of the depression.

To look to fear of Communism, hatred of Versailles, and concern about the depression is to look for the causes of Nazi success in forces that were external to Germany or at least supranational in character. Many writers have contended that Nazism was, instead, a purely German phenomenon, a reflection of the allegedly authoritarian instincts of the German people and a virtually inevitable culmination of German history. The British historian A. J. P. Taylor has written that the Third Reich rested solely on "German force and German impulse; it owed nothing to alien forces." Another British writer sees proof in Nazism that the Germans "are not good material for democracy." William L. Shirer has offered much the same view in his best-seller on *The Rise and Fall of the Third Reich*. It is certainly true that the mentality of many Germans was authoritarian, but can one accept the view that this was the major cause of the rise of Nazism to power? After all, the majority

War and Totalitarianism

of the Germans voted between 1919 and 1928 for parties that supported the democratic republic.

Several interpretations of the Nazi success have been briefly presented to this point and four more are offered in the readings that follow. The first reading is a variation on the last interpretation mentioned above, seeing in the traditionally authoritarian leadership of the German army a central element in the elevation of Hitler to the chancellorship of Germany. After considering the explanations offered above and those presented in the readings, do the best critical and analytical thinking of your own that you can. What was the role of anti-Semitism in Hitler's success? Was it a basic cause or simply the result of the Nazi victory? Did Nazism come to power chiefly because of uniquely German conditions or as a result of supranational forces and circumstances? If the latter, could a Nazi-type movement gain power in some other area of the western world, or was it peculiar to the period between the two world wars? There are enough fascinating questions about this subject to occupy many scholars for a lifetime, and yet it is a matter of continuing importance to find the best answers possible.

GORDON A. CRAIG

THE ARMY LEADERS SWUNG TO HITLER'S SIDE

Military leaders, already powerful in peacetime Germany, became the most influential makers of German policy in 1917–18. The top commanders, Paul von Hindenburg and Erich Ludendorff, had the last word on the most important issues. Within the Weimar Republic after 1919 the Army retained a large though reduced measure of influence. The fact that Hindenburg, the wartime Marshal, was President of Germany from 1925 to 1934 insured the Army leaders a hearing in the crisis of 1932–33. Indeed, a Reichswehr (Army) general, Kurt von Schleicher, was the immediate predecessor of Hitler as Chancellor (head of the Cabinet) of Germany.

Though others advised Hindenburg to appoint Hitler Chancellor and he was reluctant to do so, it was the old Marshal who named Hitler head of the Cabinet on January 30, 1933. It is important to determine the role of the Army leaders in this appointment.

The selection that follows is taken from the major book of a noted American historian of modern Germany. Gordon A. Craig served at Princeton University from 1941 to 1961 and since has taught at Stanford University. A distinguished teacher and a highly literate writer, Craig has made the political role of German military leaders a special area of competence. He has published several books, but the one from which this selection is taken has been his most significant contribution.

What exactly was the role of the Army leaders in the crisis of 1932–33? Did Hitler become Chancellor because they promoted his appointment? Or did they simply fail to block it? Were the top Army leaders in agreement on the matter? How important were they as compared with other causes of the rise of Nazism to power?

In the critical years of the Weimar Republic, as in previous periods of German history, the army played a decisive part in determining the political destiny of the nation. The most dangerous enemies of the republic realized that they could not hope to overthrow it unless they secured at least the sympathetic neutrality of the army; and Hitler for one was guided by that knowledge in all phases of his policy before 1933. Hitler set out deliberately to play upon the dissatisfaction which existed within the army, and while his promises of a restored and expanded military establishment gradually enticed the bulk of the junior officers to his support, his charges that the republican régime lacked national spirit and failed adequately to defend the interests of the state found a sympathetic response in the hearts of the officer corps in general. Thus the fateful political change of 30 January 1933 was supported, at least tacitly, by the army. . . .

The last unhappy phase in the history of the Weimar Republic was one, therefore, in which the army was more continuously and intimately involved in domestic politics than it had been under either Seeckt[1] or Groener.[2] This was made abundantly clear in the negotiations which led to the formation of the Papen[3] government. It was Schleicher who urged Hindenburg to appoint Franz won Papen as Bruening's successor, who first broached the matter to Papen himself, who nominated most of his ministerial colleagues, and who conducted the negotiations which were designed to win Hitler's forbearance as the new cabinet began its work. And in all this, as Papen himself has written, "Schleicher left . . . no doubt that he was acting as spokesman for the army, the only stable organization remaining in the State."

The first fruits of Schleicher's grand design were hardly impressive. Papen's appointment as Chancellor was received with considerable stupefaction by a country which, with reason, had never been able to take the gentleman jockey, and war-time military attaché in the United States, very seriously; and wits were quick to point out that the only qualifications for a ministerial portfolio in the new government seemed to be a background in the *Gardekürassier* Regiment or the title Freiherr (Baron). The initial criticism deepened as the consequences of Schleicher's negotiations with Hitler became apparent. In return for an equivocal promise to support the new government, Hitler had been assured that new elections for the Reichstag would be held and that the decree abolishing the S.A. would be repealed. The Reichstag was consequently dissolved on 4 June and the S.A. *Verbot* rescinded on the 15th. Hitler immediately turned his full attention to the task of scoring new gains in the forthcoming elections, and he loosed his liberated storm troopers against his opponents. A new wave of violence swept over the country, reaching its peak in riots at Altona on 17 July when fifteen persons were killed and fifty injured.

These events, which weakened whatever meagre popular support the new government possessed, did not disturb Schleicher or cause him to deviate from his course. He agreed with his fellow cabinet ministers—for he had undertaken to serve as Reichswehr Minister in Papen's government—that it would be expedient to reimpose the ban on political demonstrations and parades, even if this was likely to strain Hitler's "tolerance" to the breaking point. But at the same time, he insisted that the time had come to strike out at the Social Democrats, and in a way designed simultaneously to placate Hitler and to advance the government's plan of centralizing political authority in the country. The main stronghold of Social Democratic power since 1929 had been the Prussian government; and Prussia was currently governed by a Socialist-Centre coalition government, the Braun-Severing government, although this no longer represented a majority in the *Landtag*[4] and was ruling *ad interim*. Schleicher proposed the deposition of the Prussian ministers and

[1] Commander of the German Army, 1920–26. [Editor's note.]

[2] Minister of Defense, 1928–32. [Editor's note.]

[3] Chancellor, May 31 to November 17, 1932, following Heinrich Brüning. [Editor's note.]

[4] Prussian parliament. [Editor's note.]

From Gordon A. Craig, *The Politics of the Prussian Army, 1640–1945* (Oxford, 1955), pp. xviii, 455–459, and 461–466. Reprinted by permission of the Clarendon Press.

their replacement by a Reich Commissioner; and, to justify such highhanded action, he secured from friendly sources within the Prussian Ministry of the Interior what purported to be evidence that the Prussian department of police was under communist influence, that it had been lax in dealing with communist demonstrations and that, consequently, it was responsible for the disorders at Altona and elsewhere.

Papen was in full agreement with the proposed plan. After securing the approval of the President and ordering General Gerd von Rundstedt, commanding *Wehrkreis III*, to alert his troops for immediate action, the Chancellor and the Reichswehr Minister on 20 July informed the flabbergasted Prussian ministers that they were to be replaced by a Reich Commissioner in the person of Papen. The angry officials protested loudly but in vain, and, on the same day, were physically ejected from their offices. Neither on the 20th nor on succeeding days did anything resembling active resistance materialize, for neither the *Reichsbanner* nor the trade unions were, in the opinions of their leaders, strong enough to oppose the government's stroke, and the police could not be counted on to test their strength against that of the local garrisons.

For Papen and Schleicher, however, this well-executed coup was an empty victory. Neither it, nor Papen's success in freeing Germany from reparations at the Lausanne conference, nor even his carefully calculated withdrawal from the Disarmament conference on 23 July served to increase the reputation or the popularity of the government; and this was made unmistakably clear in the national elections of 31 July. When the votes were counted and the Reichstag seats apportioned, it was patent that the Cabinet of Barons had been rejected by an overwhelming majority of the people. The only two parties upon whom Papen could rely with any assurance—the Nationalists and the *Volkspartei*—won only forty-four seats between them. On the other hand, the nazis—whose thunder Schleicher and Papen had hoped to steal by their coup in Prussia—doubled their representation, winning 230 seats and becoming the largest party in the Reichstag. There was now no hope that Hitler would tolerate Papen further. The nazi chief burned for power and, when it was refused him in the now famous interview with Hindenburg on 13 August, he wasted no time in going on the offensive. When Papen met the Reichstag for the first time on 12 September, he was forced to dissolve it immediately, for the nazis and the communists combined to defeat him overwhelmingly in a vote of confidence. This necessitated new elections and, when they were held, in the first week of November, Papen fared little better than he had in July. Ninety per cent of the votes cast were still against the government.

In mid-October Josef Goebbels[5] had written in his diary: "The Reichswehr has already fallen away from the Cabinet. Upon what will it base itself now?" The remark was perceptive, if premature. It was only after the November elections that army support was withdrawn from Papen, and this, of course, was Schleicher's doing. The general had, without doubt, become increasingly displeased with Papen in the weeks since the July coup, for the Chancellor had not only developed an irritating habit of making up his own mind on important issues, but was also in a fair way to supplanting Schleicher in the affections of the President. But it was the November election results which raised more basic differences. The most salient feature of the elections was the sharp setback suffered by the nazis—a loss of two million votes and thirty-four Reichstag seats. To Schleicher this proved that the time had come to put into effect the second part of his programme, the operation designed to split the National Socialist party. He was aware that Gregor Strasser, the leader of that party's powerful political organization, was deeply discouraged by the election returns, and believed that they foreshadowed a precipitous decline in party fortunes. Schleicher thought that Strasser would be willing to join a new government and that he would be supported by important elements of the party, including Roehm.[6] To make this new combination possible, however, Papen would have to step down, for neither Strasser nor Roehm would be prepared to serve under him.

Papen, on the other hand, had developed a love for office which was—despite all the disclaimers which he makes in his memoirs—to persist until 1945. He had no intention of stepping down. He would, he insisted, make a last effort to secure, by negotiation with the parties, a workable parliamentary majority. If this failed, as it almost certainly would, he would summon Hitler and demand that he either demonstrate that he could obtain such a majority or that he

[5] Chief propagandist under Hitler of the N.S.D.A.P. [Editor's note.]

[6] An early patron of Hitler; head of the Nazi S. A. forces 1931–34. [Editor's note.]

enter the cabinet as Vice-Chancellor. If Hitler refused, then all attempts to observe constitutional propriety must be abandoned. The Reichstag—and if necessary the opposition parties, and the trade unions—should be dissolved and the cabinet should rule quite openly by presidential decree backed by the authority of the army.

With the President's backing, the first steps of the Papen programme were taken. The parties were canvassed and emphatically rejected the suggestion that they support the cabinet. For five days, between 19 and 24 November, Hindenburg, his secretary Meissner, and Papen conducted acrimonious negotiations with Hitler, only to receive in the end his flat refusal to accept anything but a grant of full power. After that there was nothing left for Papen but the third alternative—the open violation of the constitution; and in an interview with Hindenburg and Schleicher on 1 December, he proposed this.

The fact that the President, despite his sincere desire to remain true to his constitutional oath, gave his approval to Papen's plan, shows how completely he had fallen under the spell of the *Herrenreiter*. Hindenburg, indeed, proved wholly impervious to all of the rather disingenuous arguments which Schleicher now made in favour of legality, and he was frankly sceptical of the general's claim that he could destroy the nazis without departing from the letter of the constitution. He preferred, he said, to go on with Papen. In consequence, Schleicher was compelled to resort to the same kind of forcing play which had served to get rid of Groener and Bruening. He brought the influence of the army to bear against the Chancellor.

At a meeting of the full cabinet on 2 December Schleicher came out flatly against the Papen proposals. . . .

The Chancellor repaired to Hindenburg who listened in silence to the news. Then the President said: "My dear Papen, you will not think much of me if I change my mind. But I am too old and have been through too much to accept the responsibility for a civil war. Our only hope is to let Schleicher try his luck."

Thus Schleicher himself—rather reluctantly, since he knew that his political talent was best exercised behind the scenes—became Chancellor in the first week of December. A few days later, Goebbels wrote cheerfully in his diary: "A Jew has written a book called 'The Rise of Schleicher,' of which a huge edition is being published. A great pity, since when it appears in the shop window von Schleicher will have disappeared from the political stage." Once again the little doctor's gift of prophecy was working well. Schleicher's chancellorship, which marked the highest point of army influence in the history of the republic, was brief and inglorious. It was notable, however, in one respect. Despite its brevity, it was long enough for Schleicher and the generals who supported him to execute a remarkable volte-face. In early December they were determined that Hitler must not come to power and confident that they could prevent this. By late January they were determined that he *must* come to power and frightened lest something should occur to postpone his doing so.

The failure of Schleicher's chancellorship was made inevitable within a week of his assumption of office. He had staked everything on his ability to detach Gregor Strasser from Hitler's side, and his confidence in his influence over Strasser was, in fact, justified. He erred, however, in assuming that Strasser's defection would break up the National Socialist party; and, basically, his mistake arose from his over-estimation of Strasser's capacities and his underestimation of Hitler's political genius in moments of crisis.

On 3 December Schleicher invited Strasser to join his cabinet as Vice-Chancellor and Minister-President of Prussia. For the next five days there were heated discussions in the inner circles of the nazi party, with Strasser urging that the offer must be accepted in order to avoid new elections which might be disastrous for the party, and Goering[7] and Goebbels staunchly opposing this course as being the rankest kind of defeatism. After momentary hesitation, Hitler vetoed the Strasser policy and, on 7 December, accused the chief of the party's political organization of seeking to replace him as Leader. Strasser hotly denied the charge and, on the following day, resigned from the party. But there his resistance stopped. Far from seeking to carry all or part of the party with him, as Schleicher had expected, he washed his hands of the whole business and took his family off for a vacation in Italy.

[7] One of the leading Nazis, Hermann Goering at the end of January 1933 would become a member of the Hitler Cabinet. [Editor's note.]

Hitler, on the other hand, in an explosion of that demoniac rage which always cowed his party comrades when they were exposed to it, threatened to commit suicide if the party fell to pieces and then proceeded to smash the political organization which Strasser had ruled so long, to set up a new central party commission under Rudolf Hess, and to bully the deputies and gauleiters into new pledges of unconditional loyalty. By mid-December the party was unquestionably united behind the Leader; and that fact spelled failure for the scheme which Schleicher had elaborated in the cabinet meeting of 2 December.

The Chancellor was forced then to do what Papen had done before him—to make the dismal round of the parties, seeking support which would give him a workable majority when the Reichstag re-convened. But here his past record for deviousness told against him in his negotiations with the middle and left parties, while the promises he made in order to allay their suspicions alienated the parties of the right. Remembering the coup in Prussla, the directorate of the Social Democratic party not only rejected Schleicher's initial overtures, and advised the trade union leadership to do the same, but was openly scornful when the Chancellor promised fundamental reforms to relieve unemployment and a scheme of land settlement to alleviate the distress of the peasantry. The only tangible effect, indeed, of the last mentioned plan was to destroy what support Schleicher had in conservative circles, for, on 12 January, the Landbund[8] delivered a broadside against the government, accusing it—as it had once accused Bruening—of desiring to impose agrarian bolshevism on the eastern districts of the Reich. The persistence with which Schleicher clung to his agrarian policy—and his threat to publish details of the Osthilfe scandals of 1927–8 if the resistance of the Landbund did not cease—not only influenced the decision of the Nationalist party to withdraw its support from the government—a step announced on 20 January—but sensibly weakened Schleicher's popularity in the army, whose officer corps, after all, was still recruited from the very families which would suffer most from the execution of his projects.

Schleicher ended up then with even less party backing than his predecessor. And, this being so, he was forced to go to the President and make precisely the same request that his predecessor had made on

1 December. On 23 January he told the President that the Reichstag must be dissolved and that Germany must be ruled, under article 48 of the constitution, by what amounted to military dictatorship. Hindenburg was a very old and infirm man who suffered frequent lapses of memory, but he had no difficulty in remembering the arguments which Schleicher had used against this very solution only two months before:

On December 2 [he said] you declared that such a measure would lead to civil war. The Army and the police, in your opinion, were not strong enough to deal with internal unrest on a large scale. Since then the situation has been worsening for seven weeks. The Nazis consider themselves in a stronger position, and the left wing is more radical in its intentions than ever. If civil war was likely then, it is even more so now, and the Army will be still less capable of coping with it. In these circumstances I cannot possibly accede to your request for dissolution of the Reichstag and carte blanche to deal with the situation.

The President ordered Schleicher to go on with his search for a majority, and the Chancellor went through the motions of doing so. But Schleicher was well aware that his fall was only a matter of days away, and he felt that the time would be better spent in influencing the choice of a successor. This was, after all, a matter which vitally concerned the army, and Schleicher still claimed to speak for that body.

Practically speaking, there were only two possible successors: Hitler and Papen. Hitler, whose fortunes had seemed to be on the down-grade in January, had been strengthened by the establishment of relations with a group of Rhenish-Westphalian industrialists and bankers who assumed responsibility for the debts of his party and were openly calling for his elevation to power. The ebb-tide of party fortunes seemed to have turned, and in local elections the nazis had registered heavy successes within the past weeks. Hitler's appointment to the chancellorship would have seemed a certainty if it had not been for Hindenburg's past record of opposition to him and the President's deep affection for Papen. There was no doubt that Papen wanted office again; and, in view of Hindenburg's feelings, he had an excellent chance of getting it.

Of the two solutions Schleicher preferred the first. His reasons for this were not entirely rational and certainly by no means free of personal prejudice. But he seems to have calculated—as so many others did—that if Hitler assumed the responsibilities of office he would become more moderate in his views

8 Association representing landowning farmers. [Editor's note.]

and would be susceptible to management by other agencies, notably by the army. If, on the other hand, Papen became Chancellor, Hitler might well raise the standard of revolt, and the army would be placed in the awkward position of having to defend Papen. The general never doubted that the army would have fought cheerfully against Hitler for a Schleicher cabinet; but he refused to believe that it would do the same for Papen, or that it should be forced to do so.

In the last days of January 1933 Schleicher was desperately anxious lest a new Papen government be formed. On 27 January he asked Hammerstein to use the occasion of General von dem Bussche's customary report to the President on personnel affairs in the officer corps to sound Hindenburg out on his intentions.[9] Hammerstein did so and was severely snubbed for his pains, being told that he would be better advised to spend his time thinking of ways of improving manoeuvres rather than in meddling in political matters. However, the President added, "I have no intention whatever of making that Austrian corporal either Minister of Defence or Chancellor of the Reich." This alarmed Schleicher even farther. On the following day, when he went to the President to tell him that the cabinet was resolved to resign unless the powers requested on the 23rd were granted, he tried to argue that the formation of a new Papen government would be disastrous for Germany. The only response he received was a set speech accepting his resignation.

Until the formation of a new government, of course, Schleicher was still Chancellor and Minister of Defence and, with his friend Hammerstein, had direct command over the army. But on 29 January Schleicher learned that General Werner von Blomberg, commanding *Wehrkreis I* and currently a member of the German delegation to the Disarmament conference, had been ordered by the President to return to Berlin and to report to him personally rather than to the Bendlerstrasse (War Ministry), as custom required. This seemed to denote an intention on Hindenburg's part of removing the army from the control of its present commanders by appointing Blomberg as Minister of Defence, after he had prom-

[9] Hammerstein was Chief of Army Command, 1930–34. [Editor's note.]

ised army support to Papen. In short, if Schleicher and Hammerstein were to block Papen, they were, they thought, going to have to move fast.

The true measure of their desperation in these last days is shown by the fact that the idea of arresting the President and his entourage was frankly discussed by Schleicher's intimates. More important, at least two plain intimations of this possibility were made to Hitler. On the afternoon of 29 January Hammerstein—the man who Groener had believed would oppose a nazi seizure of power "with brutality"—was dispatched by Schleicher to ask Hitler about the state of his current negotiations with Papen and to tell him that, if he thought that Papen was planning to form a government which would exclude him, the generals would be willing "to influence the position." That same night Werner von Alvensleben, one of Schleicher's close associates, went—again at the general's request—to Goebbel's house where a group of nazi chieftains was anxiously awaiting final confirmation of Hitler's appointment as Chancellor and of the President's willingness to dissolve the Reichstag. Alvensleben took the occasion to say to Hitler: "If the Palace crowd are only playing with you, the Reichswehr Minister and the Chief of the *Heeresleitung* will have to turn out the Potsdam garrison and clean out the whole pig-sty from the Wilhelmstrasse."

These were astonishing *démarches*, so astonishing, indeed, that Hitler does not seem to have known what construction to place upon them and secretly took precautions to guard against an army *Putsch*, which might be directed against himself. The Fuehrer's suspicion, while understandable, was unjustified. At this crucial moment in German history, the army command had swung to his side. The only *Putsch* which Schleicher and Hammerstein now contemplated was one which would make certain his appointment. Such action was not, it is true, necessary; and Hitler became Chancellor on 30 January without the intervention of the Potsdam garrisons. But surely the will was as important here as the deed would have been; and Hitler himself later admitted that "if . . . the Army had not stood on our side, then we should not be standing here today." . . .

GERHARD RITTER

NAZISM AROSE FROM DEMOCRATIC RADICALISM

Did Hitler become Chancellor because the military leaders wanted it? Craig finds it significant that "at this crucial moment in German history, the army command had swung to his side." A noted German historian, Gerhard Ritter, has written on the other hand that "the rapid rise to power of the National-Socialist Party after 1931 cannot be explained by any political activity of the military."

Ritter looks for broader and deeper causes of Hitler's success, and he does not find them in the traditional conservative and authoritarian forces of Germany. He finds the introduction into Germany of popular sovereignty responsible. "Lacking any kind of critical ability, the masses saw in Hitler a savior and a prophet," Ritter writes.

Ritter, himself a conservative and a German patriot, is defending his own values of a lifetime when he defends conservativism and the traditional national forces of Germany against the allegation that they brought Hitler to power. Out of his conservatism and patriotism, Ritter participated in the wartime Resistance movement against Hitler. After 1945, as a distinguished scholar of the older generation, he reexamined his own conceptions of history and helped to reestablish and reinvigorate historical studies in Western Germany. As professor of history at Freiburg-im-Breisgau, Ritter has published many books about medieval and modern German history. The third volume of his impressive study of the role of the military in the German Empire of 1871–1918, *Staatskunst und Kriegshandwerk*, appeared in 1964.

In this selection Ritter distinguishes between the advocates of "liberalism" (which he uses in the original early-nineteenth century sense of the word) and those who favor the direct rule of the masses. Ritter finds the roots of Nazi success in materialistic "democratic radicalism." In doing so he challenges not only the historical assumptions but the political values of many western European and American scholars. Is it possible, after all, that Ritter is right? If he is, there is cause for continued alertness against the rise of a Nazi-like movement not only in Germany but elsewhere. If Hitler did not come to power because of uniquely German conditions, it might be possible for a movement like Nazism to succeed in any nation founded on a materialistic and radical democracy.

The Weimar Republic failed because it did not succeed in winning general confidence, in becoming genuinely popular through successes which could be appreciated from a distance. So the rejection of Democratic slogans became one of the essential conditions for the rise of Hitler's Party. But to attrib-

From Maurice Baumont, John H. E. Fried, Edmond Vermeil, and others, *The Third Reich* (New York: Frederick A. Praeger, Inc., 1955), pp. 389–395, 396–397, 399–400, 402–403, and 410–412. Reprinted by permission of UNESCO.

ute this rejection simply to "the Germans' lack of a sense of liberty" explains nothing; it only disguises with a grand phrase the true historical problem: the reasons why the chances of liberals have much diminished in this century, particularly in Germany after the First World War.

The desire to replace the unsettled parliamentary coalition governments with a strong and lasting authority certainly played a very large part in Hitler's rise to power. In his propaganda for such an authority Hitler never ceased to praise, as an ideal model for the constitution of the state, the army, with its definite orders and clear responsibility derived from above, not from below, from those who lead, and not from those who are led; and this won the approval of many old soldiers of the First World War, just as Mussolini did when with his Blackshirts he appealed to the instincts of the old "front-line soldiers" and "fighting men." These instincts were certainly much more developed in Germany than in Italy. Perhaps, too, the pedantic eagerness to serve with which the subalterns carried out their *Führer's* orders and plans after the establishment of the dictatorship was greater in Germany.

The great electoral successes of Hitler since 1930, however, cannot be explained by the Germans' wish to find in political life a military discipline, by a desire to be given orders and to be able to obey them. The masses who rallied to him did not at all believe that they were helping a dictator to seize power; they supported a man of the people who had their confidence and from whom they expected the fulfillment of their wishes — of a thousand vast hopes.

The same thing had already occurred in Italy, and its repetition after so few years is a striking proof of the fact that ordinary men never learn anything from history. Hitler had clearly copied from Mussolini the technique of setting up, without a *coup d'état* as such and without violating the constitution, a one party state.

In any case, the German dictatorship was not the first, but the last to be established in Europe, and it became by far the most dangerous (if the Russian Bolshevist dictatorship is ignored).

The conclusion is, therefore, that in order to examine the historical foundations of National-Socialism, one must first of all see what it was in twentieth-century Europe that gave the totalitarian state, composed of one single party, such a good opportunity of taking the place of the constitutional liberal parliamentary state. For the totalitarian state, composed of one single party, is a European, and not solely a German phenomenon.

A great deal could be written about the various causes of the decline of liberal ideas in social and political affairs. I can give only a few brief hints:

(1) First, the *changes in social and economic structure* which took place in the nineteenth and twentieth centuries must be borne in mind. Modern industrial society, a mass society of innumerable individuals united by common needs, has taken the place of the former *bourgeois* society, consisting of a layer of economically independent notables who were the great landowners and *bourgeois*.

The First World War accelerated and intensified the process of economic and social levelling, by removing differences during wartime, especially in Germany. The whole of society was ground down into a uniform mass, grey as the soldiers; it was subjected to overall state control, to a totalitarian power which deeply affected even private life. It restricted the free expression of opinion, imposed censorship on the press, cut it off from all communication with foreign countries, and made it entirely dependent on the official information office, which accustomed the people to official communiqués which only very rarely divulged the whole truth, and in many cases suppressed, mutilated, or falsified it. More or less compulsory state or war loans swallowed up private incomes, later annihilated by inflation, which practically led to ruin and the end of fiduciary currency. Those possessing real estate (*Sachwertbesitzer*) had a monopoly, all the educated middle classes were impoverished, and large sections of society became solely dependent on state salaries and pensions or on private business; innumerable people who had been independent were so no longer.

As a result of such general changes, the party system on which the liberal state was founded was modified. Under the influence of universal suffrage, the parties were no longer composed of groups of notables, of clubs whose members were men who were socially and financially independent, who knew something about politics and were interested in them. They became mass organisations, directed by the electoral machine formed by a more or less highly organised party bureaucracy. The political agent took the place of the political idealist, and planned propaganda took the place of personal conviction and persuasion.

At the same time, the style and content of publications were changed. Political education, real discussion, individual thought ceased to be important; instead, what was required was mass appeal. In order to interest the masses, they must be attracted by sensationalism. He who is best at sensationalism is also the most popular. The most effective method is always the sermon of hatred, the least effective the voice of peaceable reason, since it makes the reader think, and even requires a certain wish to learn, and some knowledge.

(2) Similarly, *political intentions* changed. In the nineteenth century the struggle (particularly in Central Europe) was for national unity and for liberty guaranteed by a constitution—that is to say, for the participation of the governed in state affairs, for an assured, liberal legal system, and for protection against arbitrary acts. These were Ideal ends, which had sprung mostly from spiritual impulses. By the end of the century they had been achieved in Italy and in Germany (with two exceptions).

In their place the economic preoccupations of modern industrial society came to the fore. The struggle for a higher standard of living became the main cause of internal political differences; the idea of liberty was eclipsed by the idea of "social justice"; Liberalism was attacked and discarded in favour of Socialism. Political thought became more and more materialistic. Instead of being preoccupied by unity and liberty, it was interested in class conflicts, material interests, and the struggle for daily bread; in foreign policy the questions of the hour were *Lebensraum*[1], the great outlets and sources of raw materials, trading profits, and the rate of exchange.

So in general, politics stopped striving towards an ideal, and the prestige of parliaments declined. Since it had now become a matter of the interests of groups of people, the personal integrity of the representatives of these people is doubted. The details of their debates on economic subjects become more abstruse and uninteresting; the great complexity of modern economy partly controlled by the state, and the large number of opposing interests represented in parliament, make definite solutions, understood

and approved by all, extremely rare. Therefore there is a great deal of discontent, and discontent breeds the summoning of a "strong man." The great groups of interests take "direct," extra-parliamentary action; there are strikes, the big workers' and employers' unions exert pressure on public opinion, there are processions, demonstrations, and mass meetings. The place of real debates is taken by announcements. Political struggles become more violent—he who has armed or semi-military partisans, ready to strike, at his call has the best chance of success.

Here, too, the World War accelerated and exaggerated this evolution. Like all great wars, it left behind it many adventurous spirits who were unable to settle down again to a *bourgeois* existence. They were nationalists, ready to serve any political adventurer who could use them for his "patriotic" activities. In *Mein Kampf* Hitler severely criticised the indiscipline of these eternal soldiers, without political aims, grouped together in bands (*Freikorps*), secret societies, and armed associations of all kinds, who sometimes supported and sometimes threatened republican governments. To him the fact that these armed bands and *Freikorps* had at times protected the republic from Communism showed nothing but unpardonable stupidity. He disapproved strongly of their Vehme[2] murders, too, because they liquidated minor traitors without daring to deal with the "great November criminals."

In fact, however, many of these toughs became members of the *Sturmtruppen*[3], and the *Führerkorps* was mostly made up of them. There is a close connection between the SA and SS terrorists and these adventurous stragglers from the First World War. The inflation which took place in 1923, as a result of the war, left many people without money and with nothing to lose, so that they were ready to become political agents.

(3) The *changes in religious life* produced the same results. Christian teaching scarcely reached the populations of industrial towns; European civilisation became more and more secular as a result of the technical progress which took place in this rationalised and "unsupernatural" world. In Germany idealist philosophy, which had been a substitute for religion in *bourgeois* society for many years, began

---

[1] Literally, "living space," but used in the general sense of territory for German expansion. [Editor's note.]

[2] The Vehme or Feme were secret and self-appointed nationalist tribunals, remotely resembling vigilantes. [Editor's note.]

[3] i.e., the Nazi S.A. forces. [Editor's note.]

to be rejected, not in favour of philosophical materialism but of the modern "philosophy of life" which was spreading throughout Europe. This "philosophy of life" influenced large sections of society, and there was much talk of the supremacy of will, of biological explanations of mankind and of society, the glorification of physical strength, and of pure vitality, instead of a higher spirituality; the intellect and the rational were despised, while strong "instincts" (*Triebe*) and the vital impulse (the *élan vital* of H. Bergson) were admired. Nietzsche's doctrine of the superman and of the will to power as the prime force in the world, envisaged at first as an aristocratic ethical system, became in popular literature the deification of brutal mankind, of will to domination, of the eternal struggle for existence, of brute strength—though not without the complicity of that philosopher who unhesitatingly set the most daring aphorisms before the world. Darwinian ideas of the "survival of the fittest," of the eternal struggle for existence of all creatures, influenced all political thought. In all countries, including those of Western Europe, the age of imperialism brought with it books extolling the doctrine of might; with no knowledge of life, wars were no longer thought to be disasters for civilisation, but rather creative crises without which there could be no historical evolution.

Marxist theories were even more widespread, although not always recognised as such—the only political reality was the conflict of material interests, and political ideals were only ideological camouflage. (That this was a serious mistake is proved by all history, including that of National-Socialism.)

The example of the romanticism of the younger generation at the beginning of the twentieth century, with its scorn of *bourgeois* security and of reason and its call for "a dangerous life" and for exciting experience (*Erlebnis*), might lead one to believe that European countries were tired of the long period of peacefulness which had brought them their material well-being. Well-being and security were both destroyed by the First World War, which reduced society to a uniformity which could be touched only by mass violence and brutality.

This complete change of the political climate gave a new and troubling reality to the theories of Wilfredo Pareto[4] about the eternal circular movement of activist *élites*, about the deceit of middle-class morality, and about the propelling force of deep feeling. The same was true of Georges Sorel's[5] theories about "violence" and the "myth" which moves the masses, without the truth of its content having any importance. During their first phase, French syndicalists wished to replace old-style parliamentary groups by the ideal leader's party and militant *élite* which would pursue the aims of combat rather than the ideals of the *bourgeois* middle classes, and thus showed the young Mussolini his first and most pressing plan of action. The large-scale destruction of the war showed the way for futurist policies (in the meaning given to them by men like Gentile, Papini, and Marinetti)[6] which refuse all connection with the authorities of the past.

(4) *New technical facilities for political propaganda* made the mobilisation of the masses much easier than it had been in the age of *bourgeoisies;* facilities such as loud-speakers, radio, a daily press rapidly printed in thousands of copies, lorries and motor-coaches which made possible the speedy deployment of political shock troops, almost limitless mass transport by railway, road, and air, so that it was possible to go proselytising from one end of the country to the other and to address a different mammoth meeting each evening. In 1922 40,000 Blackshirts formed ranks for the march on Rome, and caused a political panic simply on account of their numbers. At each of his national party congresses Hitler assembled and addressed some half a million men.

Thus did it become possible to make a reality of the theory of the sovereignty of the people, in a radical manner that was completely new. The masses could now be activated directly to become the political sovereign, and the roundabout method of the election of people's representatives to Parliament was no longer the only one.

It is clear that from the start the direct control of the "will of the people" was fundamental to democratic radicalism, unlike the Anglo-Saxon liberalism. The latter was originally founded not on the political rights of the many, but on the political privileges possessed by the various estates under feudalism, and which were perpetuated in the party groupings in modern parliaments. Groups of important people

[4] Italian elitist political philosopher, d. 1923. [Editor's note.]

[5] French syndicalist, d. 1922. [Editor's note.]

[6] Italian intellectuals of the early twentieth century who are regarded by many as forerunners of Fascism. [Editor's note.]

"represented" the people; in England these groups slowly became parties of the many during the nineteenth century.

The principle of direct sovereignty of the people, on the other hand, was in existence in the primitive democracy of the free American states in the seventeenth and eighteenth centuries. It was manifest in the town meetings of the settlers which constituted the first germs of American democracy; this principle is still in existence today, as shown by the President's position as a man on whom the nation, on whom every voter, but not Congress, can rely; before Congress his position is that of the executor of the will of the people.

Political compromise reached by discussion, the just balancing of the opposing desires and interests of different classes, groups, and individuals, belongs to the liberal parliamentary system. The nation is not regarded as a uniform mass of men, but as a collection of different individuals. The individual is important not only as a comrade of the people (*Volksgenosse*), but also as a person with claims on life and independent action.

Democratic radicalism, on the other hand, with terrible consistency, requires definite decisions instead of compromise. Sovereignty means deciding and not compromising. The best example of this rational principle is the idea, invented by Jean-Jacques Rousseau, of the "general will," an absolute idea which does not recognise any minority rights; if one opposes the general will it is because one has mistaken the general good (*Social Contract,* Book IV, chapter 2). The general will is the sworn enemy of individual intellect, of groups of individuals, because such groups are unaware of, or opposed to, the real public good; the more the individual intellect is overcome, the more probable it is that the real general will, the true interests of the people, will operate (*Social Contract,* Book II, chapter 3). Direct sovereignty of the people is infinitely preferable to any form of parliamentary government, for parliaments are the legacy of feudalism, and therefore the place in which private interests, and not the public good, struggle for supremacy (*Social Contract,* Book III, chapter 15).

Jean-Jacques Rousseau's general will became a myth at the time of the great revolution; aided by groups of individuals, it dominated parliamentary discussion and became increasingly intolerant. The peo-ple, now sovereign, is united in a popular political community (this was the most important innovation), a community of which each individual is part, although his particular rights are not protected (as Rousseau required). No appeal to higher authority is possible, because the people is sovereign, and there can be no appeal to ancient rights or privileges of the kind that was possible under the monarchy. Any one who opposes the will of the people is considered dangerously selfish, and therefore excludes himself from the community (this exclusion may then be made certain by banishment, imprisonment, or the guillotine).

How can the absolute and indivisible will of the people best be expressed? The best and simplest way, as Rousseau saw it, was the convocation of the sovereign people to a citizens' meeting, as in the classical city-state, the Swiss canton, or the American town meeting. But this form of direct democracy is of necessity limited to a very small community.

In large states there is the plebiscite which may be employed to show support for, and to be complementary to, the legislative machinery of parliament; for especially important laws, administrative decisions, and questions of foreign policy there would be a referendum. This system is cumbersome, costly, and difficult to operate, however, and does not really make possible a radical popular government.

A third method may be employed in large countries, however. The will of the people may be transferred to one man in whom confidence is reposed, who thus becomes an embodiment of the people, tangible and visible to all. Such a transference is made directly by the votes of the people, without passing through Parliament. . . .

The success of the twentieth-century dictatorships is conceivable only against this broad canvas of history. Of course they should not be considered in any way as the belated result of the French Revolution, or as having been influenced in any way by the works of Jean-Jacques Rousseau—this would be a very false interpretation of these historical remarks. Each of these dictatorships found its opportunity and its particular modern form in an extremely recent past.

Yet the latent possibility of a sudden change from radical democratic liberty to totalitarian tyranny is not modern. It grows where the great, socially disorganised, intellectually uniform masses in the modern city awaken to political consciousness, and where the former public authorities with their roots in the dim past (monarchy or parliamentary government) are destroyed or discredited. In such circumstances success seems assured if the distrust of a system of domination, already smouldering, is inflamed and a compact front is formed with a solid following. The masses are more ready to trust a living man than an anonymous institution.

Should a leader appear who is able to pass himself off as the representative of the most pure will of the people and as a real leader, then he will gain the support of the people, especially if he has a good few hard-hitting adherents. . . .

It is a very great mistake to believe that the modern function of leader of the people is in any way the heritage and continuation of the old, monarchic power of the princes. Neither Frederick the Great, Bismarck, nor Wilhelm II were the historical precursors of Adolf Hitler. His precursors were the demagogues and Caesars of modern history, from Danton to Lenin and Mussolini. It is also erroneous to see in the fanatical enthusiasm which millions of men felt for Hitler between 1930 and 1933 a continuation of the traditional veneration of Germans for their ancient princely houses. Our people's old attachment to its dynasties was, where it existed, the result of a traditional feeling; it was primarily caused by respect for a very ancient custom.

Hitler's party was, on the contrary, composed of numerous uprooted individuals whose mentality was revolutionary, who all consciously desired a new order, and who were convinced that their *Führer* was superior to any earlier leader. The characteristic of the Hitlerian movement which most strongly attracted the masses was its modernity, the fact that it was contemporary (facts which were brought out by the very far-flung technical apparatus used to gain support for the Party). Hitler's obscure, popular origins added to this attraction, and seemed an assurance that he could have nothing in common with the hated right-wing reactionaries—the great Junker land-owners, the officer class, and the great capitalists—even if he was sometimes obliged by force of circumstances to co-operate with people like Ludendorff and Hugenberg.[7] Ludendorff himself declared himself opposed to Junker and capitalist prejudice, and a public-spirited friend of the people. Hitler and his supporters always contended that the electoral alliance established between the National-Socialists, the Stahlhelm[8] group, and Hugenberg's party—the Harzburg Front of 1931—was nothing more than a tactical agreement, for Hitler detested "all reaction." And when he opened negotiations with the big industrialists once more, being short of money and desirous of rapid success, Otto Strasser and the Schwarze Front, the most convinced revolutionary elements in the Party, deserted the cause and started an open rebellion. Later he was to seize every opportunity of condemning the "selfishness" of the capitalist class and stating how much his policy favoured the workers.

In any case, he did not wish to be a conservative, either socially or politically; he wished to be a revolutionary. But what did this revolution imply? What was the difference between his dictatorship and that of other modern dictators? What was specifically German in it, what could be only explained by specifically German historical events?

If the situation is simplified somewhat, one can answer that *Volksführer* Hitler's mission in history was to accomplish that which the Emperor and his Government had been unable to accomplish in the First World War: to weld the nation into a closed, warlike community under the leadership of a really popular *Führer*, respected by all. . . .

Wilhelm II only once succeeded in getting near the heart of the nation as a whole, on 4th August 1914, when he said to the *Reichstag* assembled in the Berlin castle: "I know parties no more, I only know Germans." These words had a tremendous effect. The idea of a popular, unified political community struck the people with the same effect that the French had experienced at the festival of the Federation on 14th July 1790. Yet this was an isolated incident; the new-found community broke up in conflicts about the aims of the war and its methods, and the Emperor's rule failed so completely that the German monarchy received a death-blow.

The Germans experienced a bitter disappointment when not only was the war lost in spite of tremendous efforts, terrible economic privation, and millions of deaths, but also when the popular com-

[7] Leader of the monarchical Nationalist Party (DNVP) at the time Hitler became Chancellor; member of Hitler's Cabinet. [Editor's note.]

[8] Association of German war veterans. [Editor's note.]

munity broke up instead of becoming stronger. The Right, bellicose nationalists out for conquest, and the Socialist leaders, who were opposed to imperialism and desirous of peace, no longer saw eye to eye. They attacked one another so violently, supporters of "victorious peace" (*Siegfrieden*) and "peace by agreement" (*Verständigungsfrieden*) the "prolongers of war" (*Kriegsverlängerer*) and "defeatists," as they described each other, that the nation was split into two halves.

This bitter conflict was the decisive and perhaps fundamental occurrence which led to the rise of National-Socialism. In comparison with this, all other considerations seem to me to be of secondary importance. Hitler's party was brought to power primarily by his efforts to overcome the old and fatal conflict between the nationalist *bourgeois* parties of the right and the masses of the left, the working and lower middle classes. It was not called the "German workers' National-Socialist Party" (*Nationalsozialistische deutsche Arbeiterpartei*) in vain. The name was a programme in itself. . . .

Lacking any kind of critical ability, the masses saw in Hitler a saviour and a prophet, as he described in a voice hoarse with passion the violent brutalities committed by the victorious Powers on a defenceless Germany, as he promised that the criminals of November 1918 would be punished ("Some tens of thousands," he wrote in *Mein Kampf*, "shall one day expiate this crime against the state"); as he poured ridicule on the bungling of the "Marxist fumblers," as he pilloried the internal corruption of the "system of Weimar," or invoked the satanism of Bolshevism, or the grotesque spectre of an international conspiracy of Jews. No one asked how much this deluge of accusations contained of truth, exaggeration or slander, of wild invention of lies. We can still remember the horror with which we saw this preaching of boundless hatred echoed in the newspapers of the period, and its effect on a public opinion which was both worried and contaminated.

It is extraordinary that these speeches filled with hatred were interpreted as the preparation for a new and more fundamental popular community (*Volksgemeinschaft*). Yet they were interpreted in this way. Many people were aware of the eccentric side of Hitler's visions of the future and of the fanaticism and furious passion of his movement. His *confrères*, shadows of demagogy, partly corrupt, partly suspect, and partly plebeian, were much more

strongly criticised. It was realised that the minor leaders of the new movement were the men who had created disturbances at public meetings, and were therefore not worthy of confidence; the National-Socialist press was unreliable, its intellectual level very low, and its writings peculiar and of miserable quality. Nevertheless, the new popular community, the political and moral regeneration of the whole nation which was extolled in it, was regarded as an imposing doctrine, full of possibilities for the future.

How was such blindness possible? Was it the result of general decadence, of the disappearance of the tenets of religious morality? Did the German people lack moral instinct, and were they therefore unable to sense when a thing came from below? This lack of political and moral flair seems to be the most serious guilt with which the Germans who supported Hitler in these years can be reproached, and this reproach is not diminished by the fact that Germany was certainly not the only country to lack political and moral instinct where Hitler was concerned.

However, three factors must be taken into consideration. In the first place, calumnies, insults, and the moral abasement of the opposition are part of the normal equipment of every political struggle, and the violence with which this deplorable method is used varies only in degree. He who preaches distrust in a tottering government will always have great success in a modern mass democracy (as we have already remarked). And in Germany the political discussion was developing into a latent civil war; in a civil war strong fists are superior to all speeches and convictions. Of course, the peaceable *bourgeois* is inferior in such a sort of combat.

Secondly, it needed a high degree of moral and intellectual superiority to rest quiet and patient in such a situation as the Germans experienced in 1931–32, in the face of steadily growing millions of unemployed and of continual failures of foreign policy.

Thirdly, and more important, Hitler's demagogy was not restricted to negation alone. It gave the masses an admittedly indefinite conception of the future, but one which impressed them and aroused their enthusiasm. Hitler's criticism of existing Powers was not designed to cause despair, but to prepare the way for what he named the regeneration of the state and the people.

Nazism Arose from Democratic Radicalism   729

The "chains of Versailles," he said, will be cast off as soon as Germany is regenerated from within, as soon as the will of the people really becomes assured, and thus permits a strong and definite leadership. The German people must put an end to the reign of numerous parties, must seize power from the November criminals, and place it in the hands of a national leadership; then Germany will be so great that the victorious Powers of Versailles will be obliged to give her her "right to life" (*Lebensrecht*) without a struggle. Germany must be strong, so as to be indispensable to other countries; then she will not lack allies.

First of all, Germany must be set in order. A definite plan of action in the field of economics was hardly mentioned. But Hitler's hearers, dazzled by the vision of a new and more glorious Germany, scarcely noticed this omission. The appeal to instincts of hatred was covered up by declarations of idealist and patriotic sentiments—virile courage, discipline, selfless readiness to serve the community, the tend-ency of all forces towards one great end: spontaneous devotion to the whole, the social brotherhood of all classes.

As in Mussolini's Italy, the ideal of brotherhood at the front, where in the World War there were no party or class differences, was extremely important. Hitler also adopted the ideal of military leadership and discipline as the best means of creating an orderly state. For the people, however, to be led was to co-operate voluntarily and not to be commanded; his followers (*Gefolgschaft*) were governed by fidelity to the *Führer*, himself an official carrying out the will of the people, who undertook on his side to be faithful to his followers.

Thus was born the false image of a moral community, which concealed the future dictator's lust for power. He was able to appeal simultaneously to the highest and lowest instincts. This mixture is always the most effective in politics—good and evil, noble and vile, truth, lies, and half-truths. . . .

FRANZ NEUMANN

NAZISM AS A PRODUCT OF CAPITALISM

The idea that the masses put Hitler in power has been anathema to Communists, democratic socialists, and many democrats who are not socialists. Both Marxist and non-Marxist socialists have been especially vocal in attributing the rise of Nazism to a quite different force, to capitalism. Their interpretation has been widely accepted, because Nazism flourished in a period when economic determinism was most popular in the Western world as a theory of historical causation.

In singling out capitalism as a cause of Nazi success, Franz Neumann, like Ritter, points to a universal rather than to a uniquely German phenomenon. Neumann was a noted German labor economist before Hitler became Chancellor. Later he taught political science at Columbia University until his untimely death in an automobile accident in Europe in 1954. His book *Behemoth*, published in 1942, was regarded for more than a decade as the "standard" interpretation of the character of Nazism and the causes of its rise to power.

At this point it is well to remember Marx's prediction that proletarian revolution would occur in an advanced capitalistic society after capitalism had intensified its exploitation of the workers. To Neumann and many other socialists, Nazism and

War and Totalitarianism

Fascism (they often refer to both simply as "Fascism") fulfilled Marx's prophecy and represented an *inevitable* intensification of capitalism in crisis. If this was the case, Nazism might arise in any capitalist society. Thus, if you accept the idea that Nazism was the by-product of capitalism, it is especially important to ask whether it is an evitable end result of capitalism in general or if it was, instead, the by-product of specifically German capitalism in the unique conditions of the Great Depression.

If you accept, instead, Ritter's interpretation you might ask whether the Nazi Revolution was rather a revolt of the masses against capitalism and not a tool of crisis capitalism. Understandably socialists have refused to admit any such thing. If Nazism was a workers' revolt against advanced capitalism rather than an instrument of an intensified capitalism, then Marx was right in forecasting an eventual proletarian revolution against the capitalists but was a grotesquely mistaken prophet of the kind of revolution that would take over from capitalism. Was Nazism a tool of capitalism? Was it rather a revolt against capitalism? It is a fact that Hitler in his climb to power denounced the capitalist system. He appealed to the German workers for support and won some of them to his side. He called his movement "National" and "Socialist" (thus "Nazi"), and a number of scholars believe it succeeded as an amalgam of nationalist and socialist tendencies in Germany, tendencies that had been antithetical before Hitler's time.

The strong man of the Social Democratic party, Otto Braun, Prussian prime minister until 20 June 1932 when he was deposed by the Hindenburg-Papen *coup d'état*, attributes the failure of the party and Hitler's successful seizure of power to a combination of Versailles and Moscow. This defense is neither accurate nor particularly skilful. The Versailles Treaty naturally furnished excellent propaganda material against democracy in general and against the Social Democratic party in particular, and the Communist party unquestionably made inroads among Social Democrats. Neither was primarily responsible for the fall of the Republic, however. Besides, what if Versailles and Moscow had been the two major factors in the making of National Socialism? Would it not have been the task of a great democratic leadership to make the democracy work in spite of and against Moscow and Versailles? That the Social Democratic party failed remains the crucial fact, regardless of any official explanation. It failed because it did not see that the central problem was the imperialism of German monopoly capital, becoming ever more urgent with the continued growth of the process of monopolization. The more

monopoly grew, the more incompatible it became with the political democracy. . . .

The efficient and powerfully organized German system of our time was born under the stimulus of a series of factors brought into the forefront by the First World War. The inflation of the early '20s permitted unscrupulous entrepreneurs to build up giant economic empires at the expense of the middle and working classes. The prototype was the Stinnes empire and it is at least symbolic that Hugo Stinnes was the most inveterate enemy of democracy and of Rathenau's foreign policy.[1] Foreign loans that flowed into Germany after 1924 gave German industry the liquid capital needed to rationalize and enlarge their plants. Even the huge social-welfare program promoted by the Social Democracy indirectly strengthened the centralization and concentration of industry, since big business could far more easily assume the burden than the small or middle entrepreneur. Trusts, combines, and cartels covered the whole economy with a network of authoritarian

[1] Walther Rathenau, then German Foreign Minister, was murdered in 1922 by anti-Semitic nationalists. [Editor's note.]

From Franz Neumann, *Behemoth: The Structure and Practice of National Socialism* (Toronto, New York, and London, 1942), pp. 14–16, 30, and 34. Reprinted by permission of Professor Herbert Marcuse.

Nazism As a Product of Capitalism

organizations. Employers' organizations controlled the labor market, and big business lobbies aimed at placing the legislative, administrative, and judicial machinery at the service of monopoly capital.

In Germany there was never anything like the popular anti-monopoly movement of the United States under Theodore Roosevelt and Woodrow Wilson. Industry and finance were of course firmly convinced that the cartel and trust represented the highest forms of economic organization. The independent middle class was not articulate in its opposition, except against department stores and chains. Though the middle class belonged to powerful pressure groups, like the Federal Union of German Industries, big business leaders were invariably their spokesmen.

Labor was not at all hostile to the process of trustification. The Communists regarded monopoly as an inevitable stage in the development of capitalism and hence considered it futile to fight capital concentration rather than the system itself. Ironically enough, the policy of the reformist wing of the labor movement was not significantly different in effect. The Social Democrats and the trade unions also regarded concentration as inevitable, and, they added, as a higher form of capitalist organization. Their leading theorist, Rudolf Hilferding, summarized the position at the party's 1927 convention: "Organized capitalism means replacing free competition by the social principle of planned production. The task of the present Social Democratic generation is to invoke state aid in translating this economy, organized and directed by the capitalists, into an economy directed by the democratic state." By economic democracy the Social Democratic party meant a larger share in controlling the monopolist organizations and better protection for the workers against the ill effects of concentration.

The largest trusts in German history were formed during the Weimar Republic. The merger in 1926 of four large steel companies in western Germany resulted in the formation of the *Vereinigte Stahlwerke* (the United Steel Works). The *Vereinigte Oberschlesiche Hüttenwerke* (the United Upper Silesian Mills) was a similar combination among the steel industries of Upper Silesia. The *I.G. Farbenindustrie* (the German Dye Trust) arose in 1925 through the merger of the six largest corporations in this field, all of which had previously been combined in a pool. In 1930 the capital stock of the Dye Trust totaled 1,100,000,000 marks and the number of workers it employed reached 100,000.

At no time in the Republic (not even in the boom year of 1929) were the productive capacities of German industry fully, or even adequately, utilized. The situation was worst in heavy industry, especially in coal and steel, the very fields that had furnished the industrial leadership during the empire and that still dominated the essential business organizations. With the great depression, the gap between actual production and capacity took on such dangerous proportions that governmental assistance became imperative. Cartels and tariffs were resorted to along with subsidies in the form of direct grants, loans, and low interest rates. These measures helped but at the same time they intensified another threat. The framework of the German government was still a parliamentary democracy after all, and what if movements threatening the established monopolistic structure should arise within the mass organizations? As far back as November 1923, public pressure had forced the Stresemann cabinet to enact a cartel decree authorizing the government to dissolve cartels and to attack monopolistic positions generally. Not once were these powers utilized, but the danger to privileges inherent in political democracy remained and obviously became more acute in times of great crisis. . . .

Even before the beginning of the great depression, therefore, the ideological, economic, social, and political systems were no longer functioning properly. Whatever appearance of successful operation they may have given was based primarily on toleration by the anti-democratic forces and on the fictitious prosperity made possible by foreign loans. The depression uncovered and deepened the petrification of the traditional social and political structure. The social contracts on which that structure was founded broke down. The Democratic party disappeared; the Catholic Center shifted to the right; and the Social Democrats and Communists devoted far more energy to fighting each other than to the struggle against the growing threat of National Socialism. The National Socialist party in turn heaped abuse upon the Social Democrats. They coined the epithet, November Criminals: a party of corruptionists and pacifists responsible for the defeat in 1918, for the Versailles Treaty, for the inflation.

The output of German industry had dropped sharply. Unemployment was rising: six million were registered in January 1932, and there were perhaps two million more of the so-called invisible unemployed. Only a small fraction received unemployment insurance and an ever larger proportion received no support at all. The unemployed youth became a special problem in themselves. There were hundreds of thousands who had never held jobs. Unemployment became a status, and, in a society where success is paramount, a stigma. Peasants revolted in the north while large estate owners cried for financial assistance. Small businessmen and craftsmen faced destruction. Houseowners could not collect their rents. Banks crashed and were taken over by the federal government. Even the stronghold of industrial reaction, the United Steel Trust, was near collapse and its shares were purchased by the federal government at prices far above the market quotation. The budget situation became precarious. The reactionaries refused to support a large-scale works program lest it revive the declining power of the trade unions, whose funds were dwindling and whose membership was declining. . . .

By joining the concert of the Western European powers the Weimar government hoped to obtain concessions. The attempt failed. It was supported neither by German industry and large landowners nor by the Western powers. The year 1932 found Germany in a catastrophic political, economic, and social crisis.

The system could also operate if the ruling groups made concessions voluntarily or under compulsion by the state. That would have led to a better life for the mass of the German workers and security for the middle classes at the expense of the profits and power of big business. German industry was decidedly not amenable, however, and the state sided with it more and more.

The third possibility was the transformation into a socialist state, and that had become completely unrealistic in 1932 since the Social Democratic party was socialist only in name.

The crisis of 1932 demonstrated that political democracy alone without a fuller utilization of the potentialities inherent in Germany's industrial system, that is, without the abolition of unemployment and an improvement in living standards, remained a hollow shell.

The fourth choice was the return to imperialist expansion. Imperialist ventures could not be organized within the traditional democratic form, however, for there would have been too serious an opposition. Nor could it take the form of restoration of the monarchy. An industrial society that has passed through a democratic phase cannot exclude the masses from consideration. Expansionism therefore took the form of National Socialism, a totalitarian dictatorship that has been able to transform some of its victims into supporters and to organize the entire country into an armed camp under iron discipline. . . .

ALAN BULLOCK

HITLER AS THE KEY TO NAZI SUCCESS

Neumann as an economic determinist has found the impersonal forces of capitalism responsible for the rise of Nazism to power. Many other scholars see it as an illustration of the "great man" theory of history at work. The foundation of Hitler's success, according to Alan Bullock, was "his own energy and ability as a political leader."

Hitler's unique personal qualities—both strengths and weaknesses—are set forth in the selection that follows. It is taken from Bullock's full-length biography of the Nazi leader, the best yet published. Alan Bullock is a noted British expert on contemporary history and professor of modern history at Oxford. He is too good a scholar to attribute the success of Nazism exclusively to Hitler's personality, but he makes clear his conviction that Hitler's leadership was a prime element in shaping the character of National Socialism, in bringing it to power, and in the maintenance of its tyranny for twelve years.

When you have read the following selection, consider all of the interpretations you have now encountered about the reasons for the Nazi victory in 1933. Was it the work of one man, Adolf Hitler? Of leading Entente statesmen, makers of the Versailles Treaty? Of the men of German industry or the German army? Of the democratic system? The theories lead from the sins of one man to fundamental philosophical and theological questions about the nature of Man in general. In forming your own explanation, you must first decide which factors were relatively most important in causing the Nazi victory. Since one interpretation is not just as good as any other, your own synthesis of the factors of greatest importance demands that you find and evaluate as much evidence as possible. In going beyond these extracts you might begin by reading the full books from which these readings have been taken.

The foundation of Hitler's success was his own energy and ability as a political leader. Without this, the help would never have been forthcoming, or would have produced insignificant results. Hitler's genius as a politician lay in his unequalled grasp of what could be done by propaganda, and his flair for seeing how to do it. He had to learn in a hard school, on his feet night after night, arguing his case in every kind of hall, from the smoke-filled back room of a beer-cellar to the huge auditorium of the *Zirkus Krone*; often, in the early days, in the face of opposition, indifference or amused contempt; learning to hold his audience's attention, to win them over; most important of all, learning to read the minds of his audiences, finding the sensitive spots on which to hammer. "He could play like a virtuoso on the well-tempered piano of lower middleclass hearts," says Dr. Schacht.[1] Behind that virtuosity lay years of experience as an agitator and mob orator. Hitler came to know Germany and the German people at first hand as few of Germany's other leaders ever had. By the time he came to power in 1933 there were few towns of any size in the Reich where he had not spoken. Here was one great advantage Hitler had over nearly all the politicians with whom he had to deal, his immense practical experience of politics, not in the Chancellery or the Reichstag, but

in the street, the level at which elections are won, the level at which any politician must be effective if he is to carry a mass vote with him.

Hitler was the greatest demagogue in history. Those who add "only a demagogue" fail to appreciate the nature of political power in an age of mass politics. As he himself said: "To be a leader, means to be able to move masses."

The lessons which Hitler drew from the activities of the Austrian Social Democrats and Lueger's Christian Socialists[2] were now tried out in Munich. Success was far from being automatic. Hitler made mistakes and had much to learn before he could persuade people to take him seriously, even on the small stage of Bavarian politics. By 1923 he was still only a provincial politician, who had not yet made any impact on national politics, and the end of 1923 saw the collapse of his movement in a fiasco. But Hitler learned from his mistakes, and by the time he came to write *Mein Kampf* in the middle of the 1920s he was able to set down quite clearly what he was trying to do, and what were the conditions of success. The pages in *Mein Kampf* in which he discusses the technique of mass propaganda and po-

[1] Schacht served Hitler as Minister of Economics, 1934–37, and in other capacities. [Editor's note.]

[2] Karl Lueger was a demagogic politician at the height of his popularity during Hitler's years in Vienna before World War I. [Editor's note.]

Pp. 68–71, 372–380, 384, 385 from *Hitler: A Study in Tyranny*, Completely Revised Edition, by Alan Bullock, Copyright © 1962 by Alan Bullock. Reprinted by permission of Harper & Row, Publishers and of Odhams Press, Ltd.,

litical leadership stand out in brilliant contrast with the turgid attempts to explain his entirely unoriginal political ideas.

The first and most important principle for political action laid down by Hitler is: Go to the masses. "The movement must avoid everything which may lessen or weaken its power of influencing the masses. . . because of the simple fact that no great idea, no matter how sublime or exalted, can be realized in practice without the effective power which resides in the popular masses."

Since the masses have only a poor acquaintance with abstract ideas, their reactions lie more in the domain of the feelings, where the roots of their positive as well as their negative attitudes are implanted. . . . The emotional grounds of their attitude furnish the reason for their extraordinary stability. It is always more difficult to fight against faith than against knowledge. And the driving force which has brought about the most tremendous revolutions on this earth has never been a body of scientific teaching which has gained power over the masses, but always a devotion which has inspired them, and often a kind of hysteria which has urged them into action. Whoever wishes to win over the masses must know the key that will open the door to their hearts. It is not objectivity, which is a feckless attitude, but a determined will, backed up by power where necessary.

Hitler is quite open in explaining how this is to be achieved. "The receptive powers of the masses are very restricted, and their understanding is feeble. On the other hand, they quickly forget. Such being the case, all effective propaganda must be confined to a few bare necessities and then must be expressed in a few stereotyped formulas." Hitler had nothing but scorn for the intellectuals who are always looking for something new. "Only constant repetition will finally succeed in imprinting an idea on the memory of a crowd." For the same reason it is better to stick to a programme even when certain points in it become out of date: "As soon as one point is removed from the sphere of dogmatic certainty, the discussion will not simply result in a new and better formulation, but may easily lead to endless debates and general confusion."

When you lie, tell big lies. This is what the Jews do, working on the principle, "which is quite true in itself, that in the big lie there is always a certain force of credibility; because the broad masses of a nation are always more easily corrupted in the deeper strata of their emotional nature than consciously or voluntarily, and thus in the primitive simplicity of their minds they more readily fall victims to the big lie than the small lie, since they themselves often tell small lies in little matters, but would be ashamed to resort to large-scale falsehoods. It would never come into their heads to fabricate colossal untruths and they would not believe that others could have the impudence to distort the truth so infamously. . . . The grossly impudent lie always leaves traces behind it, even after it has been nailed down."

Above all, never hesitate, never qualify what you say, never concede an inch to the other side, paint all your contrasts in black and white. This is the "very first condition which has to be fulfilled in every kind of propaganda: a systematically one-sided attitude towards every problem that has to be dealt with. . . . When they see an uncompromising onslaught against an adversary, the people have at all times taken this as proof that right is on the side of the active aggressor; but if the aggressor should go only halfway and fail to push home his success . . . the people will look upon this as a sign that he is uncertain of the justice of his own cause."

Vehemence, passion, fanaticism, these are "the great magnetic forces which alone attract the great masses; for these masses always respond to the compelling force which emanates from absolute faith in the ideas put forward, combined with an indomitable zest to fight for and defend them. . . . The doom of a nation can be averted only by a storm of glowing passion; but only those who are passionate themselves can arouse passion in others."

Hitler showed a marked preference for the spoken over the written word. "The force which ever set in motion the great historical avalanches of religious and political movements is the magic power of the spoken word. The broad masses of a population are more amenable to the appeal of rhetoric than to any other force." The employment of verbal violence, the repetition of such words as "smash," "force," "ruthless," "hatred," was deliberate. Hitler's gestures and the emotional character of his speaking, lashing himself up to a pitch of near-hysteria in which he would scream and spit out his resentment, had the same effect on an audience. Many descriptions have been given of the way in which he succeeded in communicating passion to his listeners, so that men groaned or hissed and women sobbed involuntarily, if only to relieve the tension, caught up in the spell of powerful emotions of hatred and exaltation, from which all restraint had been removed.

It was to be years yet before Hitler was able to achieve this effect on the scale of the Berlin *Sportpalast* audiences of the 1930s, but he had already begun to develop extraordinary gifts as a speaker. It was in Munich that he learned to address mass audiences of several thousands. In *Mein Kampf* he remarks that the orator's relationship with his audience is the secret of his art. "He will always follow the lead of the great mass in such a way that from the living emotion of his hearers the apt word which he needs will be suggested to him and in its turn this will go straight to the hearts of his hearers." A little later he speaks of the difficulty of overcoming emotional resistance: this cannot be done by argument, but only by an appeal to the "hidden forces" in an audience, an appeal that the orator alone can make. . . .

The extravagant conversations recorded by Hermann Rauschning for the period 1932–1934, and by Dr. Henry Picker at the Fuehrer's H.Q. for the period 1941–1942, reveal Hitler in another favourite role, that of visionary and prophet. As the French Ambassador, André Francois-Poncet, noted, there was in Hitler much of King Ludwig II of Bavaria. The fabulous dreams of a vast empire embracing all Europe and half Asia; the geopolitical fantasies of inter-continental wars and alliances; the plans for breeding an *élite*, biologically preselected, and founding a new Order to guard the Holy Grail of pure blood; the designs for reducing whole nations to slavery—all these are the fruits of a crude, disordered, but fertile imagination soaked in the German romanticism of the late nineteenth century, a caricature of Wagner, Nietzsche, and Schopenhauer. This was the mood in which Hitler indulged, talking far into the night, in his house on the Obersalzberg, surrounded by the remote peaks and silent forests of the Bavarian Alps; or in the Eyrie he had built six thousand feet up on the Kehlstein, above the Berghof, approached only by a mountain road blasted through the rock and a lift guarded by doors of bronze. It was also the mood in which he and Himmler[3] drew up the blueprints and issued the orders for the construction of that New Order which was to replace the disintegrating liberal bourgeois world of the nineteenth century. After the outbreak of the war and the conquest of the greater part of Europe, all

[3] Leader of the Nazi S. S forces. [Editor's note.]

practical restraint upon Hitler's translation of his fantasies into brutal reality was removed. The S.S. extermination squads, the *Einsatzkommandos*, with their gas-vans and death camps; the planned elimination of the Jewish race; the treatment of the Poles and Russians, the Slav *Untermenschen*—these, too, were the fruits of Hitler's imagination.

All this combines to create a picture of which the best description is Hitler's own famous sentence: "I go the way that Providence dictates with the assurance of a sleep-walker." The former French Ambassador speaks of him as "a man possessed"; Hermann Rauschning writes: "Dostoevsky might well have invented him, with the morbid derangement and the pseudocreativeness of his hysteria"; one of the Defence Counsel at the Nuremberg Trials, Dr. Dix, quoted a passage from Goethe's *Dichtung und Wahrheit* describing the Demoniac and applied this very aptly to Hitler. With Hitler, indeed, one is uncomfortably aware of never being far from the realm of the irrational.

But this is only half the truth about Hitler, for the baffling problem about this strange figure is to determine the degree to which he was swept along by a genuine belief in his own inspiration and the degree to which he deliberately exploited the irrational side of human nature, both in himself and others, with a shrewd calculation. For it is salutary to recall, before accepting the Hitler-Myth at anything like its face value, that it was Hitler who invented the myth, assiduously cultivating and manipulating it for his own ends. So long as he did this he was brilliantly successful; it was when he began to believe in his own magic, and accept the myth of himself as true, that his flair faltered.

So much has been made of the charismatic nature of Hitler's leadership that it is easy to forget the astute and cynical politician in him. It is this mixture of calculation and fanaticism, with the difficulty of telling where one ends and the other begins, which is the peculiar characteristic of Hitler's personality: to ignore or under-estimate either element is to present a distorted picture.

The link between the different sides of Hitler's character was his extraordinary capacity for self-dramatization. "This so-called *Wahnsystem*, or capacity for self-delusion," Sir Nevile Henderson, the British Ambassador, wrote, "was a regular part of his technique. It helped him both to work up his own passions and to make his people believe anything that he might think good for them." Again and again one is struck by the way in which, having once decided rationally on a course of action, Hitler would whip himself into a passion which enabled him to bear down all opposition, and provided him with the motive power to enforce his will on others. The most obvious instance of this is the synthetic fury, which he could assume or discard at will, over the treatment of German minorities abroad. When it was a question of refusing to listen to the bitter complaints of the Germans in the South Tyrol, or of uprooting the German inhabitants of the Baltic States, he sacrificed them to the needs of his Italian and Russian alliances with indifference. So long as good relations with Poland were necessary to his foreign policy he showed little interest in Poland's German minority. But when it suited his purpose to make the "intolerable wrongs" of the Austrian Nazis, or the Germans in Czechoslovakia and Poland, a ground for action against these states, he worked himself into a frenzy of indignation, with the immediate—and calculated—result that London and Paris, in their anxiety for peace, exerted increased pressure on Prague or Warsaw to show restraint and make further concessions to the German demands.

One of Hitler's most habitual devices was to place himself on the defensive, to accuse those who opposed or obstructed him of aggression and malice, and to pass rapidly from a tone of outraged innocence to the full thunders of moral indignation. It was always the other side who were to blame, and in turn he denounced the Communists, the Jews, the Republican Government, or the Czechs, the Poles, and the Bolsheviks for their "intolerable" behaviour which forced him to take drastic action in self-defense.

Hitler in a rage appeared to lose all control of himself. His face became mottled and swollen with fury, he screamed at the top of his voice, spitting out a stream of abuse, waving his arms wildly and drumming on the table or the wall with his fists. As suddenly as he had begun he would stop, smooth down his hair, straighten his collar and resume a more normal voice.

This skilful and deliberate exploitation of his own temperament extended to other moods than anger. When he wanted to persuade or win someone over he could display great charm. Until the last days of his life he retained an uncanny gift of personal magnetism which defies analysis, but which many who met him have described. This was connected with the curious power of his eyes, which are persistently said to have had some sort of hypnotic quality. Similarly, when he wanted to frighten or shock, he showed himself a master of brutal and threatening language, as in the celebrated interviews with Schuschnigg[4] and President Hacha.[5]

Yet another variation in his roles was the impression of concentrated will-power and intelligence, the leader in complete command of the situation and with a knowledge of the facts which dazzled the generals or ministers summoned to receive his orders. To sustain this part he drew on his remarkable memory, which enabled him to reel off complicated orders of battle, technical specifications and long lists of names and dates without a moment's hesitation. Hitler cultivated this gift of memory assiduously. The fact that subsequently the details and figures which he cited were often found to contain inaccuracies did not matter: it was the immediate effect at which he aimed. The swiftness of the transition from one mood to another was startling: one moment his eyes would be filled with tears and pleading, the next blazing with fury, or glazed with the faraway look of the visionary.

Hitler, in fact, was a consummate actor, with the actor's and orator's facility for absorbing himself in a role and convincing himself of the truth of what he was saying at the time he said it. In his early years he was often awkward and unconvincing, but with practice the part became second nature to him, and with the immense prestige of success behind him, and the resources of a powerful state at his command, there were few who could resist the impression of the piercing eyes, the Napoleonic pose and the "historic" personality.

Hitler had the gift of all great politicians for grasping the possibilities of a situation more swiftly than his opponents. He saw, as no other politician did, how to play on the grievances and resentments of the German people, as later he was to play on French and British fear of war and fear of Communism. His insistence upon preserving the forms of legality in the struggle for power showed a brilliant under-

[4] Head of the Austrian Government at the time Hitler decided to annex Austria in 1938. [Editor's note.]

[5] President of Czechoslovakia when Hitler carried out the German occupation of Bohemia and Moravia in March 1939. [Editor's note.]

standing of the way to disarm opposition, just as the way in which he undermined the independence of the German Army showed his grasp of the weaknesses of the German Officer Corps.

A German word, *Fingerspitzgefühl*—"finger-tip feeling"—which was often applied to Hitler, well describes his sense of opportunity and timing.

No matter what you attempt [Hitler told Rauschning on one occasion], if an idea is not yet mature you will not be able to realize it. Then there is only one thing to do: have patience, wait, try again, wait again. In the subconscious, the work goes on. It matures, sometimes it dies. Unless I have the inner, incorruptible conviction: *this is the solution,* I do nothing. Not even if the whole Party tries to drive me into action.

Hitler knew how to wait in 1932, when his insistence on holding out until he could secure the Chancellorship appeared to court disaster. Foreign policy provides another instance. In 1939 he showed great patience while waiting for the situation to develop after direct negotiations with Poland had broken down and while the Western Powers were seeking to reach a settlement with Soviet Russia. Clear enough about his objectives, he contrived to keep his plans flexible. The date he fixed for the invasion of Czechoslovakia, 1 October 1938, is one of the few instances in which Hitler committed himself to a definite time-table, out of fury at the way the Czechs had scored off him on 28 May. Much more characteristic was his action in the case of the annexation of Austria and the occupation of Prague, where he made the final decision on the spur of the moment.

Until he was convinced that the right moment had come Hitler would find a hundred excuses for procrastination. His hesitation in such cases was notorious: his refusal to make up his mind to stand as a Presidential candidate in 1932, and his attempt to defer taking action against Roehm and the S.A. in 1934, are two obvious examples. Once he had made up his mind to move, however, he would act boldly, taking considerable risks, as in the reoccupation of the Rhineland in 1936, or the invasion of Norway and Denmark just before the major campaign in the west.

Surprise was a favourite gambit of Hitler's, in politics, diplomacy and war: he gauged the psychological effect of sudden, unexpected hammer-blows in paralysing opposition. An illustration of his appreciation of the value of surprise and quick decision, even when on the defensive, is the second presidential campaign of 1932. It had taken Goebbels weeks to persuade Hitler to stand for the Presidency at all. The defeat in the first ballot brought Goebbels to despair; but Hitler, now that he had committed himself, with great presence of mind dictated the announcement that he would stand a second time and got it on to the streets almost before the country had learned of his defeat. In war the psychological effect of the *blitzkrieg* was just as important in Hitler's eyes as the strategic: it gave the impression that the German military machine was more than life-size, that it possessed some virtue of invincibility against which ordinary men could not defend themselves.

No régime in history has ever paid such careful attention to psychological factors in politics. Hitler was a master of mass emotion. To attend one of his big meetings was to go through an emotional experience, not to listen to an argument or a programme. Yet nothing was left to chance on these occasions. Every device for heightening the emotional intensity, every trick of the theatre was used. The Nuremberg rallies held every year in September were masterpieces of theatrical art, with the most carefully devised effects. "I had spent six years in St. Petersburg before the war in the best days of the old Russian ballet," wrote Sir Nevile Henderson, "but for grandiose beauty I have never seen a ballet to compare with it." To see the films of the Nuremberg rallies even today is to be recaptured by the hypnotic effect of thousands of men marching in perfect order, the music of the massed bands, the forest of standards and flags, the vast perspectives of the stadium, the smoking torches, the dome of searchlights. The sense of power, of force and unity was irresistible, and all converged with a mounting crescendo of excitement on the supreme moment when the Fuehrer himself made his entry. Paradoxically, the man who was most affected by such spectacles was their originator, Hitler himself, and, as Rosenberg[6] remarks in his memoirs, they played an indispensable part in the process of self-intoxication.

Hitler had grasped as no one before him what could be done with a combination of propaganda and terrorism. For the complement to the attractive power

---

[6] A leading Nazi racist "philosopher." [Editor's note.]

of the great spectacles was the compulsive power of the Gestapo,[7] the S.S., and the concentration camp, heightened once again by skilful propaganda. Hitler was helped in this not only by his own perception of the sources of power in a modern urbanized mass-society, but also by possession of the technical means to manipulate them. This was a point well made by Albert Speer, Hitler's highly intelligent Minister for Armaments and War Production, in the final speech he made at his trial after the war.

Hitler's dictatorship [Speer told the court] differed in one fundamental point from all its predecessors in history. His was the first dictatorship in the present period of modern technical development, a dictatorship which made complete use of all technical means for the domination of its own country.

Through technical devices like the radio and the loudspeaker, eighty million people were deprived of independent thought. It was thereby possible to subject them to the will of one man. . . .

Earlier dictators needed highly qualified assistants, even at the lowest level, men who could think and act independently. The totalitarian system in the period of modern technical development can dispense with them; the means of communication alone make it possible to mechanize the lower leadership. As a result of this there arises the new type of the uncritical recipient of orders. . . . Another result was the far-reaching supervision of the citizens of the State and the maintenance of a high degree of secrecy for criminal acts.

The nightmare of many a man that one day nations could be dominated by technical means was all but realized in Hitler's totalitarian system.

In making use of the formidable power which was thus placed in his hands Hitler had one supreme, and fortunately rare, advantage: he had neither scruples nor inhibitions. He was a man without roots, with neither home nor family; a man who admitted no loyalties, was bound by no traditions, and felt respect neither for God nor man. Throughout his career Hitler showed himself prepared to seize any advantage that was to be gained by lying, cunning, treachery, and unscrupulousness. He demanded the sacrifice of millions of German lives for the sacred cause of Germany, but in the last year of the war was ready to destroy Germany rather than surrender his power or admit defeat.

Wary and secretive, he entertained a universal dis-

<hr>

[7] Hitler's secret police. [Editor's note.]

trust. He admitted no one to his counsels. He never let down his guard, or gave himself away. This is reflected in the almost total absence of any correspondence apart from official letters such as those he wrote to Mussolini. Hitler rarely committed himself to paper. "He never," Schacht wrote, "let slip an unconsidered word. He never said what he did not intend to say and he never blurted out a secret. Everything was the result of cold calculation." . . .

Cynical though he was, Hitler's cynicism stopped short of his own person: he came to believe that he was a man with a mission, marked out by Providence, and therefore exempt from the ordinary canons of human conduct.

Hitler probably held some such belief about himself from an early period. It was clear enough in the speech he made at his trial in 1924, and after he came out of prison those near him noticed that he began to hold aloof, to set a barrier between himself and his followers. After he came to power it became more noticeable. It was in March, 1936, that he made the famous assertion already quoted: "I go the way that Providence dictates with the assurance of a sleep-walker." In 1937 he told an audience at Würzburg:

However weak the individual may be when compared with the omnipotence and will of Providence, yet at the moment when he acts as Providence would have him act he becomes immeasurably strong. Then there streams down upon him that force which has marked all greatness in the world's history. And when I look back only on the five years which lie behind us, then I feel that I am justified in saying: That has not been the work of man alone.

Just before the occupation of Austria, in February, 1938, he declared in the Reichstag:

Above all, a man who feels it his duty at such an hour to assume the leadership of his people is not responsible to the laws of parliamentary usage or to a particular democratic conception, but solely to the mission placed upon him. And anyone who interferes with this mission is an enemy of the people.

It was in this sense of mission that Hitler, a man who believed neither in God nor in conscience ("a Jewish invention, a blemish like circumcision"), found both justification and absolution. He was the Siegfried come to reawaken Germany to greatness, for whom morality, suffering and "the litany of private virtues" were irrelevant. It was by such dreams that he sustained the ruthlessness and determination of his will. So long as this sense of mission was balanced by the cynical calculations of the politician, it represented a source of strength, but success was fatal. When half Europe lay at his feet and all need of restraint was removed, Hitler abandoned himself entirely to megalomania. He became convinced of his own infallibility. But when he began to look to the image he had created to work miracles of its own accord—instead of exploiting it—his gifts deteriorated and his intuition deluded him. Ironically, failure sprang from the same capacity which brought him success, his power of self-dramatization, his ability to convince himself. His belief in his power to work miracles kept him going when the more sceptical Mussolini faltered. Hitler played out his "world-historical" role to the bitter end. But it was this same belief which curtained him in illusion and blinded him to what was actually happening, leading him into that arrogant overestimate of his own genius which brought him to defeat. The sin which Hitler committed was that which the ancient Greeks called *hybris*, the sin of overweening pride, of believing himself to be more than a man. If ever a man was destroyed by the image he had created it was Adolf Hitler. . . .

4

RESPONSIBILITY FOR THE SECOND WORLD WAR

In the view of Alan Bullock, Hitler was destroyed by the image he had created for himself. In more prosaic terms, others have contended that he was destroyed by a war that he forced upon Europe in 1939. A few authors, however, have tended to place the blame for the outbreak of World War II on leaders of other nations, or at least to make them share the burden of guilt.

Any attempt to explain why the Second World War occurred must take into account the conditions left in the wake of the war of 1914–18. One of the results of the collapse in 1917 and 1918 of the three great empires of Central-Eastern Europe—Russia, Austria-Hungary, and Germany—was the resurrection of Poland as a unified nation. The Polish state was given territory that was taken from Germany by the Treaty of Versailles, including the so-called "Polish Corridor." This was a strip of land following the Vistula River to the Baltic. Its population contained a mixture of Germans and Poles. It was given to Poland so that the resurrected state could have the "free access to the sea" that Wilson had promised Poland in his Fourteen Points. In further fulfillment of Wilson's promise, the German city of Danzig at the mouth of the Vistula was taken from Germany and made into a Free City under the League of Nations, and Poland was granted special rights in Danzig by the League. The creation of the Polish Corridor separated East Prussia from Germany proper. Both this and the loss of Danzig caused German resentment against Versailles and against Poland.

When war began in 1939 the *immediate* causes were: (1) Hitler's insistence that the Polish provisions of the Versailles Treaty be revised; (2) the support Hitler gained from Stalin in the Nazi-Soviet Pact of August 23, 1939; (3) Poland's unwillingness to meet Hitler's demands; and (4) the support given Poland by Great Britain and France. Each of these has been treated as the prime immediate cause of the war by one historian or another. Most scholars have placed the overwhelming responsibility upon Hitler or Nazi-Germany more generally. The reasoning has been simple and straightforward: no demands, no crisis; no willingness to resort to force to satisfy the demands, no war.

To many historians this interpretation is too simple and quite inadequate. Quite possibly there would have been no Second World War if the Polish-German problem had been the only unsettling legacy of the peace settlement after World War I. A more basic and general flaw of the peace settlement was that it did not accurately reflect the real balance of power in Europe. It was made possible by the American aid that had been given to the Entente Powers, by the defeat of Germany, and by the chaos Russia was experiencing in the Civil War of 1917–21 following the Bolshevik Revolution. But all three of these circumstance were only temporary. American troops (and those of Britain as well) were almost entirely withdrawn from Europe by 1920, leaving the French to try to preserve the settlement as best they could. The military defeat of Germany was followed neither by a dismemberment of the country nor by a general military occupation by the victors, and as Germany patched up her wounds she soon stood forth again as the strongest nation in Europe, notwithstanding the Versailles Treaty. Finally, by 1928 the Soviet Union was as strong as tsarist Russia had been in 1914, and the Five Year Plans of 1928–1941 made it at least as powerful as Germany. Stalin by 1939 had the power to help upset the settlement of 1919–21, which had been made without consulting the Soviet leaders (and even against their opposition in the case of Poland's eastern frontier).

By the late 1930's the small states that emerged as independent in 1918–19 in Central-Eastern Europe, from Finland down through Yugoslavia, were powerless to withstand either Nazi Germany or Communist Russia if these two recovered giants decided to use force directly against their smaller neighbors. For several years it did not seem that this would happen. Instead the U.S.S.R. sought to subvert them internally by supporting their Communist parties, and Nazi Germany tried to gain influence over them through economic and diplomatic means. Then in March, 1938, Hitler sent German troops into Austria and incorporated that small German-populated nation into the "Third Reich." During the summer of 1938 he intensified his propaganda against Czechoslovakia, which contained a sizeable German-speaking minority in the Sudetenland. At the Munich Conference the leaders of Britain and France, Neville Chamberlain and Edouard Daladier, agreed to German annexation of the Sudetenland. This was the high point of the French and British policy of appeasement, through which they hoped to avoid war by satisfying Hitler's demands. But in March 1939 Hitler used force to gain control over the remnants of Czechoslovakia and after that directed his demands at Poland.

In evaluating responsibility for the outbreak of war in 1939 it is of central importance to decide whether Hitler's demands were reasonable, moderate, and virtually satisfied by August 1939, or whether his ambitions were irrational, sweeping, and possibly insatiable. If the first was the case, possibly the Poles, British, and French should have followed the policy of appeasement in the crisis of 1939. If the latter was the case, they had already practiced appeasement too long and acted properly in August 1939 in resisting Hitler's demands.

The role of the U.S.S.R. in the coming of World War II is even more a matter of dispute. Distrusting Communist Russia, the French and British did not try to win Stalin to a common stand to obstruct the eastward expansion of Nazi Germany before 1939. Even then they refused to agree to his price for Soviet support—expansion of Soviet influence in Central-Eastern Europe. Hitler was ready to pay the price, in spite of his loud denunciations of Communism and the U.S.S.R. over a period of two decades, and on August 23 the Nazi-Soviet Pact was negotiated in Moscow.

In the Communist interpretation, Stalin's approval of the Nazi-Soviet Pact was a necessary act of self-preservation for the U.S.S.R. Communist historians and political leaders alike have contended that the capitalistic powers—France and Britain, backed up by the United States—deliberately were encouraging Hitler to expand eastward in the hope that Germany and Soviet Russia would become locked in combat. Stalin later laid down the line for Communist scholars when he stated that "the war arose in reality as the *inevitable* result of the development of the world economic and political forces on the basis of monopoly capitalism." (Italics added.) Winston Churchill, on the other hand, more than once observed that "there never was a war in all history easier to prevent by timely action." Many western historians assign Stalin a large share of blame for his failure to take timely action with the West in 1939 to block Hitler's designs on Poland. Indeed, some argue that through the Nazi-Soviet Pact Stalin gave the green light to aggression and that this agreement was comparable to the "blank check" that Germany gave Austria-Hungary in 1914.

The results of the decisions of 1939 continue to be felt. The importance of understanding why the war came is clear. Did it begin as a result of a deliberate design? If so, by whose design? Or was it the unintended by-product of blunder? If so, whose blunder? The readings that follow should help you develop your own tentative interpretation. To understand how the conflict that began in 1939 was broadened into a global war will require additional reading.

THE NUREMBERG JUDGMENT

EUROPE FORCED INTO WAR

In 1945–46 the East-West alliance that defeated the Axis Powers had not yet fully disintegrated into the "Cold War." Soviet, French, British, and American jurists then sat in judgment on Germany's war leaders in the International Military Tribunal in Nuremberg. They developed an interpretation of responsibility for the outbreak of war in 1939, and in doing so they heard dozens of witnesses for and against the defendants, received depositions from thousands of others, and drew upon tons of German records that Allied armies had confiscated in 1945. The judges wrote history as well as a legal judgment. Indeed, they based their legal judgment squarely on the history they wrote. Their view of history is presented in the following selection from the Nuremberg judgment of October 1, 1946.

Study this material critically and carefully. Was the Nuremberg historical verdict affected by the fact that no Germans were among the judges? By the fact that Italians and Poles were not present as either judges or defendants? By the fact that the U.S.S.R. was represented among the prosecution and the judges? By the fact that Great Britain, France, and the United States made up—with the U.S.S.R.—the prosecution and the judges?

During the years immediately following Hitler's appointment as Chancellor, the Nazi Government set about reorganizing the economic life of Germany, and in particular the armament industry. This was done on a vast scale and with extreme thoroughness.

It was necessary to lay a secure financial foundation for the building of armaments, and in April 1936, the defendant Goering was appointed coordinator for raw materials and foreign exchange, and empowered to supervise all state and party activities in these fields. In this capacity he brought together the War Minister, the Minister of Economics, the Reich Finance Minister, the President of the Reichsbank, and the Prussian Finance Minister to discuss problems connected with war mobilization, and on the 27th May 1936, in addressing these men, Goering opposed any financial limitation of war production and added that "all measures are to be considered from the standpoint of an assured waging of war.". . .

The first acts of aggression referred to in the indictment are the seizure of Austria and Czechoslovakia; and the first war of aggression charged in the indictment is the war against Poland begun on the 1st September 1939.

Before examining that charge it is necessary to look more closely at some of the events which preceded these acts of aggression. The war against Poland did not come suddenly out of an otherwise clear sky; the evidence has made it plain that this war of aggression, as well as the seizure of Austria and Czechoslovakia, was premeditated and carefully prepared, and was not undertaken until the moment was thought opportune for it to be carried through as a definite part of the preordained scheme and plan.

For the aggressive designs of the Nazi Government were not accidents arising out of the immediate political situation in Europe and the world; they were a deliberate and essential part of Nazi foreign policy.

From *Nazi Conspiracy and Aggression: Opinion and Judgment*, published by the Office of United States Chief of Counsel for Prosecution of Axis Criminality (Washington, 1947), pp. 12–13, 16–21, 27–34.

From the beginning, the National Socialist movement claimed that its object was to unite the German people in the consciousness of their mission and destiny, based on inherent qualities of race, and under the guidance of the Fuehrer.

For its achievement, two things were deemed to be essential: The disruption of the European order as it had existed since the Treaty of Versailles, and the creation of a Greater Germany beyond the frontiers of 1914. This necessarily involved the seizure of foreign territories.

War was seen to be inevitable, or at the very least, highly probable, if these purposes were to be accomplished. The German people, therefore, with all their resources, were to be organized as a great political-military army, schooled to obey without question any policy decreed by the State.

In "Mein Kampf" Hitler had made this view quite plain. It must be remembered that "Mein Kampf" was no mere private diary in which the secret thoughts of Hitler were set down. Its contents were rather proclaimed from the house tops. It was used in the schools and universities and among the Hitler youth,[1] in the SS and the SA, and among the German people generally, even down to the presentation of an official copy to all newly married people. By the year 1945 over six and one-half million copies had been circulated. . . .

"Mein Kampf" is quite explicit in stating where the increased territory is to be found:

Therefore we National Socialists have purposely drawn a line through the line of conduct followed by prewar Germany in foreign policy. We put an end to the perpetual Germanic march towards the south and west of Europe, and turn our eyes towards the lands of the east. We finally put a stop to the colonial and trade policy of the prewar times, and pass over to the territorial policy of the future. But when we speak of new territory in Europe today, we must think principally of Russia and the border states subject to her.

"Mein Kampf" is not to be regarded as a mere literary exercise, nor as an inflexible policy or plan incapable of modification.

Its importance lies in the unmistakable attitude of aggression revealed throughout its pages.

Evidence from captured documents has revealed

[1]Nazi youth organization. [Editor's note.]

that Hitler held four secret meetings to which the Tribunal proposes to make special reference because of the light they shed upon the question of the common plan and aggressive war. . . .

They are obviously careful records of the events they describe, and they have been preserved as such in the archives of the German Government, from whose custody they were captured. Such documents could never be dismissed as inventions, nor even as inaccurate or distorted; they plainly record events which actually took place.

It will perhaps be useful to deal first of all with the meeting of the 23d November 1939, when Hitler called his supreme commanders together. A record was made of what was said, by one of those present. At the date of the meeting, Austria and Czechoslovakia had been incorporated into the German Reich, Poland had been conquered by the German armies, and the war with Great Britain and France was still in its static phase. The moment was opportune for a review of past events. Hitler informed the commanders that the purpose of the conference was to give them an idea of the world of his thoughts, and to tell them his decision. He thereupon reviewed his political task since 1919, and referred to the secession of Germany from the League of Nations, the denunciation of the Disarmament Conference, the order for rearmament, the introduction of compulsory armed service, the occupation of the Rhineland, the seizure of Austria, and the action against Czechoslovakia. He stated:

One year later, Austria came; this step also was considered doubtful. It brought about a considerable reinforcement of the Reich. The next step was Bohemia, Moravia, and Poland. This step also was not possible to accomplish in one campaign. First of all, the western fortification had to be finished. It was not possible to reach the goal in one effort. It was clear to me from the first moment that I could not be satisfied with the Sudeten German territory. That was only a partial solution. The decision to march into Bohemia was made. Then followed the erection of the Protectorate and with that the basis for the action against Poland was laid, but I wasn't quite clear at that time whether I should start first against the east and then in the west or vice versa . . . Basically I did not organize the armed forces in order not to strike. The decision to strike was always in me. Earlier or later I wanted to solve the problem. Under pressure it was decided that the east was to be attacked first.

This address, reviewing past events and reaffirming the aggressive intentions present from the beginning, puts beyond any question of doubt the character of

War and Totalitarianism

the actions against Austria and Czechoslovakia, and the war against Poland.

For they had all been accomplished according to plan; and the nature of that plan must now be examined in a little more detail.

At the meeting of the 23d November 1939, Hitler was looking back to things accomplished; at the earlier meetings now to be considered, he was looking forward, and revealing his plans to his confederates. The comparison is instructive.

The meeting held at the Reich Chancellery in Berlin on the 5th November 1937 was attended by Lieutenant Colonel Hossbach, Hitler's personal adjutant, who compiled a long note of the proceedings, which he dated the 10th November 1937 and signed.

The persons present were Hitler, and the defendants Goering, von Neurath, and Raeder, in their capacities as Commander in Chief of the Luftwaffe, Reich Foreign Minister, and Commander in Chief of the Navy respectively, General von Blomberg, Minister of War, and General von Fritsch, the Commander in Chief of the Army.

Hitler began by saying that the subject of the conference was of such high importance that in other States it would have taken place before the Cabinet. He went on to say that the subject matter of his speech was the result of his detailed deliberations, and of his experiences during his $4\frac{1}{2}$ years of government. He requested that the statements he was about to make should be looked upon in the case of his death as his last will and testament. Hitler's main theme was the problem of living space, and he discussed various possible solutions, only to set them aside. He then said that the seizure of living space on the continent of Europe was therefore necessary, expressing himself in these words:

It is not a case of conquering people but of conquering agriculturally useful space. It would also be more to the purpose to seek raw material producing territory in Europe directly adjoining the Reich and not overseas, and this solution would have to be brought into effect for one or two generations . . . The history of all times—Roman Empire, British Empire—has proved that every space expansion can only be effected by breaking resistance and taking risks. Even set-backs are unavoidable; neither formerly nor today has space been found without an owner; the attacker always comes up against the proprietor.

He concluded with this observation:

The question for Germany is where the greatest possible conquest could be made at the lowest cost.

Nothing could indicate more plainly the aggressive intentions of Hitler, and the events which soon followed showed the reality of his purpose. It is impossible to accept the contention that Hitler did not actually mean war; for after pointing out that Germany might expect the opposition of England and France, and analyzing the strength and the weakness of those powers in particular situations, he continued:

The German question can be solved only by way of force, and this is never without risk . . . If we place the decision to apply force with risk at the head of the following expositions, then we are left to reply to the questions "when" and "how." In this regard we have to decide upon three different cases.

The first of these three cases set forth a hypothetical international situation, in which he would take action not later than 1943 to 1945, saying:

If the Fuehrer is still living then it will be his irrevocable decision to solve the German space problem not later than 1943 to 1945. The necessity for action before 1943 to 1945 will come under consideration in cases 2 and 3.

The second and third cases to which Hitler referred show the plain intention to seize Austria and Czechoslovakia, and in this connection Hitler said:

For the improvement of our military-political position, it must be our first aim in every case of entanglement by war to conquer Czechoslovakia and Austria simultaneously in order to remove any threat from the flanks in case of a possible advance westwards.

He further added:

The annexation of the two States to Germany militarily and politically would constitute a considerable relief, owing to shorter and better frontiers, the freeing of fighting personnel for other purposes, and the possibility of reconstituting new armies up to a strength of about twelve divisions.

This decision to seize Austria and Czechoslovakia was discussed in some detail; the action was to be taken as soon as a favorable opportunity presented itself.

The military strength which Germany had been building up since 1933 was now to be directed at the two specific countries, Austria and Czechoslovakia.

The defendant Goering testified that he did not believe at that time that Hitler actually meant to attack

Austria and Czechoslovakia, and that the purpose of the conference was only to put pressure on von Fritsch to speed up the rearmament of the Army.

The defendant Raeder testified that neither he, nor von Fritsch, nor von Blomberg, believed that Hitler actually meant war, a conviction which the defendant Raeder claims that he held up to the 22d August 1939. The basis of this conviction was his hope that Hitler would obtain a "political solution" of Germany's problems. But all that this means, when examined, is the belief that Germany's position would be so good, and Germany's armed might so overwhelming, that the territory desired could be obtained without fighting for it. It must be remembered toQ that Hitler's declared intention with regard to Austria was actually carried out within a little over 4 months from the date of the meeting, and within less than a year the first portion of Czechoslovakia was absorbed, and Bohemia and Moravia a few months later. If any doubts had existed in the minds of any of his hearers in November 1937, after March of 1939 there could no longer be any question that Hitler was in deadly earnest in his decision to resort to war. The Tribunal is satisfied that Lieutenant Colonel Hossbach's account of the meeting is substantially correct, and that those present knew that Austria and Czechoslovakia would be annexed by Germany at the first possible opportunity. . . .

By March 1939 the plan to annex Austria and Czechoslovakia, which had been discussed by Hitler at the meeting of the 5th November 1937, had been accomplished. The time had now come for the German leaders to consider further acts of aggression, made more possible of attainment because of that accomplishment.

On the 23d May 1939, a meeting was held in Hitler's study in the new Reich Chancellery in Berlin. Hitler announced his decision to attack Poland and gave his reasons, and discussed the effect the decision might have on other countries. In point of time, this was the second of the important meetings to which reference has already been made, and in order to appreciate the full significance of what was said and done, it is necessary to state shortly some of the main events in the history of German-Polish relations.

As long ago as the year 1925 an Arbitration Treaty between Germany and Poland had been made at Locarno, providing for the settlement of all disputes between the two countries. On the 26th January 1934, a German-Polish declaration of nonaggression was made, signed on behalf of the German Government by the defendant von Neurath. On the 30th January 1934, and again on the 30th January 1937, Hitler made speeches in the Reichstag in which he expressed his view that Poland and Germany could work together in harmony and peace. On the 20th February 1938, Hitler made a third speech in the Reichstag in the course of which he said with regard to Poland:

And so the way to a friendly understanding has been successfully paved, an understanding which, beginning with Danzig, has today, in spite of the attempts of certain mischief makers, succeeded in finally taking the poison out of the relations between Germany and Poland and transforming them into a sincere, friendly cooperation. Relying on her friendships, Germany will not leave a stone unturned to save that ideal which provides the foundation for the task which is ahead of us—peace.

On the 26th September 1938, in the middle of the crisis over the Sudetenland, Hitler made the speech in Berlin which has already been quoted, and announced that he had informed the British Prime Minister that when the Czechoslovakian problem was solved there would be no more territorial problems for Germany in Europe. Nevertheless, on the 24th November of the same year, an OKW directive was issued to the German armed forces to make preparations for an attack upon Danzig; it stated:

The Fuehrer has ordered: (1) Preparations are also to be made to enable the Free State of Danzig to be occupied by German troops by surprise.

In spite of having ordered military preparations for the occupation of Danzig, Hitler, on the 30th January 1939, said in a speech in the Reichstag:

During the troubled months of the past year, the friendship between Germany and Poland has been one of the reassuring factors in the political life of Europe.

Five days previously, on the 25th January 1939, von Ribbentrop[2] said in the course of a speech in Warsaw:

Thus Poland and Germany can look forward to the future with full confidence in the solid basis of their mutual relations.

Following the occupation of Bohemia and Moravia by Germany on the 15th March 1939, which was

[2] Foreign Minister in the Nazi regime, 1938–45. [Editor's note.]

a flagrant breach of the Munich Agreement, Great Britain gave an assurance to Poland on the 31st March 1939, that in the event of any action which clearly threatened Polish independence, and which the Polish Government accordingly considered it vital to resist with their national forces, Great Britain would feel itself bound at once to lend Poland all the support in its power. The French Government took the same stand. It is interesting to note in this connection, that one of the arguments frequently presented by the defense in the present case is that the defendants were induced to think that their conduct was not in breach of international law by the acquiescence of other powers. The declarations of Great Britain and France showed, at least, that this view could be held no longer.

On the 3d April 1939, a revised OKW[3] directive was issued to the armed forces, which after referring to the question of Danzig made reference to Fall Weiss (the military code name for the German invasion of Poland) and stated:

The Fuehrer has added the following directions to Fall Weiss: (1) Preparations must be made in such a way that the operation can be carried out at any time from the 1st September 1939 onwards. (2) The High Command of the Armed Forces has been directed to draw up a precise time-table for Fall Weiss and to arrange by conferences the synchronized timings between the three branches of the Armed Forces.

On the 11th of April 1939, a further directive was signed by Hitler and issued to the armed forces, and in one of the annexes to that document the words occur:

Quarrels with Poland should be avoided. Should Poland, however, adopt a threatening attitude toward Germany, "a final settlement" will be necessary, notwithstanding the pact with Poland. The aim is then to destroy Polish military strength, and to create in the east a situation which satisfies the requirements of defense. The Free State of Danzig will be incorporated into Germany at the outbreak of the conflict at the latest. Policy aims at limiting the war to Poland, and this is considered possible in view of the internal crisis in France, and British restraint as a result of this.

In spite of the contents of those two directives, Hitler made a speech in the Reichstag on the 28th of April 1939, in which, after describing the Polish Government's alleged rejection of an offer he had made with regard to Danzig and the Polish Corridor, he stated:

I have regretted greatly this incomprehensible attitude of the Polish Government, but that alone is not the decisive fact; the worst is that now Poland like Czechoslovakia a year ago believes, under the pressure of a lying international campaign, that it must call up its troops, although Germany on her part has not called up a single man, and had not thought of proceeding in any way against Poland. . . . The intention to attack on the part of Germany which was merely invented by the international Press . . .

It was 4 weeks after making this speech that Hitler, on the 23d May 1939, held the important military conference to which reference has already been made. Among the persons present were the defendants Goering, Raeder, and Keitel.[4] The adjutant on duty that day was Lieutenant Colonel Schmundt, and he made a record of what happened, certifying it with his signature as a correct record.

The purpose of the meeting was to enable Hitler to inform the heads of the armed forces and their staffs of his views on the political situation and his future aims. After analyzing the political situation and reviewing the course of events since 1933, Hitler announced his decision to attack Poland. He admitted that the quarrel with Poland over Danzig was not the reason for this attack, but the necessity for Germany to enlarge her living space and secure her food supplies. He said:

The solution of the problem demands courage. The principle by which one evades solving the problem by adapting oneself to circumstances is inadmissible. Circumstances must rather be adapted to needs. This is impossible without invasion of foreign states or attacks upon foreign property.

Later in his address he added:

There is therefore no question of sparing Poland, and we are left with the decision to attack Poland at the first suitable opportunity. We cannot expect a repetition of the Czech affair. There will be war. Our task is to isolate Poland. The success of the isolation will be decisive. . . . The isolation of Poland is a matter of skillful politics.

Lieutenant Colonel Schmundt's record of the meeting reveals that Hitler fully realized the possibility of Great Britain and France coming to Poland's assistance. If, therefore, the isolation of Poland could not be achieved, Hitler was of the opinion that Germany should attack Great Britain and France first, or at any rate should concentrate primarily on the war in the West, in order to defeat Great Britain and France quickly, or at least to destroy their effectiveness.

[3]Armed Forces Supreme Command. [Editor's note.]

[4]Keitel was Chief of the Supreme Command of the Armed Forces under Hitler, 1938–45. [Editor's note.]

Nevertheless, Hitler stressed that war with England and France would be a life and death struggle, which might last a long time, and that preparations must be made accordingly.

During the weeks which followed this conference, other meetings were held and directives were issued in preparation for the war. The defendant von Ribbentrop was sent to Moscow to negotiate a non-aggression pact with the Soviet Union.

On the 22d August 1939 there took place the important meeting of that day, to which reference has already been made. The prosecution have put in evidence two unsigned captured documents which appear to be records made of this meeting by persons who were present. The first document is headed: "The Fuehrer's speech to the Commanders in Chief on the 22nd August 1939 . . ." The purpose of the speech was to announce the decision to make war on Poland at once, and Hitler began by saying:

It was clear to me that a conflict with Poland had to come sooner or later. I had already made this decision in the spring, but I thought that I would first turn against the West in a few years, and only afterwards against the East . . . I wanted to establish an acceptable relationship with Poland in order to fight first against the West. But this plan, which was agreeable to me, could not be executed since essential points have changed. It became clear to me that Poland would attack us in case of a conflict with the West.

Hitler then went on to explain why he had decided that the most favorable moment had arrived for starting the war. "Now," said Hitler, "Poland is in the position in which I wanted her . . . I am only afraid that at the last moment some Schweinhund[5] will make a proposal for mediation . . . A beginning has been made for the destruction of England's hegemony."

This document closely resembles one of the documents put in evidence on behalf of the defendant Raeder. This latter document consists of a summary of the same speech, compiled on the day it was made, by one Admiral Boehm, from notes he had taken during the meeting. In substance it says that the moment had arrived to settle the dispute with Poland by military invasion, that although a conflict between Germany and the West was unavoidable in the long run, the likelihood of Great Britain and France coming to Poland's assistance was not great,

and that even if a war in the West should come about, the first aim should be the crushing of the Polish military strength. It also contains a statement by Hitler that an appropriate propaganda reason for invading Poland would be given, the truth or falsehood of which was unimportant, since "the Right lies in Victory."

The second unsigned document put in evidence by the prosecution is headed: "Second Speech by the Fuehrer on the 22d August 1939," and it is in the form of notes of the main points made by Hitler. Some of these are as follows:

Everybody shall have to make a point of it that we were determined from the beginning to fight the Western Powers. Struggle for life or death . . . destruction of Poland in the foreground. The aim is elimination of living forces, not the arrival at a certain line. Even if war should break out in the West, the destruction of Poland shall be the primary objective. I shall give a propagandist cause for starting the war—never mind whether it be plausible or not. The victor shall not be asked later on whether we told the truth or not. In starting and making a war, not the Right is what matters, but Victory . . . The start will be ordered probably by Saturday morning. (That is to say, the 26th August.)

In spite of it being described as a second speech, there are sufficient points of similarity with the two previously mentioned documents to make it appear very probable that this is an account of the same speech, not as detailed as the other two, but in substance the same.

These three documents establish that the final decision as to the date of Poland's destruction, which had been agreed upon and planned earlier in the year, was reached by Hitler shortly before the 22d August 1939. They also show that although he hoped to be able to avoid having to fight Great Britain and France as well, he fully realized that there was a risk of this happening, but it was a risk which he was determined to take.

The events of the last days of August confirm this determination. On the 22d August 1939, the same day as the speech just referred to, the British Prime Minister wrote a letter to Hitler, in which he said:

Having thus made our position perfectly clear, I wish to repeat to you my conviction that war between our two peoples would be the greatest calamity that could occur.

On the 23d August, Hitler replied:

The question of the treatment of European problems on a

[5]Literally, a swineherd's dog; in German, more or less like saying "some bastard" or "some rascal." [Editor's note.]

peaceful basis is not a decision which rests with Germany, but primarily on those who since the crime committed by the Versailles Dictate have stubbornly and consistently opposed any peaceful revision. Only after a change of spirit on the part of the responsible Powers can there be any real change in the relationship between England and Germany.

There followed a number of appeals to Hitler to refrain from forcing the Polish issue to the point of war. These were from President Roosevelt on the 24th and 25th August; from His Holiness the Pope on the 24th and 31st August; and from M. Daladier, the Prime Minister of France, on the 26th August. All these appeals fell on deaf ears.

On the 25th August, Great Britain signed a pact of mutual assistance with Poland, which reinforced the understanding she had given to Poland earlier in the year. This coupled with the news of Mussolini's unwillingness to enter the war on Germany's side, made Hitler hesitate for a moment. The invasion of Poland, which was timed to start on the 26th August, was postponed until a further attempt had been made to persuade Great Britain not to intervene. Hitler offered to enter into a comprehensive agreement with Great Britain, once the Polish question had been settled. In reply to this, Great Britain made a countersuggestion for the settlement of the Polish dispute by negotiation. On the 29th August, Hitler informed the British Ambassador that the German Government, though skeptical as to the result, would be prepared to enter into direct negotiations with a Polish emissary, provided he arrived in Berlin with plenipotentiary powers by midnight of the following day, August 30. The Polish Government were informed of this, but with the example of Schuschnigg and Hácha before them, they decided not to send such an emissary. At midnight on the 30th August the defendant von Ribbentrop read to the British Ambassador at top speed a document containing the first precise formulation of the German demands against Poland. He refused, however, to give the Ambassador a copy of this, and stated that in any case it was too late now, since no Polish plenipotentiary had arrived.

In the opinion of the Tribunal, the manner in which these negotiations were conducted by Hitler and von Ribbentrop showed that they were not entered into in good faith or with any desire to maintain peace, but solely in the attempt to prevent Great Britain and France from honoring their obligations to Poland.

Parallel with these negotiations were the unsuccessful attempts made by Goering to effect the isolation of Poland by persuading Great Britain not to stand by her pledged word, through the services of one Birger Dahlerus, a Swede. Dahlerus, who was called as a witness by Goering, had a considerable knowledge of England and of things English, and in July 1939 was anxious to bring about a better understanding between England and Germany, in the hope of preventing a war between the two countries. He got into contact with Goering as well as with official circles in London, and during the latter part of August, Goering used him as an unofficial intermediary to try and deter the British Government from their opposition to Germany's intentions toward Poland. Dahlerus, of course, had no knowledge at the time of the decision which Hitler had secretly announced on the 22d August, nor of the German military directives for the attack on Poland which were already in existence. As he admitted in his evidence, it was not until the 26th September, after the conquest of Poland was virtually complete, that he first realized that Goering's aim all along had been to get Great Britain's consent to Germany's seizure of Poland.

After all attempts to persuade Germany to agree to a settlement of her dispute with Poland on a reasonable basis had failed, Hitler, on the 31st August, issued his final directive, in which he announced that the attack on Poland would start in the early morning of the 1st September, and gave instructions as to what action would be taken if Great Britain and France should enter the war in defense of Poland.

In the opinion of the Tribunal, the events of the days immediately preceding the 1st September 1939, demonstrate the determination of Hitler and his associates to carry out the declared intention of invading Poland at all costs, despite appeals from every quarter. With the ever increasing evidence before him that this intention would lead to war with Great Britain and France as well, Hitler was resolved not to depart from the course he had set for himself. The Tribunal is fully satisfied by the evidence that the war initiated by Germany against Poland on the 1st September 1939, was most plainly an aggressive war, which was to develop in due course into a war which embraced almost the whole world, and resulted in the commission of countless crimes, both against the laws and customs of war, and against humanity.

Europe Forced into War

RAYMOND J. SONTAG

AN AMERICAN HISTORIAN'S CASE AGAINST HITLER

The Nuremberg judgment placed the blame for World War II upon Germany. In the years that followed, as the Cold War developed and both Moscow and the West published collections of documents to support their antithetical interpretations, many authors broadened the Nuremberg definition of responsibility. Others, particularly German scholars, narrowed it to focus the responsibility upon Hitler rather than upon "Germany." Unlike their counterparts after World War I, most German historians after 1945 made no attempt to put the primary blame for the war of 1939–45 on the leaders of other countries. Most concurred in the view expressed by Hermann Mau and Helmut Krausnick in a book published in 1953: "Hitler had ordered the attack knowing that he was risking a world war." This theme is developed with care by Raymond J. Sontag in the selection that follows.

Professor of History at the University of California (Berkeley), Sontag won justified acclaim in the 1930's for a balanced account of the coming of World War I. It was especially fitting that a man of his competence in German diplomatic history was selected in 1946 to serve as United States representative on an American-British-French board of editors that was to select and publish captured documents of the German Foreign Office. Professor Sontag served as chief American editor from 1946 to 1949. With James A. Beddie, Sontag edited the documents the Department of State published in 1948 on *Nazi-Soviet Relations, 1939–1941*. Under able successors the documents on Germany's 1939 diplomacy were completely published in 1956. They provided a basis for an article by Sontag in *Foreign Affairs*, from which this reading is taken. Clearly and without resort to emotionalism, Sontag argues that Hitler pressed his Polish demands until he pushed himself and Europe into war.

Hitler freely admitted [before September, 1939] that his successes in the foreign field had been won by bluff. The conviction was general in Europe that the First World War had dangerously undermined European society and that another war would bring the structure to ruin, with Communism as the only gainer. The Soviet Union, sharing this conviction, was eager to stand clear so that it would not be involved in the general ruin. By exploiting fear of war Hitler had won much. He was confident that still more must be won by diplomacy before he could safely embark on war with the West.

Some day, Hitler recognized, Britain and France would be tempted to set limits to German power, even by war. In preparation for that day, he argued, Germany must not only strain her resources in military preparations; she must also win territory sufficient to feed her people during a long war—for war with the Western democracies would be both long and hard. Colonies would be of no value; their resources would be lost by blockade just when they were needed. The territory must be won in Eastern Europe. There, German skill could increase agricultural production, and the non-German population

From Raymond J. Sontag, "The Last Months of Peace, 1939," *Foreign Affairs*, XXXV (April, 1957), pp. 508–515, 519–524. Excerpted by special permission from *Foreign Affairs*, April, 1957. Copyright by the Council on Foreign Relations, Inc., New York.

would provide a labor pool for farm and factory. The moment was, he believed, auspicious. Russia could not interfere: the purges had shaken the country and deprived the Red Army of its leaders; Stalin must fear a victorious army no less than military defeat. Fear of Russia would hold Poland on the side of Germany so long as exactions from Poland were counterbalanced by concessions to Polish territorial greed. Italy and Japan were so completely estranged from the Western democracies that they must follow the German lead. British and especially French rearmament was only beginning, and was encountering opposition unavoidable where the press was unmuzzled. Above all, Britain and France were ruled by men who had already retreated before the threat of war. Hitler was convinced that they lacked the resolution to precipitate a war or conduct it to the death.

The moves of March 1939 were, like the annexation of Austria and the Sudeten districts of Czechoslovakia, merely preliminary to the task of winning "living space." They would provide better frontiers and advanced military bases in the east, jumping-off places for future action. They would not bring the enlarged agricultural base needed for the future long war of annihilation with the Western democracies. Hitler made no diplomatic or military preparations which would suggest that even local opposition of any importance was anticipated. In one sense he envisioned the moves of March 1939 as the logical completion of the campaign against Czechoslovakia; in another sense, they were moves preparatory to the winning of the desired agricultural base.

In the early morning hours of March 15, 1939, after a stormy interview with Hitler, President Hácha wearily signed away the independence of what was left of Czechoslovakia. German troops had already crossed the frontier, and by afternoon Hitler was in Prague. The following Monday, March 20, the Lithuanian Foreign Minister was received by Ribbentrop and told that Memel must be surrendered to Germany. Even before this demand was accepted on Thursday, the next move was made.

On Tuesday, March 21, Ribbentrop asked the Polish Ambassador, Lipski, to call on him. The Ambassador said that the German protectorate over Slovakia had hit Poland hard. Ribbentrop hinted that the status of Slovakia was not necessarily final and might be subject to discussion if German-Polish relations developed satisfactorily. It was Hitler's hope, Rib-

bentrop continued, that such would be the case; but the Führer was troubled by anti-German feeling in Poland. The Poles must surely recognize that unless they cooperated with Germany they would be absorbed by Communist Russia. It was necessary to put German-Polish relations on a sound and lasting basis. To this end, Danzig must return to Germany, and Germany must be granted extra-territorial rail and road connections between the Reich and East Prussia. Then Hitler would be prepared to guarantee the Polish Corridor, and then it would be possible to deal with the Slovak question to the satisfaction of all. Ribbentrop suggested that Lipski take these proposals to Warsaw. Possibly the Polish Foreign Minister, Beck, would come to Berlin to discuss them; Hitler would warmly welcome such a discussion.

Lipski did go to Warsaw, and while he was away Hitler informed his army commander that a military solution of the problem of Danzig was not desired, because this would drive Poland into the arms of Britain; the use of Slovakia as a bargaining counter to win Polish agreement was contemplated. While he did not wish to solve the Polish question militarily unless especially favorable political conditions arose, Hitler continued, plans should be made, with the objective of beating the Poles so thoroughly that they would not be a political factor for some decades. He would absent himself from Berlin, leaving the conduct of negotiations with Lipski to Ribbentrop.

The Polish reply was presented by Lipski on Sunday, March 26. In form it was most conciliatory, but it did not meet the German demands. Ribbentrop, from his discussion with Lipski, drew the conclusion that this was not the Polish Government's last word and that Poland merely wished to escape as cheaply as possible. The next day, he applied pressure. The Polish reply, he said, could not be regarded as a basis for a settlement; German-Polish relations were, therefore, deteriorating rapidly. Lipski promised to do what he could to overcome the difficulties. Two days later, the German representative in Danzig was told that Poland was not to be provoked. Polish reluctance would be worn down by attrition tactics, and Danzig should adopt a sphinxlike attitude. Ribbentrop was of the opinion that the climax of the crisis had been reached.

Already signs were multiplying that the crisis was not, in fact, at its climax, and that Prague, Memel and Danzig had violently shaken world diplomatic alignments. In Britain and France the annihilation of

Czechoslovakia produced a strong popular reaction against the policy of appeasement. Chamberlain[1] and Daladier[2] had wavered and then fallen in with the popular mood. Recognition of the German action in Czechoslovakia was refused, and the British and French Ambassadors in Berlin were ordered home for consultation. When there were rumors of new German moves in Central Europe, there was a flurry of diplomatic activity from which emerged, on March 31, a declaration by Chamberlain in the House of Commons that Britain and France would aid Poland in resisting any action clearly threatening Polish independence. Hard on this declaration, the Polish Foreign Minister arrived in London, and at the conclusion of his visit Chamberlain stated on April 6 that a permanent alliance would be negotiated between Britain and Poland. Moreover, Chamberlain offered similar guarantees to states of southeastern Europe, and these offers met with a sympathetic reception despite German reminders that "the shelter of the umbrella" had been no protection for Abyssinia, Austria, Czechoslovakia or the Spanish Republicans.

More ominous, negotiations began in mid-April for drawing the Soviet Union into what the Germans called the British encirclement program; someone kept the German Embassy in London fully and promptly informed of these negotiations. Finally, even the United States Government assumed a more active rôle. At the onset of the March crisis, the German chargé in Washington warned that the Roosevelt Administration was determined to support Britain and France in any war with Germany and that, while American opinion was opposed to war, this opposition would collapse on the first news of air attacks on British or French cities. On April 15, President Roosevelt appealed directly to Hitler and Mussolini, asking for assurance against armed attack on a long list of states.

Even within the Axis, the occupation of Prague produced a violent reaction. As usual, the Italian Government had received no advance notice of the German action, and repetition intensified Italian resentment against such cavalier treatment. Now, however, the Italians were not only humiliated; they were frightened. Austria and Czechoslovakia were completely under German control, and Hungary was a dependent of the Reich. As a reliable infor-

mant told the Germans, "people are saying that in the end the old Hapsburg Empire, this time under the swastika flag, will reappear on the Adriatic." German assurances that the Mediterranean, including the Adriatic, was an Italian sphere of influence, did not disarm Italian fears. On Good Friday, Mussolini moved to solidify the Italian position by seizing Albania, and he did not forewarn Germany. Meanwhile, more and more clearly the Italian suggestion that Germans in the South Tyrol be resettled in Germany was changing to a firm demand. Italian policy was assuming an unaccustomed and potentially dangerous independence of German leadership.

There is no evidence that all this activity caused Hitler any alarm, and much evidence that he continued confident of success. As the weeks passed, German policy towards Poland changed, and by May 23 Hitler was resolved to attack her at the first suitable opportunity; but this was to be an isolated operation, from which other Powers would remain aloof.

By April 3, when Beck[3] arrived in London, it was already obvious that the German plan to hold Poland away from Britain had failed. On the same day, the high command of the Wehrmacht[4] was instructed to prepare plans for an attack on Poland in such a way that the operation could begin at any time from September 1. In the amplification of these instructions issued on April 11, the war with Poland was still described as a possibility to be avoided if possible; in any case, every precaution must be taken to limit the war to Poland only. The proposal made by Ribbentrop to Lipski was withdrawn on April 6; German missions abroad were instructed not to discuss the proposal or the Polish counteroffer.

The war of nerves was begun, with full confidence of victory. Ribbentrop was convinced that "not one British soldier would be mobilized in the event of a German-Polish conflict." Göring and Hitler expressed the same conviction. Public excitement, the Nazis argued, had pushed Beck, Chamberlain and Daladier into foolish threats and promises, but, as Hitler said, "one could only yell for a certain time." When passions cooled, and reason reasserted itself, it would become obvious that the German position was overwhelmingly strong. In the German view,

[1] Prime Minister in Great Britain, 1937–40. [Editor's note.]

[2] French Premier, 1938–40. [Editor's note.]

[3] Polish Foreign Minister, 1932–39. [Editor's note.]

[4] German Armed Forces. [Editor's Note.]

War and Totalitarianism

British and French rearmament had only begun, and the German West Wall was impregnable; therefore no effective help could come to Poland from the west. Russia would not fight, and in any case the Poles knew that the Russians, if they ever entered their country, would never leave. There were even signs that reason, as the Nazis understood reason, was returning. The French and British Ambassadors returned to their posts in Berlin; and the latter, Nevile Henderson, promised that he would not cease to work for a favorable solution. The German chargé in Warsaw reported that responsible Poles wished to keep the way open for a rapprochement, although they could do nothing because of the excited state of public opinion. The German chargé in Moscow stressed Soviet "mistrust and reserve" in relations with the West, and on April 17 the Soviet Ambassador in Berlin suggested that so far as the U.S.S.R. was concerned, Nazi-Soviet relations could easily be improved. And so Hitler was probably quite honest when he said that he "had a great deal of time for theatres and concerts" and that he "regarded the whole course of events calmly."

Through four weeks after Chamberlain's promise of assistance to the Poles, the Germans kept their own counsel. Then, on Friday, April 28, Hitler spoke. The British encirclement policy and the Polish military agreement had, he said, destroyed the Anglo-German naval agreement of 1935 and the German-Polish political understanding of 1934. With irony verging on ridicule, he dismissed Roosevelt's peace appeal as meaningless. About Russia he said nothing. The reaction abroad to the speech, as reported by German representatives, was heartening. The comment of the chargé in Paris (the German Ambassadors to Britain and France had not yet returned to their posts) was typical: "It is fairly generally recognized that the tone of the speech was moderate, serious and dignified, and that the German demands are by no means incapable of being met."

A week after Hitler's speech the strength of the German position was dramatized by a meeting in Milan between Ribbentrop and the Italian Foreign Minister, Ciano. In the communiqué issued at the conclusion of the meeting, on May 7, emphasis was placed on the "perfect identity of views" between Germany and Italy, and on the intention of the two Governments to conclude a political and military pact — the pact which was grandiloquently to be called "The Pact of Steel."

Actually, the pact which was announced on May 7 and concluded on May 22 was thought a poor and temporary substitute for the alliance of Germany, Italy and Japan for which the Germans had been pressing. The Japanese were willing to conclude an alliance against Russia; they were as yet unwilling to promise military assistance against Britain and the United States. Since the alliance was wanted by Hitler as a means of bringing the British to a more "reasonable" attitude, the proposal of an alliance against Russia was rejected. As an alternative, Ribbentrop touched lightly in his discussion with Ciano on the possibility of improving relations with the Soviet Union. Ciano thought such a move desirable; but felt that for domestic political reasons Mussolini would not wish too great an improvement.

At this stage in the developing crisis, the Germans also showed no great eagerness to strengthen their position by bidding for the support of the Soviet Union, despite clear indications of the importance which the British and French attached to a political agreement with the U.S.S.R. When Dirksen[5] returned to his post in London he reported that failure to achieve agreement with Russia would shake the position of the British. Similarly, on his return to Paris, Welczeck[6] reported that "even right-wing circles are convinced that without Russia there would be no possibility of effectively stemming the German advance in the East."

The Russians did their best to elicit a German offer. On May 3 Molotov replaced Litvinov as Foreign Secretary and the Soviet chargé in Berlin intimated that the change could facilitate improvement in Nazi-Soviet relations. Two weeks later he again suggested that an improvement in relations would not be difficult to achieve. The German Government did bring Schulenburg, the Ambassador in Moscow, home for consultation; but he returned to Russia with instructions only to suggest the reopening of economic negotiations which had been interrupted earlier in the year. Schulenburg talked with Molotov for over an hour on May 20, but found him unwilling to reopen the economic discussions until a "political basis" had been found. After some wavering, the German Government decided to make no definite political proposals.

On May 23, Hitler reviewed the international situa-

[5]German Ambassador to Great Britain. [Editor's note.]
[6]German Ambassador to France. [Editor's note.]

tion with his military advisers. Now, two months after his first demands on Poland, he had enlarged his objective. Poland was to be attacked at the first suitable opportunity, and destroyed. "It is not Danzig that is at stake. For us it is a matter of expanding our living space in the East and making food supplies secure and also solving the problem of the Baltic States." The campaign against Poland could be a success only if Britain and France stood aside. There were indications that "Russia might disinterest herself in the destruction of Poland," but to restrain Russia it might be necessary to have closer ties with Japan. In any case, the task was to isolate Poland, and there must not be a simultaneous showdown with France and Britain. That showdown would come, but later. It would be a hard, and probably a long fight, involving the very existence of Germany; it was time to begin preparations for that fight. He was, therefore, setting up a small planning staff, which would work in complete secrecy, and which would study all aspects of the problem of preparing for the life and death battle with Britain. He gave no date for the war with the West, but in response to a question from Göring he stated that the armaments program would be completed by 1943 or 1944. . . .

One cannot say with certainty that Hitler was forced to revise his policy towards Russia by recognition that time was running out. What is certain is that while Hitler had ordered efforts to secure even a trade agreement stopped on June 29, and while opinion within the German Government was still fluctuating two weeks later, the pace was rapidly accelerated in the days following the uproar in Britain over the supposed offer of a huge loan to Germany by the Chamberlain government. The official in charge of the economic negotiations, Schnurre, wrote privately on August 2 that, from about July 23, he had at least one conversation daily about Russia with Ribbentrop who was also constantly exchanging views with Hitler. "The Foreign Minister is concerned to obtain some result in the Russian question as soon as possible, not only on the negative side (disturbing the British negotiations) but also on the positive side (an understanding with us)."

During the weeks which followed, the Nazis were driven, step by step, to meet every Soviet demand. The first step, on July 26, was a long dinner conversation, extending past midnight, between Schnurre, the Soviet chargé and the Soviet trade representative. Emphasizing that he was speaking on Ribbentrop's instructions, Schnurre declared that there was

no real conflict of interest between Germany and the U.S.S.R. at any point from the Baltic to the Black Sea and on to the Far East, and said he "could imagine a far-reaching arrangement of mutual interests" in all these areas. However, he warned, the opportunity to effect such an arrangment would be lost if the U.S.S.R. allied itself with Britain. The Russians expressed surprise and pleasure at these remarks; they reciprocated Schnurre's desire for improved relations, but emphasized that improvement could come only slowly.

A week later, on August 2, Ribbentrop intervened directly. In conversation with the Soviet chargé, he reiterated the German conviction that a far-reaching political agreement was possible and "dropped a gentle hint at our coming to an understanding with Russia on the fate of Poland." The chargé tried to elicit information on the concrete terms Ribbentrop had in mind; the latter said he was quite ready to be explicit when the Soviet Government stated that it also wished to put relations on a new basis.

During the days which followed, the German representatives repeatedly sought to draw from the Russians a definite statement of willingness to enter negotiations on political problems, but without success. At last, on August 10, Schnurre came to the point. He stressed the impossibility of any agreement if the U.S.S.R. concluded a military pact with Britain. Beyond that, however, he made it plain that war against Poland impended, and that a demarcation of spheres of interest in Poland was desirable before war came. This produced results. Two days later, the chargé reported that his government was interested in a discussion of political problems, including Poland, and wished the negotiations to take place in Moscow.

To Hitler it seemed that the road ahead was now clear. In a conference at Obersalzberg on August 14 he stated categorically that Russia would keep out of the war. Britain would, in the end, draw back: "the men I got to know in Munich are not the kind that start a new World War." Without Britain, France would not move.

That evening, Ribbentrop telegraphed new proposals to Schulenburg, proposals which he wished Stalin to receive in as exact a form as was possible without putting an incriminating document into Soviet hands. He proposed a linking of the Soviet and German economies, "which are complementary in every sphere." He proposed political cooperation. He affirmed "that there is no question between the Baltic Sea and the Black Sea which cannot be settled to the complete satisfaction of both countries." To secure speedy agreement, he was prepared to come to Moscow himself "to lay the foundations for a final settlement of German-Russian relations."

By then, the September 1 deadline was less than three weeks away and the propaganda campaign preparatory to war with Poland was already approaching its strident climax. Foreign observers in Berlin were freely predicting that the question of Danzig if not the fate of Poland would be settled before the month was over. Hitler encouraged these prophets. In the past he had carefully concealed his plan of action from the indiscreet Italians. This time, he was very explicit. War against Poland might come any day, he told Ciano, and would come by the end of August unless Poland not only surrendered Danzig but altered "her general attitude."

German need was Russian opportunity. Even while they had suggested ever more plainly their desire for a political agreement with Germany, the Russians had continued their negotiations with the British and French. At the time that he had announced the opening of trade negotiations with Germany, Molotov had also suggested the sending of an Anglo-French military mission to Moscow as a means of speeding agreement with the Western democracies. The discussions of this mission with the Soviet military leaders were begun on the very day, August 12, that the Germans were told of Soviet willingness to begin political discussions. Now, on August 15, when Schulenburg presented Ribbentrop's proposal that he come to Moscow, Molotov stressed the need for "adequate preparation" before the arrival of so distinguished a visitor and asked whether Germany was prepared to conclude a nonaggression pact and to influence Japanese policy in the direction of better relations with the Soviet Union.

Two days later—and even this short interval seemed long to Ribbentrop—Schulenburg was back with fresh instructions. Germany would conclude a nonaggression pact. Germany was willing to influence Japanese policy in the desired direction. But speed was essential because "of the possibility of the occurrence, any day, of serious events." Ribbentrop was prepared to come to Moscow by airplane at any time after August 18. Molotov refused to be hurried,

and laid out a timetable: first the economic agreement must be concluded; then "after a short interval" a political agreement could be made; however, there might now be an exchange of drafts of the proposed political agreement, and the Soviet Government would await with interest the German draft.

Promptly, Schulenburg received new instructions, which he executed in two interviews with Molotov on August 19. With only the thinnest covering of diplomatic verbiage, the Russians were told that war was imminent and that a delineation of spheres of influence was essential before the fighting started. In the first interview Molotov refused to set a date for Ribbentrop's visit. In the second, Molotov (apparently on new instructions from Stalin) agreed that Ribbentrop might come on August 26 or 27. Meanwhile, in Berlin, the trade agreement was finally signed.

Hitler now intervened with a letter to Stalin. Polish presumption, said Hitler, had produced intolerable tension which might lead to war any day. There was no time to lose. He asked that Ribbentrop be received on August 22, or at the latest on August 23; Ribbentrop would have full powers to draw up and sign the nonaggression pact and the political agreement. The letter was delivered on August 21. On the same day Stalin replied, agreeing to the arrival of Ribbentrop on August 23. That night, the German Government issued a communiqué telling of the impending conference for the purpose of concluding a nonaggression pact.

The final card had been played. It was a costly move. At the end of May, consideration for Soviet interests in Poland had been the highest price mentioned for a pact with the U.S.S.R. As late as August 16 Ribbentrop offered, so far as the Baltic States were concerned, only a joint guarantee of their independence. Now, in the pact of August 23, Finland, Estonia and Latvia were to be an exclusively Soviet sphere of influence. Russia was also to receive a large share of Poland. As for southeastern Europe, the Soviet claim to Bessarabia was acknowledged, while "the German side declares complete political désintéressement in these territories." In the search for "living space," a search which had seemed so easy in the spring, Hitler had been forced to surrender his claim to hegemony in the Baltic and in southeastern Europe.

The cost was high, but again Hitler was confident that he could now crush Poland without provoking general war. On August 22, before Ribbentrop reached Moscow, Hitler called his military leaders together once more. Most of what he said was an elaborate demonstration of the necessity for war with Poland, together with instructions for the ruthless conduct of the war. So far as Britain and France were concerned, his arguments were those he had used so often before: neither had really rearmed, both were obsessed by the frightful risks entailed by war, neither had strong leaders. He said the German attack would probably be launched on Saturday, August 26.

Momentarily, Hitler's optimism seemed justified by reports of the confusion caused in Britain and France by the Nazi-Soviet pact. On Wednesday, August 23, the attack on Poland was definitely set for Saturday, and on August 24 the first of the moves by which war was to be provoked was made by the Germans in Danzig. On August 25, however, there came two heavy blows: the Anglo-Polish Mutual Assistance Agreement was signed, and Mussolini made it plain that he would not intervene if Germany became involved in war with France and Britain. In the evening, the order to attack was cancelled.

There followed a week of desperate manoeuvring. Much has been written of the "offers" made by Hitler in those last days of peace, but it is now clear that the offers were intended only to shake the determination of the British Government. Hitler had gone too far to retreat, and time had run out. On September 1, the German invasion began, with Hitler still vainly hoping that the political leaders of Britain and France would, at the last moment, lose their nerve.

Over and over, through the spring and summer of 1939 the British and French Governments had said they would fight if Germany attacked Poland. These warnings went unheeded. In justification for his refusal to heed the warnings from London and Paris, Hitler invariably came back to the same arguments: Britain and France were militarily unprepared for war, and certainly for a war to protect Poland; they had threatened before, and had drawn back at the end; the men in power in 1939 were the same men whose will had collapsed in face of firm resistance. As he repeatedly boasted, he had bluffed and won before; what he had done when Germany was weak, he could do again with confidence now that Germany was strong.

These boasts had an increasingly hollow sound from the last week of July. But by then the whole world had come to regard the question of Danzig as a decisive test of strength. Through the years since 1933 he had advanced from one victory to another by convincing his opponents that if they did not surrender he would annihilate them and, if necessary, bring what Bonnet called the house of Europe crashing in ruins. Now Hitler was confronted by the despised Poles; they not only remained steady through the war of nerves, but, despite all provocation, they avoided rash action which would place the onus of aggression on them. If they were able to defy him with impunity, the tide which had carried him from success to success would turn. In a last desperate effort to break the will of his opponents, he promised the hated Communists more for neutrality than he could win from war against Poland. Even under this pressure the courage of the Poles did not collapse. Retreat was now more impossible than ever. And so the diplomatic moves of March, intended at the outset only to advance Germany another stage along the road to supremacy in Europe, led inexorably, step by step, to war against the West in which the very existence of Germany was at stake.

A. J. P. TAYLOR

BRITISH BLUNDER RATHER THAN HITLER'S DESIGN

The previous two readings have emphasized German and more specifically Hitler's responsibility for the outbreak of war in 1939. The one that follows challenges that interpretation. It is taken from a book published in 1961 by a distinguished British historian.

The author, A. J. P. Taylor, was a Fellow of Magdalen College at Oxford when he published this interpretation. In books on nineteenth-century Italy, Imperial Germany's acquisition of colonies in the 1880's, Bismarck, the course of German history, the Habsburg monarchy, and diplomatic history, Taylor had made himself known before 1961 for his research, his vivid and sometimes surprising interpretations, and his terse and ironical style, drawing heavily upon cynicism and paradox. It was usually said of Taylor's works, even before 1961, that they were "thought provoking," which they were. The book of 1961 stirred more controversy than any of Taylor's other works. It is inaccurate to say simply that the book is "pro-German" or "pro-Hitler." In his early pages Taylor briefly seems to imply that Germany should have been dismembered into separate states in 1919; that a Germany left united, as if by some kind of geopolitical natural law, inevitably would reassert the power it had briefly established with the surrender of Soviet Russia at Brest-Litovsk early in 1918. But Taylor, who in the Chamberlain era opposed appeasement of Nazi Germany, in his 1961 treatment frequently justifies Hitler's demands and criticizes British policy.

A more extreme interpretation was developed late in 1961 by an American writer, David L. Hoggan, who published in German a book entitled *The Forced War: Causes and Authors of the Second World War*. Hoggan's thesis went far beyond Taylor's, but was like Taylor's in that it put responsibility on Great Britain. It argued that British foreign policy in 1938–39 deliberately sought, finally with success, "to involve Germany in a new World War." Hoggan argued that "Halifax's war policy, which had the secret blessings of Roosevelt and Stalin," frustrated last-minute efforts for a peaceful solution of the German-Polish problem. Hitler set his forces in motion on September 1, 1939, only when he was "left with no other choice," "only after he had reached the decision that war with Poland was in any case unavoidable."

Hoggan was an unknown historian, and few serious scholars in either Germany or the United States were likely to pay much attention to his extreme views. Taylor, on the other hand, wrote at the peak of a career that had brought him international reputation. His arguments must be given serious consideration. Is Taylor's writing persuasive? More important, is his evidence convincing? What evidence, if any, has he left out? In absolving Hitler of sole responsibility, was he really trying to put the blame squarely upon the German people as a whole? Was he angry at Prime Minister Chamberlain because he did not give in to Hitler's demands in 1939 or because he failed to conclude a pact with the U.S.S.R.?

The leading authors to whom we turn for accounts of the origins of the second World war—Namier, Wheeler-Bennett, Wiskemann in English, Baumont in French—all published their books soon after the war ended; and all expressed views which they had held while the war was on, or even before it began. Twenty years after the outbreak of the first World war, very few people would have accepted without modification the explanations for it given in August 1914. Twenty years and more after the outbreak of the second World war nearly everyone accepts the explanations which were given in September 1939. . . .

If the evidence had been sufficiently conflicting, scholars would soon have been found to dispute the popular verdict, however generally accepted. This has not happened; and for two apparently contradictory reasons—there is at once too much evidence and too little. The evidence of which there is too much is that collected for the trials of war-criminals in Nuremberg. Though these documents look imposing in their endless volumes, they are dangerous material for a historian to use. They were collected, hastily and almost at random, as a basis for lawyers' briefs. This is not how historians would proceed. . . .

If we seek instead for evidence assembled in a more detached and scholarly way, we discover how much worse off we are than our predecessors who studied the origins of the first World war. . . .

In principle and doctrine, Hitler was no more wicked and unscrupulous than many other contemporary statesmen. In wicked acts he outdid them all. The policy of Western statesmen also rested ultimately on force—French policy on the army, British policy on sea-power. But these statesmen hoped that it would not be necessary to use this force. Hitler intended to use his force, or would at any rate threaten to use it. If Western morality seemed superior, this was largely because it was the morality of

the *status quo;* Hitler's was the immorality of revision. There was a curious, though only superficial, contradiction in Hitler between aims and methods. His aim was change, the overthrow of the existing European order; his method was patience. Despite his bluster and violent talk, he was a master in the game of waiting. He never made a frontal attack on a prepared position—at least never until his judgement had been corrupted by easy victories. Like Joshua before the walls of Jericho, he preferred to wait until the forces opposing him had been sapped by their own confusions and themselves forced success upon him. He had already applied this method to gain power in Germany. He did not "seize" power. He waited for it to be thrust upon him by the men who had previously tried to keep him out. In January 1933 Papen and Hindenburg were imploring him to become Chancellor; and he graciously consented. So it was to be in foreign affairs. Hitler did not make precise demands. He announced that he was dissatisfied; and then waited for the concessions to pour into his lap, merely holding out his hand for more. Hitler did not know any foreign countries at first hand. He rarely listened to his foreign minister, and never read the reports of his ambassadors. He judged foreign statesmen by intuition. He was convinced that he had taken the measure of all *bourgeois* politicians, German and foreign alike, and that their nerve would crumble before his did. This conviction was near enough to the truth to bring Europe within sight of disaster. . . .

The watershed between the two World wars extended over precisely two years. Post-war ended when Germany reoccupied the Rhineland on 7 March 1936; pre-war began when she annexed Austria on 13 March 1938. From that moment, change and upheaval went on almost without interruption until the representatives of the Powers, victorious in the scond World war, met at Potsdam in July 1945. Who first raised the storm and launched the march of events? The accepted answer is clear:

From *The Origins of the Second World War* by A. J. P. Taylor, pp. 8, 13–14, 71–72, 131–132, 195–196, 209–211, 213–216, 218–220, 250, 263–264, 268–269, 272–278. Copyright © 1961 by A. J. P. Taylor. Reprinted by permission of Atheneum Publishers and Hamish Hamilton, Ltd.

War and Totalitarianism

it was Hitler. The moment of his doing so is also accepted: it was on 5 November 1937. We have a record of the statements which he made that day. It is called "the Hossbach memorandum," after the man who made it. This record is supposed to reveal Hitler's plans. Much play was made with it at Nuremberg; and the editors of the *Documents on German Foreign Policy* say that "it provides a summary of German foreign policy in 1937–38." It is therefore worth looking at in detail. Perhaps we shall find in it the explanation of the second World war; or perhaps we shall find only the source of a legend.

That afternoon Hitler called a conference at the Chancellery. It was attended by Blomberg, the minister of war; Neurath, the foreign minister; Fritsch, commander-in-chief of the army; Raeder, commander-in-chief of the navy; and Goering, commander-in-chief of the air force. Hitler did most of the talking. He began with a general disquisition on Germany's need for *Lebensraum*. He did not specify where this was to be found—probably in Europe, though he also discussed colonial gains. But gains there must be. "Germany had to reckon with two hate-inspired antagonists, Britain and France. . . . Germany's problem could only be solved by means of force and this was never without attendant risk." When and how was there to be this resort to force? Hitler discussed three "cases." The first "case" was "period 1943–1945." After that the situation could only change for the worse; 1943 must be the moment for action. Case 2 was civil war in France; if that happened, "the time for action against the Czechs had come." Case 3 was war between France and Italy. This might well occur in 1938; then "our objective must be to overthrow Czechoslovakia and Austria simultaneously." None of these "cases" came true; clearly therefore they do not provide the blueprint for German policy. Nor did Hitler dwell on them. He went on to demonstrate that Germany would gain her aims without a great war; "force" apparently meant to him the threat of war, not necessarily war itself. The Western Powers would be too hampered and too timid to intervene. "Britain almost certainly, and probably France as well, had written off the Czechs and were reconciled to the fact that this question of Germany would be cleared up in due course." No other Power would intervene. "Poland—with Russia in her rear—will have little inclination to engage in war against a victorious Germany." Russia would be held in check by Japan.

Hitler's exposition was in large part daydreaming, unrelated to what followed in real life. Even if seriously meant, it was not a call to action, at any rate not to the action of a great war; it was a demonstration that a great war would not be necessary. Despite the preliminary talk about 1943–1945, its solid core was the examination of the chances for peaceful triumphs in 1938, when France would be preoccupied elsewhere. Hitler's listeners remained doubtful. The generals insisted that the French army would be superior to the German even if engaged against Italy as well. Neurath doubted whether a Mediterranean conflict between France and Italy were imminent. Hitler waved these doubts aside: "he was convinced of Britain's non-participation, and therefore he did not believe in the probability of belligerent action by France against Germany." There is only one safe conclusion to be drawn from this rambling disquisition: Hitler was gambling on some twist of fortune which would present him with success in foreign affairs, just as a miracle had made him Chancellor in 1933. There was here no concrete plan, no directive for German policy in 1937 and 1938. Or if there were a directive, it was to wait upon events. . . .

The losses of territory to Poland were, for most Germans, the indelible grievance against Versailles. Hitler undertook a daring operation over this grievance when he planned cooperation with Poland. But there was a way out. The actual Germans under Polish rule might be forgotten—or withdrawn; what could not be forgiven was the "Polish corridor" which divided East Prussia from the Reich. Here, too, there was a possible compromise. Germany might be satisfied with a corridor across the corridor—a complicated idea for which there were however many precedents in German history. German feeling could be appeased by the recovery of Danzig. This seemed easy. Danzig was not part of Poland. It was a Free City, with its own autonomous administration under a High Commissioner, appointed by the League of Nations. The Poles themselves, in their false pride as a Great Power, had taken the lead in challenging the League's authority. Surely, therefore, they would not object if Germany took the League's place. Moreover, the problem had changed since 1919. Then the port of Danzig had been essential to Poland. Now, with the creation of Gdynia by the Poles, Danzig needed Poland more than the Poles needed Danzig. It should then be easy to arrange for the safeguarding of Poland's economic interests, and yet to recover Danzig for the Reich. The stumbling-block would be removed; Germany and Poland could act together in the Ukraine.

On 24 October [1938] Ribbentrop first aired these proposals to Lipski, the Polish ambassador. If Danzig and the Corridor were settled, there could then be "a joint policy towards Russia on the basis of the Anti-Comintern Pact." Hitler was even franker when Beck, the Polish foreign minister, visited him in January 1939: "The divisions which Poland stationed on the Russian frontier saved Germany just so much military expenditure." Of course, he added, "Danzig is German, will always remain German, and will sooner or later become part of Germany." If the question of Danzig were settled, he would be ready to guarantee the Corridor to Poland. Hitler may have been cheating the Poles over Danzig all along—demanding its return as the preliminary to their destruction. But Polish ambitions in the Ukraine were of long standing; Danzig seemed a triviality in comparison. Beck "made no secret of the fact that Poland had aspirations directed towards the Soviet Ukraine," when Ribbentrop visited Warsaw on 1 February.

Nevertheless, the Poles did not respond to Hitler's offer. Blindly confident in their own strength and contemptuous of Czech softness, they were determined not to yield an inch; this, they believed, was the only safe method of doing business with Hitler. Moreover—a point which Hitler never understood—though they would not cooperate with Soviet Russia against Germany, they were almost equally resolved not to cooperate with Germany against Soviet Russia. They regarded themselves as an independent Great Power; and forgot that they had gained their independence in 1918 only because both Russia and Germany had been defeated. Now they had to choose between Germany and Russia. They chose neither. Only Danzig prevented cooperation between Germany and Poland. For this reason, Hitler wanted to get it out of the way. For precisely the same reason, Beck kept it in the way. It did not cross his mind that this might cause a fatal breach. . . .

On 21 March Lipski called on Ribbentrop and protested against the German behaviour over Slovakia—it "could only be regarded as a blow against Poland." Ribbentrop was in a weak position; and he knew it. To protect himself, he paraded grievances

in his turn. Polish newspapers, he complained, were behaving badly: "a gradual stiffening in German-Polish relations was becoming apparent." Danzig must return to the Reich—this would rivet Poland to the German side. Then there could be a German guarantee for the Corridor, a nonaggression treaty for 25 years, and "a common policy" in the Ukraine. Lipski was sent off to place this offer before Beck. Co-operation with Poland was still the German aim; Danzig merely the security for it. Hitler himself thought this. On 25 March he issued a directive:

The Führer *does not* wish to solve the Danzig question by force. He does not wish to drive Poland into the arms of Britain by this.

A possible military occupation of Danzig could be contemplated *only* if L[ipski] gave an indication that the Polish Government could not justify voluntary cession of Danzig to their own people and that a *fait accompli* would make a solution easier to them.

Hitler's objective was alliance with Poland, not her destruction. Danzig was a tiresome preliminary to be got out of the way. As before, Beck kept it in the way. So long as Danzig stood between Poland and Germany, he could evade the embarrassing offer of a German alliance, and so, as he thought, preserve Polish independence.

Beck's calculations worked, though not precisely as he intended. On 26 March Lipski returned to Berlin. He brought with him a firm refusal to yield over Danzig, though not a refusal to negotiate. Until this moment everything had gone on in secret, with no public hint of German-Polish estrangement. Now it blazed into the open. Beck, to show his resolve, called up Polish reservists. Hitler, to ease things along as he supposed, allowed the German press to write, for the first time, about the German minority in Poland. There were rumours of German troop-movements towards the Polish frontier, just as there had been similar rumours of German movements against Czechoslovakia on 21 May 1938. These new rumours were equally without foundation. They seem to have been started by the Poles. They were however aided on their way by some German generals who claimed to be opponents of Hitler. These generals "warned" the British government. With what object? So that Great Britain would deter Hitler by threatening him with war? Or so that she would cheat him of his war by making the Poles yield over Danzig? Perhaps it was a combination of the two,

War and Totalitarianism

with an inclination towards the second. At any rate, these generals briefed the correspondent of the *News Chronicle* who was just being expelled from Germany; and on 29 March he, in turn, sounded the alarm at the foreign office. He found willing listeners. After the occupation of Prague and the supposed threat to Rumania, the British were ready to believe anything. They did not give a thought to Danzig. They supposed that Poland herself was in imminent danger, and likely to succumb. No alarm, it is true, came from the British ambassador in Berlin. But the foreign office had been misled by him on previous occasions, or so it thought; now it preferred the reports of journalists. Immediate action seemed necessary if Polish nerve were to be strengthened and the "peace front" saved.

On 30 March Chamberlain drafted with his own hand an assurance to the Polish government:

If . . . . any action were taken which clearly threatened their independence, and which the Polish Government accordingly felt obliged to resist with their national forces, His Majesty's Government and the French Government would at once lend them all the support in their power.

That afternoon Beck was discussing with the British ambassador how to implement his proposal of a week earlier for a general declaration, when a telegram from London was brought in. The ambassador read out Chamberlain's assurance. Beck accepted it "between two flicks of the ash off his cigarette." Two flicks; and British grenadiers would die for Danzig. Two flicks; and the illusory great Poland, created in 1919, signed her death-warrant. The assurance was unconditional: the Poles alone were to judge whether it should be called upon. . . .

British policy had, without design, made Danzig the decisive question for 1939, just as, with more deliberation, it presented the Sudeten Germans as the decisive question in 1938. But with this difference. The Sudeten German question was asked of the Czechs and the French. It was they who were pressed to make concessions, or to face the risk of war. In 1939 the British were themselves at question, faced with the choice between resistance or conciliation. British ministers preferred the second course. They were still the men of peace who had rejoiced at the settlement of Munich. They still hated the prospect of war; still hoped to find a way out by means of negotiation. Moreover, with mounting Japanese pressure in the Far East, they had increas-

ing desire to turn their backs on Europe. Besides, in taking a stand over Danzig they were on peculiarly weak ground. Danzig was the most justified of German grievances: a city of exclusively German population which manifestly wished to return to the Reich and which Hitler himself restrained only with difficulty. The solution, too, seemed peculiarly easy. Halifax[1] never wearied of suggesting that Danzig should return to German sovereignty, with safeguards for Polish trade.

Hitler wanted this also. The destruction of Poland had been no part of his original project. On the contrary, he had wished to solve the question of Danzig so that Germany and Poland could remain on good terms. Was Polish obstinacy then the only thing which stood between Europe and a peaceful outcome? By no means. Previously Danzig might have been settled without implying any upheaval in international relations. Now it had become the symbol of Polish independence; and, with the Anglo-Polish alliance, of British independence as well. Hitler no longer wished merely to fulfill German national aspirations or to satisfy the inhabitants of Danzig. He aimed to show that he had imposed his will on the British and on the Poles. They, on their side, had to deny him this demonstration. All parties aimed at a settlement by negotiation, but only after victory in a war of nerves. There is, of course, an alternative explanation. Some, or all, of the parties may have been driving deliberately for war. There can hardly be any who believe this of Poland; few, even in Germany, who now believe that the British were planning the "encirclement" of Germany in order to impose again the "slavery" of Versailles. Many however believe that Hitler was a modern Attila, loving destruction for its own sake and therefore bent on war without thought of policy. There is no arguing with such dogmas. Hitler was an extraordinary man; and they may well be true. But his policy is capable of rational explanation; and it is on these that history is built. The escape into irrationality is no doubt easier. The blame for war can be put on Hitler's Nihilism instead of on the faults and failures of European statesmen—faults and failures which their public shared. Human blunders, however, usually do more to shape history than human wickedness. At any rate, this is a rival dogma which is worth developing, if only as an academic exercise. . . .

[1] British Foreign Secretary, 1938–40. [Editor's note.]

British Blunder Rather Than Hitler's Design

The economic advance of Soviet Russia, on the other hand, obsessed Hitler. It was indeed startling. During the ten years between 1929 and 1939, while the manufacturing production of Germany increased by 27 per cent and that of Great Britain by 17 per cent, Soviet Russia's increased by 400 per cent; and the process was only beginning. By 1938 Soviet Russia was the second industrial Power in the world, ranking only after the United States. She had still far to go: her population was still impoverished, her resources were hardly tapped. But Germany had not much time if she were to escape being overshadowed, and still less if she hoped to seize the Soviet Ukraine. Here again, it would have made sense for Hitler to plan a great war against Soviet Russia. But, though he often talked of such a war, he did not plan it. German armaments were not designed for such a war. Hitler's rearmament in width was only intended to reinforce a diplomatic war of nerves. Even the rearmament in depth which the German generals wanted would only have equipped Germany for a long-drawn-out war of exhaustion on the Western front such as was fought during the first World war. The Germans had to improvise furiously when they went to war against Soviet Russia in June 1941; and they failed to achieve a quick decisive victory there largely because they had altogether neglected to prepare transport for a war of this nature. In the end, it is hard to tell whether Hitler took the project of war against Soviet Russia seriously; or whether it was an attractive illusion with which he hoped to mesmerise Western statesmen. If he took it seriously, this makes the actual war of 1939—not a war against Soviet Russia, but a war against the Western Powers, with Germany and Soviet Russia halfway towards an alliance—more inexplicable than ever. Or rather the old, simple explanation reasserts itself. The war of 1939, far from being premeditated, was a mistake, the result on both sides of diplomatic blunders.

Hitler contributed little to the course of diplomacy between April and August 1939. As on previous occasions, he was content to prepare and to wait, confident that the obstacles would somehow disintegrate before him. The example of the Czech crisis was always in his mind. There he had been faced with a strong Czech army and an apparently firm alliance between France and Czechoslovakia. In the end the French gave way, and the Czechs also. It would be the same over Poland. He said of the Western statesmen: "Our opponents are poor creatures [little worms]. I saw them at Munich." He

no longer troubled himself about the French. He knew that they would go wherever the British led them, though acting as a brake on the road to war. This time the British would have to decide more directly; and he expected them to decide for concession. Did he also expect the Poles to give way without war? This is harder to answer. On 3 April the armed forces were told to be ready to attack Poland at any time after 1 September, together with an assurance that this would happen only if Poland were isolated—an assurance which Hitler repeated in rather wilder form on 23 May. But these preparations were necessary whether Hitler planned to get his way by war or by threats. They tell us nothing of his real intentions; and probably he had not settled them himself. The war of nerves was enough to be going on with. Here Hitler laid down his challenge clearly. On 28 April he repudiated both the non-aggression Pact with Poland of 1934 and the Anglo-German Naval Agreement of 1935. On the same day he addressed the Reichstag. He recited his offers to Poland, and denounced Polish provocation: the Germans wished to settle the question of Danzig by free negotiation, the Poles answered by relying on force. He was ready to make a new agreement, but only if the Poles changed their attitude—that is, if they gave way over Danzig and abandoned their alliance with Great Britain. He spoke of the British in very different terms: praised the British Empire as "an inestimable factor of value for the whole of human economic and cultural life"; rejected the idea of destroying it as "nothing but the effluence of human wanton destructiveness"; and looked forward warmly to a new agreement when the British had come to their senses. Here, too, the price was the same: concession over Danzig and abandonment of the alliance with Poland. Having thus stated his terms, Hitler withdrew into silence. He was beyond the reach of ambassadors, Ribbentrop almost as much so. There were no further diplomatic exchanges with Poland before the outbreak of war, and none directly with Great Britain until the middle of August.

Decision therefore rested with the British; or rather it was dictated to them by the Anglo-Polish alliance. . . .

Hitler's later behaviour suggests that he had not made up his mind as decisively as he indicated on 23 May. To the very last minute he was battering away for the Polish offer which never came. Maybe he did not expect the Polish nerve to break of itself;

but he expected the Western Powers to do the breaking for him, as they had done predominantly with Beneš[2] in 1938. He did not foresee exactly how the nerve of the Western Powers would crumble or precisely what effect this would have on the Poles. Nor was it of much moment to him whether the Poles then gave way without war or were left to be destroyed in isolation; the result would be much the same either way. On the larger point—the crumbling of Western nerve—he never doubted. There are also indications that, as the summer wore on, he began to foresee how this would come about. A collapse of the Anglo-Franco-Soviet negotiations would, he thought, do the trick. . . .

However one spins the crystal and tries to look into the future from the point of view of 23 August 1939, it is difficult to see what other course Soviet Russia could have followed. The Soviet apprehensions of a European alliance against Russia were exaggerated, though not groundless. But, quite apart from this—given the Polish refusal of Soviet aid, given too the British policy of drawing out negotiations in Moscow without seriously striving for a conclusion—neutrality, with or without a formal pact, was the most that Soviet diplomacy could attain; and limitation of German gains in Poland and the Baltic was the inducement which made a formal pact attractive. . . .

At any rate the bomb had exploded. Hitler was radiant, confident that he had pulled off the decisive stroke. On 22 August he entertained his leading generals to the wildest of his speeches. "Close your hearts to pity. Act brutally." This rigmarole was not a serious directive for action—no formal record was kept. Hitler was glorying in his own skill. Tucked away in the speech was a hard core. "Now the probability is great that the West will not intervene." As well, Hitler was talking for effect. A report of the speech reached the British embassy almost at once; whether intentionally or not, the so-called German "resistance" did Hitler's work for him. On 23 August Hitler took a further step. He fixed the attack on Poland for 4.40 a.m. on 26 August. This, too, was play-acting to impress the generals and, through them, the Western Powers. The German timetable could operate only from 1 September. Before then an attack on Poland was possible only if she had already surrendered. But technical considerations no longer seemed to matter: the Nazi-Soviet pact was

[2] President of Czechoslovakia, 1935–38, until after the Munich Conference. [Editor's note.]

assumed to have cleared the way for a diplomatic collapse on the part of the Western Powers. . . .
In England, however, events did not come up to Hitler's expectation. Quite the reverse. Parliament met on 24 August, and unanimously applauded what it supposed to be the government's firm stand. Hitler began to have doubts: evidently more was needed to extract from the British government the concessions on which he still counted. On 24 August Hitler flew to Berlin. On his instructions, Goering called in the Swede Dahlerus, and sent him off to London with an unofficial appeal for British mediation. This was an ingenious trap: if the British refused, Hitler could claim that he had never made a move; if they yielded, they would be compelled to put pressure on Poland. The same evening Hitler held a meeting with Goering, Ribbentrop, and the principal generals. Should they go on with the attack on Poland, now due to begin within thirty-six hours? Hitler declared that he would make a further attempt to detach the Western Powers from their Polish allies. The attempt took the form of a "last offer," communicated to Henderson shortly after noon on 25 August. Germany, Hitler declared, was determined "to abolish the Macedonian conditions on her eastern frontier." The problems of Danzig and the Corridor must be solved—though he still did not say how. Once these problems were out of the way, Germany would make "a large, comprehensive offer"; she would guarantee the British Empire, accept an agreed limitation of armaments, and renew the assurance that her frontier in the west was final. Henderson was impressed, as usual. Hitler, he reported, spoke "with great earnestness and apparent sincerity." Later writers have all dismissed Hitler's offer as fraudulent; and so in a sense it was. The immediate object was to isolate Poland. Yet the offer also represented Hitler's permanent policy: though he wanted a free hand to destroy conditions in the east which enlightened Western opinion had also pronounced intolerable, he had no ambitions directed against Great Britain and France. . . .

Thus the two sides circled round each other like wrestlers seeking advantage before the clinch. The British offered to arrange direct negotiations between Germany and Poland if Hitler would promise to behave peacefully; Hitler replied that there would be no war if he got his way over Danzig. Later writers have argued that Hitler's reply was dishonest; that he was concerned to isolate Poland, not to avoid war. This may well be true. But the offer by the British government was dishonest also: there was no chance of extracting concessions from the Poles once the danger of war was removed, and the British knew it. . . .

The deadlock lasted until 29 August. Then it was broken by Hitler. He was in the weaker position, though the British did not know it. There was not much time left before 1 September for him to pull off diplomatic success. At 7.15 p.m. he made to Henderson a formal offer and a formal demand: he would negotiate directly with Poland if a Polish plenipotentiary arrived in Berlin the following day. This was a retreat from the position Hitler had rigorously asserted since 26 March—that he would never again deal directly with the Poles. Though Henderson complained that the demand was perilously near an ultimatum, he was eager to accept it; it constituted in his opinion the "sole chance of preventing war." Henderson pressed the demand on his own government; he urged the French government to advise an immediate visit by Beck; he was most insistent of all with the Polish ambassador Lipski. Lipski took no notice—apparently he did not even report Hitler's demand to Warsaw. The French government responded as clearly in the opposite direction—they told Beck to go to Berlin at once. But the decision rested with the British government. Here was the proposal which they had always wanted and which they had repeatedly hinted at to Hitler: direct negotiations between Poland and Germany. Hitler had now done his part; but they could not do theirs. They had the gravest doubt whether the Poles would thus present themselves in Berlin at Hitler's behest. Kennedy[3] reported Chamberlain's feeling to Washington: "Frankly he is more worried about getting the Poles to be reasonable than the Germans." The British gnawed over the problem throughout 30 August. Finally they hit on a sort of solution. They passed Hitler's demand on to Warsaw at 12.25 a.m. on 31 August—that is to say, twenty-five minutes after the German ultimatum, if such it were, had expired. The British had been correct in their apprehension of Polish obstinacy. Beck, when informed of Hitler's demand, at once replied: "if invited to Berlin he would of course not go, as he had no intention of being treated like President Hácha." Thus the British, by acting too late, could still claim that they had offered something which they knew they could not deliver: a Polish plenipotentiary in Berlin.

[3] United States Ambassador in London. [Editor's note.]

Hitler had not anticipated this. He had expected that negotiations would start; and he then intended them to break down on Polish obstinacy. On his instructions detailed demands were at last prepared. These were principally the immediate return of Danzig, and a plebiscite in the Corridor—the very terms which the British and French governments had themselves long favoured. But, failing a Polish plenipotentiary, the Germans had difficulty in making their terms known. At midnight on 30 August Henderson brought to Ribbentrop the news that a Polish plenipotentiary was not coming that day. Ribbentrop had only the rough draft of the proposed German terms, scribbled over with Hitler's emendations. It was not in a condition to be shown to Henderson; and Ribbentrop had instructions from Hitler not to do so. He therefore read the terms over slowly. Later a myth grew up that he had "gabbled" them, deliberately cheating Henderson with terms that were only for show. In fact Henderson got the gist clearly, and was impressed. Taken at their face value, he thought, they were "not unreasonable." On his return to the British embassy, he summoned Lipski at 2 a.m., and urged him to seek an interview with Ribbentrop at once. Lipski took no notice, and went back to bed.

The Germans were now anxious that their terms had not gone properly on record with Henderson. They once more employed Dahlerus as an allegedly unofficial emissary. Goering, claiming to be acting in defiance of Hitler, showed the terms to Dahlerus, who in turn telephoned them to the British embassy about 4 a.m. Since Goering knew that all telephone conversations were monitored by at least three government agencies (one of them his own), his defiance of Hitler was of course a fiction. The next morning Goering abandoned it. Dahlerus was given a copy of the German terms, and took it round to the British embassy. Henderson again summoned Lipski, who refused to come. Dahlerus and Ogilvie-Forbes, the British counsellor of embassy, were dispatched to see Lipski. He remained unmoved. He refused to look at the German terms. When Dahlerus was out of the room, Lipski protested against introducing this intermediary, and said: "He would stake his reputation that German morale was breaking and that the present regime would soon crack. . . . This German offer was a trap. It was also a sign of weakness on the part of the Germans." In a further effort to break through the crust of obstinacy, Dahlerus telephoned to Horace

Wilson[4] in London. The German terms, he said, were "extremely liberal"; it was "'obvious to us' [Dahlerus? Goering? Henderson?] that the Poles were obstructing the possibilities of a negotiation." Wilson realised that the Germans were listening-in; he told Dahlerus to shut up and put down the receiver.

The precaution came too late. Every move of the last few hours had been as public as if it had been announced in the newspapers. The telephone calls between Henderson and Lipski, and between Dahlerus and Henderson, the comings and goings between the British and Polish embassies — all these were known to the Germans. They were undoubtedly known to Hitler. What conclusion could he possibly draw? Only the conclusion that he had succeeded in driving a wedge between Poland and her Western allies. This was true in regard to the French government. It was true in regard to Henderson. He wrote late on 31 August: "On German offer war would be completely unjustifiable. . . . Polish Government should announce tomorrow, in the light of German proposals which have now been made public, their intention to send a Plenipotentiary to discuss in general terms these proposals." Hitler was not to know that Henderson no longer carried the weight in London which he had carried the year before. But even the British government were losing patience with the Poles. Late on the night of 31 August Halifax telegraphed to Warsaw: "I do not see why the Polish Government should feel difficulty about authorising Polish Ambassador to accept a document from the German Government." Given another twenty-four hours, and the breach would be wide open. But Hitler had not got the twenty-four hours. He was the prisoner of his own time-table. With his generals watching sceptically, he could not again call off the attack of Poland unless he had something solid to show; and this was still denied him by the Poles. The breach between Poland and her allies gave him a chance. He had to gamble on it.

At 12.40 p.m. on 31 August Hitler decided that the attack should proceed. At 1 p.m. Lipski telephoned, asking for an interview with Ribbentrop. The Germans, who had intercepted his instructions, knew that he had been told not to enter into "any concrete negotiations." At 3 p.m. Weizsäcker tele-

phoned Lipski to ask whether he was coming as a plenipotentiary. Lipski replied: "No, in his capacity as an ambassador." This was enough for Hitler. The Poles, it seemed, were remaining obstinate; he could go forward to the gamble of isolating them in war. At 4 p.m. the orders for war were confirmed. At 6.30 p.m. Lipski at last saw Ribbentrop. Lipski said that his government were "favourably considering" the British proposal for direct Polish-German negotiations. Ribbentrop asked whether he was a plenipotentiary. Lipski again answered No. Ribbentrop did not communicate the German terms; if he had tried to do so, Lipski would have refused to receive them. Thus ended the only direct contact between Germany and Poland since 26 March. The Poles had kept their nerve unbroken to the last moment. At 4.45 a.m. on the following morning the German attack on Poland began. At 6 a.m. German aeroplanes bombed Warsaw.

Here was a clear *casus foederis* for both Great Britain and France. Their ally had been wantonly attacked; it only remained for them to declare war on the aggressor. Nothing of the kind happened. Both governments addressed a pained remonstrance to Hitler, warning him that they would have to go to war unless he desisted. Meanwhile they waited for something to turn up; and something did. On 31 August Mussolini, carefully following the precedent of the previous year, proposed a European conference: it should meet on 5 September and should survey all causes of European conflict, with the precondition that Danzig should return to Germany in advance. The two Western governments were favourable to the proposal when it first reached them. But Mussolini had got his timing wrong. In 1938 he had three days in which to avert war; in 1939 less than twenty-four hours, and this was not enough. By 1 September, when the Western governments replied to Mussolini, they had to postulate that fighting must first stop in Poland. Nor was that all. While Bonnet[5] was enthusiastic for Mussolini's proposal, in Great Britain public opinion took charge. The House of Commons was restive when Chamberlain explained that Germany had merely been "warned"; it expected something more solid next day. Halifax, swinging as usual with the national mood, insisted that the conference could be held only if Germany withdrew from all Polish territory. The Italians knew that it was hopeless to place such a demand before

[4] Confidential adviser to Prime Minister Chamberlain. [Editor's note.]

[5] French Foreign Minister, 1938–39. [Editor's note.]

Hitler; they dropped the conference without further effort.

Yet both the British and French governments, the French especially, went on believing in a conference which had vanished before it was born. Hitler had initially replied to Mussolini that, if invited to a conference, he would give his answer at midday on 3 September. Therefore Bonnet, and Chamberlain with him, strove desperately to postpone a declaration of war until after that time, even though the Italians no longer intended to invite Hitler or anyone else. Bonnet conjured up the excuse that the French military wanted the delay in order to carry through mobilisation, undisturbed by German air attack (which, they knew, would not occur anyway—the German air force was fully employed in Poland). Chamberlain conjured up no excuse except that the French wanted delay and that it was always difficult to work with allies. In the evening of 2 September he was still entertaining the House of Commons with hypothetical negotiations: "If the German Government should agree to withdraw their forces then His Majesty's Government would be willing to regard the position as being the same as it was before the German forces crossed the Polish frontier. That is to say, the way would be open to discussion between the German and Polish Governments on the matters at issue." This was too much even for loyal Conservatives. Leo Amery[6] called to Arthur Greenwood,[7] acting leader of the Opposition: "Speak for England," a task of which Chamberlain

[6] Conservative member of the House of Commons. [Editor's note.]

[7] Labor member of the House of Commons. [Editor's note.]

was incapable. Ministers, led by Halifax, warned Chamberlain that the government would fall unless it sent an ultimatum to Hitler before the House met again. Chamberlain gave way. The objections of the French were overruled. The British ultimatum was delivered to the Germans at 9 a.m. on 3 September. It expired at 11 a.m., and a state of war followed. When Bonnet learnt that the British were going to war in any case, his overriding anxiety was to catch up with them. The time of the French ultimatum was advanced, despite the supposed objections of the General Staff: it was delivered at noon on 3 September and expired at 5 p.m. In this curious way the French who had preached resistance to Germany for twenty years appeared to be dragged into war by the British who had for twenty years preached conciliation. Both countries went to war for that part of the peace settlement which they had long regarded as least defensible. Hitler may have projected a great war all along; yet it seems from the record that he became involved in war through launching on 29 August a diplomatic manoeuvre which he ought to have launched on 28 August.

Such were the origins of the second World war, or rather of the war between the three Western Powers over the settlement of Versailles; a war which had been implicit since the moment when the first war ended. Men will long debate whether this renewed war could have been averted by greater firmness or by greater conciliation; and no answer will be found to these hypothetical speculations. Maybe either would have succeeded, if consistently followed; the mixture of the two, practised by the British government, was the most likely to fail. . . .

HUGH R. TREVOR-ROPER

HITLER'S PLAN FOR WAR REAFFIRMED

A. J. P. Taylor's treatment of the roles of Hitler and British leaders in the outbreak of war in 1939 set off a scholarly war in Great Britain. Is it possible that his chief motive in publishing his book in 1961 was to reawaken historical debate about the coming of World War II?

This and other possible motives are suggested by Hugh R. Trevor-Roper in the following selection, which gives most of a substantial review of the Taylor book. Whatever the historian's motive, limits imposed by scholarly methodology—most importantly, respect for critically established evidence—must not be disregarded by a responsible scholar. Trevor Roper contends that Taylor clearly disregarded scholarly canons.

Trevor-Roper is Regius Professor of Modern History at Oxford University. Was he in this review simply defending his own position against implied attack by the Taylor volume? In his colorful account of *The Last Days of Hitler* (1947) and other writings, Trevor-Roper had interpreted Hitler as a man possessed by a demonic spirit or psychic disorder, whose guilt for the outbreak of the Second World War was unique and beyond question. How convincing is Trevor-Roper's critique of Taylor's account? How convincing is Taylor's interpretation in the light of Trevor-Roper's criticism and of the total evidence at your disposal?

It is over twenty years since the war began. A generation has grown up which never knew the 1930's, never shared its passions and doubts, was never excited by the Spanish civil war, never boiled with indignation against the "appeasers," never lived in suspense from Nuremberg Rally to Nuremberg Rally, awaiting the next hysterical outburst, the next clatter of arms, from the megalomaniac in Berlin. Those of us who knew those days and who try to teach this new generation are constantly made aware of this great gulf between us. How can we communicate across such a gulf the emotional content of those years, the mounting indignation which finally convinced even the "appeasers" themselves that there could be no peace with Hitler, and caused the British people, united in pacifism in 1936, to go, in 1939, united into war? For it was not the differing shades of justice in Germany's claims upon the Rhineland, Austria, the Sudetenland, Prague, and Danzig which caused men who had swallowed the first of these annexations to be increasingly exasperated by those which followed and take up arms against the last. It was a changing mood, a growing conviction that all such claims were but pretexts under which Hitler pursued not justice or self-determination for Germany but world-conquest, and that, now or never, he must be stopped. And even across the gulf such a mood must be conveyed by those who teach history to those who learn it: for it is an element in history no less important than the mere facts.

Or is it? Mr. A. J. P. Taylor, it seems, does not think

so. He sees the gulf all right, and he wishes to speak to those on the other side of it; but in order to do so, he has decided to lighten the weight he must carry with him. Stripping himself of all personal memories, and thus making himself, in this respect, as naked as they are, he has jumped nimbly across the gulf and now presents himself to them as the first enlightened historian of the future, capable of interpreting the politics of the 1920's and 1930's without any reference to the emotions they engendered, even in himself. Their sole guide, he tells them, must be the documents, which he will select and interpret for them; and indeed, by selection and interpretation, he presents them with a new thesis, illustrated (we need hardly say) with all his old resources of learning, paradox, and *gaminerie*.

The thesis is perfectly clear. According to Mr. Taylor, Hitler was an ordinary German statesman in the tradition of Stresemann[1] and Brüning,[2] differing from them not in methods (he was made Chancellor for "solidly democratic reasons") nor in ideas (he had no ideas) but only in the greater patience and stronger nerves with which he took advantage of the objective situation in Europe. His policy, in so far as he had a policy, was no different from that of his predecessors. He sought neither war nor annexation of territory. He merely sought to restore Germany's "natural" position in Europe, which had been artificially altered by the Treaty of Versailles: a treaty

[1] German Foreign Secretary, 1923–29. [Editor's note.]
[2] German Chancellor, 1930–32. [Editor's note.]

H. R. Trevor-Roper, "A. J. P. Taylor, Hitler, and the War," *Encounter,* XVII (July, 1961), 88–96. Reprinted by permission of Professor Trevor-Roper, literary agent (A. D. Peters), and the editors of *Encounter*.

which, for that reason, "lacked moral validity from the start.". . .

The war, "far from being premeditated, was a mistake, the result on both sides of diplomatic blunders."

Hitler's own share of these diplomatic blunders was, it seems, very small. He "became involved in war," we are told, "through launching on August 29th a diplomatic manoeuvre which he ought to have launched on August 28th." The blunders of the Western statesmen were far more fundamental. . . .

. . . If only Chamberlain had not lost his nerve in 1939! If only he had shown equal "skill and persistence" in enabling Hitler to detach Danzig and the Polish Corridor, how happy we should all be! Germany would have recovered its "natural" position, "morality" would have triumphed, and everyone would be happy in the best of possible worlds.

Such, in brief, is Mr. Taylor's thesis. It is not surprising that it has been hailed with cries of delight in neo-Nazi or semi-Nazi circles in Germany. It is more surprising that the book has been greeted by the fashionable Grub Street of England as the highest achievement of British historiography. Mr. Taylor has been compared with Gibbon and Macaulay; his failure to secure worthy promotion has caused astonishment. The anonymous oracle of the *Times Literary Supplement* has predicted finality for the result of his "methodical and impeccable logic." In the *Observer*, Mr. Sebastian Haffner (who recently published a panegyric of that "greatest Roman of them all," Dr. Goebbels) has declared the book "an almost faultless masterpiece" in which "fairness reigns supreme"; and his cosy, middlebrow colleagues in rival papers, hypnotised by a reputation which they are unqualified to test, have obediently jollied their readers along in harmony with the blurb. However, let us not all be hypnotised. Before hurling ourselves down the Gadarene slope, let us ask of Mr. Taylor's thesis, not, Is it brilliant? Is it plausible? but, Is it true? By what rules of evidence, by what philosophy of interpretation is it reached?

Perhaps we may begin by noting Mr. Taylor's general philosophy. Mr. Taylor, it seems, does not believe that human agents matter much in history. His story is "a story without heroes, and perhaps even without villains." "In my opinion," he explains, "statesmen are too absorbed by events to follow a

preconceived plan. They take one step and the next follows from it." If they achieve anything, it is by accident, not design: "all statesmen aim to win: the size of their winnings often surprises them." The real determinants of history, according to Mr. Taylor, are objective situations and human blunders. Objective situations consist of the realities of power; human intelligence is best employed in recognising these realities and allowing events to conform with them; but as human intelligence seldom prevails in politics, the realities generally have to assert themselves, at greater human cost, through the mess caused by human blunders. This doctrine (if I have correctly expressed it) seems remarkably like Mr. E. H. Carr's "realist" doctrine, advanced in his book *The Twenty Years' Crisis* (1938)—see the *first* edition—a book rightly described by Mr. Taylor as "a brilliant argument in favour of appeasement."

Once we accept this general theory, the next stage is easy. All we have to do is to ask ourselves, at what point do we make our calculation of reality? This then provides us with a *datum*. Mr. Taylor takes as his *datum* the spring of 1918. At that time Germany was victorious in the West and triumphant in the East. This, he implies, was the "natural" situation: the Allied victory later in 1918 was artificial—or at least it was made artificial (or, in his words, deprived of "moral validity") by the failure of the Allies to carve Germany up before making peace. This omission left Germany still potentially the greatest power in Europe, naturally tending to revert to the "real" position of January 1918. All that intelligent German statesmen had to do, or indeed could do, was to work hand-in-glove with this "historical necessity"—to their profit. All that Allied statesmen could do was to yield to the same necessity—to their loss. In this sense Hitler and Chamberlain were intelligent statesmen.

But is this general philosophy true? Do statesmen really never make history? Are they, all of them, always "too absorbed by events to follow a preconceived plan"? Was this true of Richelieu, of Bismarck, of Lenin? In particular, was it true of Hitler? Was Hitler really just a more violent Mr. Micawber sitting in Berlin or Berchtesgaden and waiting for something to turn up: something which, thanks to historic necessity, he could then turn to advantage? Certainly Hitler himself did not think so. He regarded himself as a thinker, a practical philosopher, the demiurge of a new age of history. And since he published a blueprint of the policy which he intended to carry out, ought we not at least to look at this blueprint just in case it had some relevance to his policy? After all, the reason why the majority of the British people reluctantly changed, between 1936 and 1939, from the views of Neville Chamberlain and Mr. Taylor to the views of Winston Churchill was their growing conviction that Hitler meant what he said: that he was aiming—*so oder so,* as he used to say—at world-conquest. A contemporary conviction that was strong enough to change the mood of a nation from a passionate desire for peace to a resolute determination on war surely deserves some respect from the historian. A historian who totally ignores it because, twenty years later, he can interpret some of the documents in an opposite sense runs the risk of being considered too clever by half.

Let us consider briefly the programme which Hitler laid down for himself. It was a programme of Eastern colonisation, entailing a war of conquest against Russia. If it were successfully carried out, it would leave Germany dominant in Eurasia and able to conquer the West at will. In order to carry it out, Hitler needed a restored German army which, since it must be powerful enough to conquer Russia, must also be powerful enough to conquer the West if that should be necessary. And that might be necessary even before the attack on Russia. For in order to reach Russia, Hitler would need to send his armies through Poland; and in order to do this— whether by the conquest of Poland or in alliance with it—he would need to break the bonds of treaty and interest which bound the new countries of Eastern Europe, the creatures of Versailles, to their creators, Britain and France. Hitler might be able to break those bonds without war against the West, but he could not be sure of it: it was always possible that a war with the West would be necessary before he could march against Russia. And in fact this is what happened.

Now this programme, which Hitler ascribed to himself, and which he actually carried out, is obviously entirely different from the far more limited programme which is ascribed to him by Mr. Taylor, and which he did not carry out. How then does Mr. Taylor deal with the evidence about it? He deals with it quite simply, either by ignoring it or by denying it as inconsistent with his own theories about statesmen in general and Hitler in particular: theories (one must add) for which he produces no evidence at all.

Take the inconvenient fact of Hitler's avowed programme of a great Eastern land-empire. In spite of some casual admission, Mr. Taylor effectively denies that Hitler had any such programme. Hitler, he says, "was always the man of daring improvisations: he made lightning decisions and then presented them as the result of long-term policy." Hitler's *Table Talk,* he says airily (as if this were the only evidence for such a programme), "was delivered far in occupied territory during the campaign against Soviet Russia, and *then* Hitler dreamed of some fantastic empire which would rationalise his career of conquest." [My italics here, and in all quotations below.] But why does Mr. Taylor believe, or rather pretend, that it was only in 1942, after his Russian conquests, that Hitler dreamed of an Eastern Empire? His programme had been stated, as clearly as possible, in 1924, in *Mein Kampf,* and on numerous other occasions since. Mr. Taylor hardly ever refers to *Mein Kampf* and never to the other occasions. In 1939, he admits, some people "attributed" to Hitler "grandiose plans which *they claimed* to have discovered by reading *Mein Kampf* in the original (Hitler forbade its publication in English)." The implication is that such plans are not to be found in *Mein Kampf* and that those who "claimed to have discovered" them had not really read, or been able to read, an untranslated work. But the fact is that those plans are unmistakably stated in *Mein Kampf* and that all the evidence of the 1930's showed that Hitler still intended to carry them out. I may add (since Mr. Taylor includes me among those who have ascribed to Hitler "preconceived plans" which he never pursued) that I myself read *Mein Kampf* in the original in 1938, and that I read it under the impact of Munich and of the remarkable prophecies of Sir Robert Ensor,[3] who had read it and who insisted that Hitler meant what he said. By absolutely refusing to face this evidence, and contemptuously dismissing those who have faced it, Mr. Taylor contrives to reach the preposterous conclusion that men like Ensor, who correctly forecast Hitler's future programme from the evidence, were really wrong, and that men like Chamberlain, who did not read the evidence and were proved totally wrong by events, were really right. His sole justification of this paradox is that he has accepted as an axiom a characterisation of Hitler as a "traditional" statesman pursuing limited aims. Mr. Taylor's Hitler cannot have held such views, and therefore the inconvenient fact that the real Hitler uttered such views

[3] British historian. [Editor's note.]

with remarkable consistency for twenty years and actually put them into practice, is simply puffed aside. When Hitler, in 1941, finally launched that conquest of Russia which, as he himself said, was "the be-all and end-all of Nazism," Mr. Taylor easily explains it away. "By 1941," he says, "Hitler had lost his old gift of patience": he "gratuitously" deviated from his former course; and at the mere thought of such an unaccountable fall from grace, Mr. Taylor promptly ends his book.

Nor is this the only perversion of evidence to which Mr. Taylor has to resort, in order to represent Hitler as a "traditional" statesman. The traditional statesmen *did not seek*, as Hitler did, to incorporate the Sudeten Germans in the Reich. Traditional statesmen demanded the frontiers of 1914; but Hitler, again and again, repudiated the frontiers of 1914 as a contemptible ambition. They looked back, at most, to the war-aims of 1914; he repudiated those war-aims. Even the "natural" position of January 1918, after the huge gains of Brest-Litovsk, was insufficient for Hitler. The treaty of Brest-Litovsk gave Germany the Ukraine as a colony of exploitation, a capitalist colony. But Hitler always made it quite clear that he spurned such a colony: he wanted the Ukraine as a colony of settlement. "I should deem it a crime," he said, "if I sacrificed the blood of a quarter of a million men merely for the conquest of natural riches to be exploited in a capitalist way. The goal of the *Ostpolitik* is to open up an area of settlement for a hundred million Germans." All this is pushed aside by Mr. Taylor with the remark,

when Hitler lamented, "If only we had a Ukraine . . ." he seemed to suppose there were no Ukrainians. Did he propose to exploit, or exterminate them? *Apparently he never considered the question.*

As if Hitler had not made his answer perfectly plain! As if he had any scruples about transporting or even exterminating populations! What about the European Jews? But that episode is conveniently forgotten by Mr. Taylor. It does not fit the character of a traditional German statesman who "in principle and doctrine, was no more wicked and unscrupulous than many other contemporary statesmen."

If Mr. Taylor's cardinal assumptions about Hitler's character and purpose are, to say the least, questionable, what are we to say of his use of evidence to illustrate them? Here he states his method with admirable clarity. "It is an elementary part of historical discipline," he says, "to ask of a document

not only what is in it but why it came into existence." With this maxim we may agree, only adding that since the contents of a document are objective evidence while its purpose may be a matter of private surmise, we must not rashly subject the former to the latter. Sometimes a man may say the truth even in a document called forth by tactical necessity. At all events, we are not entitled, in defence of an already paradoxical general theory, to assume that he is lying simply because it may not be tactically necessary for him, at that moment, to utter nothing but the truth.

Now let us take a few instances. On November 5th, 1937, Hitler summoned his war-leaders to the Chancellery and made a speech which, he said, in the event of his death was to be regarded as his "last will and testament." That suggests that he was not talking irresponsibly. The official record of this speech is the so-called "Hossbach Memorandum" which was used at Nuremberg as evidence of Hitler's plans for the gradual conquest of Europe. In it Hitler declared that the aim of German policy must be the conquest of *Lebensraum* in Europe, "but we will not copy liberal capitalist policies which rely on exploiting colonies. It is not a case of conquering people but of conquering agriculturally useful space." That seems clear enough. Then Hitler went on to consider the means of making such requests. "German politics," he said "must reckon with two hateful enemies, England and France, to whom a strong German colossus in the centre of Europe would be intolerable." Moreover, he admitted, these two hateful enemies would probably, at some stage, resist him by force: "the German question can only be solved by way of force, and this is never without risk." He then proceeded to discuss hypothetical possibilities. Since the hypothetical circumstances did not in fact arise, we need not dwell on them. The essential points are that the risk of European war must be faced by 1943 – 5, for "after that we can only expect a change for the worse," and that "our *first* aim" must be, at the first convenient opportunity, "to conquer Czechoslovakia and Austria simultaneously." This first conquest he hoped to achieve without war, for "in all probability England and perhaps also France have already silently written off Czechoslovakia." It could and should therefore be attempted as soon as circumstances make it possible in order that the later, more real risk could be faced before 1943 – 5. But there was to be no doubt about the nature of the conquest. It was not to be (as Mr. Taylor always maintains) the reduction of Austria and Czechoslovakia to the role of satellites: it was to be, in Hitler's own words, "the annexation of the two states to Germany, militarily and politically." The idea of satellite states in Eastern Europe, Hitler said in a secret speech delivered only a fortnight later, was one of the futile notions of "traditional" German politicians, and he dismissed it as "idiotic" (wahnsinnig). Finally, it is clear that conquered Austria and Czechoslovakia cannot themselves have constituted the *Lebensraum* which was the ultimate objective. Austria and Czechoslovakia were to be stepping-stones, "in all probability" secured without war, towards larger conquests which would entail a greater risk.

Such was Hitler's "testament" of November 1937. Its content is clear and logical and it has been taken seriously by all historians—until Mr. Taylor comes along and tells us that we have all been hoodwinked. For was not this document produced at Nuremberg? All documents produced at Nuremberg, he says, are "loaded," and "anyone who relies on them finds it almost impossible to escape from the load with which they are charged." So Mr. Taylor gives us a sample of his method of using such documents. Why, he asks, was the speech made? "The historian," he observes, "must push through the *cloud of phrases*" (so much for Hitler's perfectly clear statements) "to the *realities* beneath." The speech, he notes, was not made to Nazis but to generals and admirals, and its purpose was clearly to demand greater rearmament. With this we can agree. But Mr. Taylor does not stop there. In order to persuade these "conservative" war-leaders of the necessity of further rearmament, Hitler (he says) had to overcome the economic opposition of Dr. Schacht. His speech therefore "*had no other purpose*" than "to isolate Schacht from the other conservatives"; the dates 1943–5 (to which Hitler consistently kept) "*like all such figures, really meant* 'this year, next year, sometime. . .'"; and the content of a speech which Hitler himself described as his political testament (but Mr. Taylor does not quote that description) is dismissed as "daydreaming unrelated to what followed in real life." Why Hitler should be expected to speak more "realistically" on military matters to Nazis at a froth-blowers' meeting than to hard-headed war-leaders who would have to organise and carry out his programme is not clear. Presumably it is "an elementary part of historical discipline" to assume that.

A second example of Mr. Taylor's "historical discipline" is provided by his treatment of the crisis leading to the outbreak of war in 1939. By now Austria and Czechoslovakia had been "annexed to Germany, militarily and politically," and Hitler had turned the heat upon Poland. According to Mr. Taylor, Hitler really only wanted the German city of Danzig, but since geography prevented him from obtaining it except by the coercion of Poland, he was forced, reluctantly, to apply such coercion and prepare military plans. Of course (according to Mr. Taylor) he did not intend to execute these plans. His military plans were "only intended to reinforce the diplomatic war of nerves." Unfortunately the British Government, misled after Hitler's occupation of Prague into thinking that he aimed at far larger conquests, had imprudently guaranteed Poland and thus threatened Hitler with European war if he sought this next "natural," "moral" aim by any but peaceful means. However, Hitler was a match for this. By making his pact with Russia, he effectively countered the British guarantee, and therefore, pushing, like Mr. Taylor, "through the cloud of phrases to the realities beneath," he ignored its empty words and relied, as a rational man, on "the crumbling of Western nerve." Unfortunately, in this case, he miscalculated. Britain, quixotically faithful to the "phrases" of the guarantee, and deluded by the idea that Hitler, if given a free hand, would not stop at Danzig, ignored all the "realities" of the situation and made war, "war for Danzig."

Such is Mr. Taylor's version of the Polish crisis. In defence of it he finds it necessary here, too, to charm away some important documents, and once again it is instructive to watch the exorcist at work. On May 23rd, 1939, Hitler again summoned his war-leaders. He told them, according to Mr. Taylor, who quotes no other words of the document, "there will be war. Our task is to isolate Poland. . . . It must not come to a simultaneous showdown with the West." "This," comments Mr. Taylor, "seems clear enough"; but he then dismisses even this evidence by saying authoritatively that "when Hitler talked to his generals, he talked for effect, not to reveal the workings of his mind." So that is that. Three months later, with the signature of the Nazi-Soviet Pact, Hitler again addressed his generals, and again Mr. Taylor is content to quote only one sentence from the speech: "now the probability is great that the West will not intervene." Apart from that "hard core," the rest of the speech, he says, can be ignored, as Hitler "was talking for effect." After all, by the Nazi-Soviet Pact, Hitler considered that "he had prevented war, not brought it on." So, once again, Hitler's mere "phrases" dissolve on contact with Mr. Taylor's "realities."

But why should we suppose, as an axiom, that Hitler, when briefing his generals on the eve of a possible war, talked only for effect? Why should we not suppose that he intended them to be ready (as they were) for the real future? And why should we altogether overlook some very clear statements which he made to them? For if we look at the full texts of these two speeches, we find that Mr. Taylor has made certain remarkable omissions.

In the first of these two speeches Hitler began by insisting that the next step towards Germany's goal could not be taken "without the invasion of foreign states or attacks upon foreign property," and that although bloodless victories had been won in the past, "further successes cannot be obtained without the shedding of blood." "*Danzig*," he went on, in words from which Mr. Taylor has firmly averted his eyes, "*is not the subject of the dispute at all. It is a question of expanding our living-space in the East*." Moreover, he looked clearly forward to the prospect of war with the West. "The Polish problem," he said, "is inseparable from conflict with the West." For all that, "we are left with the decision to attack Poland at the first opportunity. We cannot expect a repetition of the Czech affair." Of course Hitler hoped to avoid a simultaneous conflict with the West, but he did not rely on any such hope: "the *Führer* doubts the possibility of a peaceful settlement with England. We must prepare ourselves for the conflict." The remaining two-thirds of the document deal with the problems of war with Britain, "the driving-force against Germany." All this is totally ignored by Mr. Taylor: it cannot have been the "hard core" of any argument used by *his* Hitler: therefore, he declares, it was mere froth, uttered for "effect."

In the second speech Hitler similarly made clear statements which Mr. Taylor does not quote. For instance, immediately after the "hard core," the single sentence which he does quote, about the probability that the West will be frightened out of intervention by the Nazi-Soviet Pact, come the words, "*we must accept the risk with reckless resolution*"; and Hitler then went on to explain how Germany, thanks to Russian supplies, could withstand a Western blockade. His only fear, he said, was that "at the last moment some *Schweinhund* will make a proposal for mediation": a proposal, perhaps, which might have fobbed him off with Danzig which, as he had admitted, was "not the subject of the dispute at all." No: Hitler was now resolved on war, even if the West did come in.

I shall give a propagandist cause for starting the war: never mind if it be plausible or not. The victor shall not be asked afterwards whether he told the truth or not.

As for the West, "even if war should break out in the West, the destruction of Poland shall be the primary objective." Which indeed was exactly what happened. By last-minute diplomatic manoeuvres Hitler naturally sought to detach the West, but when that could not be done, he went ahead, with his eyes open, into a European war which, though larger than he had hoped, he still reckoned on winning.

I have said enough to show why I think Mr. Taylor's book utterly erroneous. In spite of his statements about "historical discipline," he selects, suppresses, and arranges evidence on no principle other than the needs of his thesis; and that thesis, that Hitler was a traditional statesman, of limited aims, merely responding to a given situation, rests on no evidence at all, ignores essential evidence, and is, in my opinion, demonstrably false. This casuistical defence of Hitler's foreign policy will not only do harm by supporting neo-Nazi mythology: it will also do harm, perhaps irreparable harm, to Mr. Taylor's reputation as a serious historian.

5

PROSPECTS FOR THE FUTURE: FIRE IN THE ASHES?

Totalitarianism, the two World Wars, and the threat of nuclear warfare have been more devastating to the European spirit than to the material possessions of Europe. One of Europe's greatest assets in the period 1871–1914 was its self-confidence, its faith in the future. That faith was lost by many Europeans during the days of trial for the Allies and defeat for the Axis powers in World War II. Others lost what faith they had retained when Communist regimes were established in Central-Eastern Europe after 1945 under the shadows of Soviet tanks. Still others who retained any confidence at all in Europe's future were severely chastened by the turn history had taken.

The material and human devastation of Europe at the end of World War II was apparent everywhere on the Continent, from the ruined factories of Stalingrad to the bombed cities of Germany, Italy, France, the Low Countries, and Great Britain. The vast numbers of human casualties included millions of helpless and innocent Jews, for whom light had been extinguished in Nazi death camps, as well as other millions who had at least found the chance to meet death while fighting for something dear to them. The political structure of many European nations was in shambles. The European economy was disrupted and many Europeans were dependent for sheer biological survival upon American economic aid. In terms of world power Europe counted for less than it had at any time since the age of Columbus and Magellan. Before 1914 Western Europeans had spoken rather contemptuously of Turkey as "the sick man of Europe." For several years after 1945 Europe itself might have been aptly described as "the sick man of the contemporary world."

For many Europeans in the 1920's Communism had been the last best hope of mankind, but by 1948 if not earlier that dream had failed. In 1948 many former Communists were saying with the novelist Arthur Koestler: "The Soviet Union has deceived our fondest hopes and shown us tragically in what treacherous quicksand an honest revolution can flounder." In the same year, George Orwell, the British novelist who had looked with hope to Communism in the 1930's, published his famous 1984. In it he sought to warn the Western world against the perils of continued drift toward collectivization, but the degree of confidence Orwell felt for European Civilization was suggested by the words he had one of the characters in his novel speak: "If you want a picture of the future, imagine a boot stamping on a human face—forever."

For many intellectuals who lost faith in Communism, the worst feature of Communist totalitarianism—whether Stalinist or Titoist or Maoist—was its thought control. Milovan Djilas, who had helped found Communist rule in Yugoslavia, was one of these. After breaking with Tito, Djilas wrote as follows: "History will pardon Communists for much, establishing that they were forced into many brutal acts because of circumstances and the need to defend their existence. But the stifling of every divergent thought, the exclusive monopoly over thinking for the purpose of defending their personal interests, will nail the Communists to a cross of shame in history."

Even some European intellectuals who refused to denounce Communism seemed to have little illusion that it would bring an ideal future. Jean-Paul Sartre, the French existentialist, concluded that man should "act without hope," and his companion, Simone de Beauvoir, wrote: "Man fulfills himself within the transitory or not at all."

The only hope held out by Sartre's rival in postwar French philosophy, Albert Camus, was that of rolling the rock of Sisyphus up the hill over and over again, even though it would fall back down each time.

In the midst of the extremely mobid atmosphere of postwar Germany, the novelist Gottfried Benn saw the limits of human possibilities in a similar light, but with a certain sardonic confidence: "And so what is that situation like? Desperate? Send me up some fresh supplies of libido and a guaranteed pre-Spenglerian civilization. The exploration of outer space hasn't yet reached the stage where we could start to feel something again at the sight of the stars." And he added: "no more above, no more below, the center is damaged, the compass needle and the quarters of heaven are no longer valid, but the species is rampant and keeps going by means of pills."

But there were other Europeans during the immediate postwar years who were not content to face the future "on pills," who did not minimize the problems at hand but who did not despair of Europe's future. Among these were several realistic dreamers who had preached the need for European union since the 1920's. The advocates of a "United States of Europe" and more modest plans for the integration of Europe believed that Europeans must at least partly sacrifice their proud national sovereignties if they were to face the future with any real basis for confidence. These men had found few followers before 1939. By 1948, confronted by the expansion of Communist power and forced to acknowledge the eclipse of their individual nations, a number of practical-minded political and economic leaders were ready to try to build a united Europe. Starting hesitantly, the movement to unify at least western and central Europe achieved more success by the late 1950's than most intelligent Europeans could have hoped for in 1948. The work of unification was still far from complete in the late 1960's, but in the intervening years the various approaches to European cooperation did more than facilitate Europe's economic recovery and strengthen it militarily; they provided a movement that could capture the devotion and reawaken the hopes of many Europeans who saw little else of a secular nature in which they could believe.

With physical recovery and slow adjustment to Cold War realities, the European spirit made a qualified comeback during the 1950's. Yet, as late as 1961 the German existentialist, Karl Jaspers, held out relatively little hope for human beings, unless they could transcend the previous frailties of human kind. Writing in *The Future of Mankind*, Jaspers asserted: "An altogether novel situation has been created by the atom bomb. Either all mankind will physically perish or there will be a change in the moral-political condition of man."

Such restricted possibilities for the years ahead were being prophesied with less and less frequency by European intellectuals in the 1960's. Some regained a large part of the old self-confidence that seemed to have been destroyed when the Second World War ended in 1945. Twenty years later, on May 2, 1965, a British specialist in contemporary history, Walter Laqueur, could write optimistically in the *New York*

Times Book Review about Europe and question the future prospects for Africa and Asia:

Since the early years of the century, whole libraries have been written about the great and growing importance of Africa and Asia. The efforts of the "emergent forces" to build up their countries ought to be followed with sympathy. But neither the cause of historical truth nor that of the emergent nations will be served by fanciful statements about their economic prospects, their cultural promise and their political futures.

Europe has been written off many times before but it has shown a surprising power of recovery. . . . Culturally, its pull on the rest of the world is at present stronger than ever before . . . . So far as there is no retreat into chaos and neobarbarism among the newly emergent nations, Western political ideas, Western cultural impulses, Western scientific and technological discoveries will be the agents of progress in the forseeable future.

Europe, concluded Laqueur, remains the "most promising of continents." The prospects for Europe had considerably improved since the mid-1950's. It remains to be seen whether Laqueur's optimistic view of 1965 was a sound one.

Obviously it will be more difficult for you to make a decision about the future of European Civilization than it has been to resolve conflicting interpretations about the past. The underlying problem in making historical interpretations is the gathering of evidence. Even about the past the evidence is partial rather than complete. About the future, direct evidence is totally lacking.

And yet for students of Western Civilization evidence about the future cannot possibly be totally lacking, because the forces of the past have momentum that carries them forward into the future. Using all sources of information at your disposal and exercising your best powers of criticism and imagination, try to imagine what will happen to *Europe* during the next ten years. Then try to imagine what will happen to *European Civilization.* Compare your ideas with those of fellow students. Write your ideas down and file them away. They will make interesting reading a decade hence.

GEOFFREY BARRACLOUGH

A GLOOMY VIEW OF EUROPE'S PROSPECTS

The following selection is taken from a book published by a British historian, Geoffrey Barraclough, some ten years after the end of World War II. Both as a Britisher and as a student of German history, Barraclough had reason to be acutely aware of the shrinkage of traditional Europe's place in the world in the twentieth century. As a student of medieval history he was accustomed to look at the trends of centuries rather than to become engulfed by the details of a decade or two. He was much influenced by Arnold Toynbee's approach to history as the study of the rise and fall of civilizations. Barraclough has taught history in Merton College at Oxford, St. John's College at Cambridge, the University of Liverpool, and the University of London. He has been President of the Historical Association of Great Britain. The author of several books, he expanded several of the ideas you will encounter in this selection in a 1964 volume entitled *An Introduction to Contemporary History*.

Barraclough takes a gloomy view of Europe's present and future. Though pessimistic about traditional Europe, he is more optimistic about the prospects of European Civilization as taken over and modified in "both American and Russian civilisation." How sound is Barraclough's conclusion that we need "a new view of the European past, adapted to the new perspectives in which the old Europe stands in a new age of global politics and global civilisation"? Is the proper view of history one that mirrors the reality of the past as accurately as possible? Or should it be one that is designed to help the reader accept the present? Or should it be something else, one that prepares readers to build the future that the historian desires or expects?

The extraordinary recovery since 1945 shows that Europe cannot, even at this late date, simply be written off as an extinct volcano. But two facts point to a fundamental change. "Modern history," as we know it, seemed to be given unity by two things: first, what is called "the expansion of Europe," and secondly the predominance of the European powers. Both are too obvious and well known to require elucidation: what is important is that they no longer hold good. For three centuries, following the voyages of Columbus, Da Gama and Magellan, the shadow of European hegemony moved across the oceans; between 1815 and 1914 the world entered a new era of global integration under the compulsion of western technology, and seemed to be receiving a European imprint, not merely in material things, the cotton shirts of Lancashire and the shoddy trousers of Dewsbury, railways, electricity, architecture, but also in political organisation and political ideas. Predominance and leadership were in the hands of the European powers. To-day that is no longer true. Down to 1914, it seemed that the relations of the European powers would settle the future of the world, and that European expansion was simply carrying the principle of Balance of Power, on which the relations of the European states were based, into the other continents. In fact, well before 1914 that had ceased to be the case. When the tottering Ottoman empire was admitted to the European Concert in 1856, and when, a little later, the United States and Japan were recognized as

"great powers," in addition to the six nations which happened at the time to be the strongest in Europe, it was clear that world-leadership was no longer a European privilege. To-day, after the war of 1939–45, two great powers survive: Russia and the United States, both with European roots and origins but neither at this date essentially European—and following at a distance there is the British commonwealth, the sinews of which also lie outside Europe. The rest, as we have seen, have sunk to provincial status. It is too early yet to speak with certainty; but the indications are that in the late twentieth or in the twenty-first century Europe is destined to enjoy (if that is the right word) something not unlike the colonial status which in the eighteenth and nineteenth centuries it imposed on Africa, much of Asia and the New World. Already the Soviet Union and the United States have their European satellites; already eastern Europe can only defend itself with Russian help against American domination, and western Europe can only defend itself with American aid against Russia.

The German historian, Ludwig Dehio, in what is probably the most remarkable and prescient study of modern history to appear since the war, has shown how and by what stages the old "historic core" of Europe (as it is sometimes called) was overtaken, dwarfed and is now in effect divided between the two great flanking powers in east and west. As his analysis makes clear, the struggle of first one power

From Geoffrey Barraclough, *History in A Changing World* (Norman, Okla., 1956), pp. 207–210, 214–220. Reprinted by kind permission of the University of Oklahoma Press and of Basil Blackwell Ltd.

and then another to secure hegemony in Europe forced the defenders of European liberty to call in the aid of outside powers, or to mobilize for their defence non-European or extra-European resources. Napoleon's attempt to unite Europe in a French empire was defeated not by the efforts of his opponents and victims in the heart of Europe, but by the resistance of the two great flanking-powers, England and Russia. And it is evident, however high we rate the defensive effort of Great Britain in 1940, that Hitler was defeated by the overseas resources of the U.S.A., on the one hand, and, on the other hand, by the Asiatic resources which Soviet Russia drew from its empire beyond the Urals. These wars, fought on European soil, devastated Europe, with the result that the extra-European powers drew ahead. The war of 1914–18 resulted, as everyone knows, in the economic and financial supremacy of the U.S.A. But another result, though less obvious, is no less significant. The successive defeats of successive powers seeking hegemony in Europe meant that European national divisions were not only preserved but increased. Few people In Europe would regret that result; few would prefer unity under French or German hegemony to the relative liberty assured by a system of small counterbalancing powers, none strong enough to enforce its will against a combination of the others. The diversity of the nations, it is usually held, has been the source of the richness of European culture and civilisation. But if we emphasize that important fact, we must recognize also that these divisions meant, and were bound to mean, weakness in the face of outside powers. They were one of the main reasons why the U.S.A. and the U.S.S.R. drew ahead. Even to-day, though in area far smaller, in population Europe (excluding the U.S.S.R.) is considerably larger than either Russia or the United States of America. The present population of Europe is around 400 million. Western Europe alone, including western but excluding eastern Germany, to-day contains over 275 million people; yet Russia's population is only about 220 million and that of the United States less than 165 million. There is therefore no absolute European numerical inferiority. And in addition, relative to its size, Europe can still claim to rank as the most highly industrialized continent of the globe. If, therefore, Europe has been overtaken and outstripped politically by the U.S.A. and the U.S.S.R., this is due in part at least to conditions within Europe itself. It was because Europe failed to solve its own problems, that it lost its predominance. Hence, in considering the position of Europe to-day, we must take into account not merely the change in world-conditions, but also the changes in European conditions. . . .

Disruptive forces there certainly are; but there are constructive forces also. No one could maintain that there is in Europe to-day that gradual exhaustion of creative energy which was so obvious in the decline of the Roman Empire.

What is obvious, on the other hand, is the dilemma of Europe—a dilemma which is nowhere more evident than in the contemporary projects for European union. If, as is commonly agreed, one of the prime causes of the decline of Europe is its lack of unity, then it seems too obvious for further discussion that the answer to that siuation lies in federation. And yet the prospects of voluntary federation, so far as can be judged, are not very great, and I imagine most historians would be more impressed by the obstacles in the way of European union to-day than by the possibilities. To discuss those obstacles in detail is none of my business. But it is worth while—and, I think, important—to insist that they do not (as is too easily assumed) consist simply in a short-sighted, selfish inability to subordinate national interests to a greater, common good. No doubt, there are many such interests at play—not all of them lightly to be dismissed. But the real issue goes deeper, and it may perhaps best be put in the form of a comparison with Greece. In ancient Greece, in its greatest age, the independent city-states—Athens, Corinth, Sparta—were essential elements. Take away the independence of those city-states, and it is difficult, if not impossible, to see how what was of enduring value in Greek civilisation could have been secured. In other words, the independence of the city-states had the same roots as Greek civilisation itself; it was ineradicable so long as that civilisation lasted. May we not say the same of the European nations? Or is it not at least a consideration which no serious, thoughtful person would simply dismiss? Back in 1924, in an address to an American audience, the Dutch historian, Jan Huizinga, a great European if ever there was one, put the position far better than I can. "I do not know," he said,

whether Americans can fully realize the necessity there is for Europe of preserving its division into many nations, and the fervent desire of all and any of these to maintain their specific national existence. I do not mean this politically so much as culturally . . . It would be quite natural for you to say: why should not the European nations, after so many centuries of bitter strife, in the long run be merged into one vast unit? . . . Still, political harmony and concord is not the one thing the world stands in need of. However indispensable to civilization peace and order may be, real civilization is not contained in them. They may even be a danger to it, should they be promoted by equalizing and levelling. What we envy you is your unity, not your uniformity. We Europeans feel too keenly that no nation, however prosperous or great, is fit to bear the burden of civilization alone. Each in his turn is called upon, in this wonderful world, to speak his word, and find a solution which just his particular spirit enables him to express. Civilization is safeguarded by diversity. Even the smallest facets in the many-sided whole may sometimes catch the light and reflect it.

Those words of Huizinga—you may say that they are only one element of the story, but just for that reason they reveal what I have called the "dilemma" of Europe. On the one side, industrialisation—which in foreseeable time will not be checked or halted—seems, with its extending scale of operations, to demand and necessitate ever greater unification: unification, indeed, in which a European union, even if it embraced the whole of Europe, might still prove to be an inadequate economic unit. And with unification, standardisation and uniformity. On the other side, the maintenance of diversity, and what an English historian has called "resistance" to "drab technological (or 'technocratic') universalism." And this is only one of the dilemmas with which Europe is faced. Europe's problem, it is often said, is that it has too much history; it cannot escape from the toils of its own traditions, break away from the past, and make a new start. But, on the other hand, may it not be answered—and has it not often been said—that the alleged "bankruptcy" of Europe is precisely due to the fact that European man has lost his historical roots, and become "an exile from his own past"? Here again—and I will not burden you with further examples—Europe is saddled with a dilemma which neither the U.S.A. nor the U.S.S.R. yet knows in the same intensity. It has rightly been said that, if Russia and America have forged ahead of Europe, it is not because either possesses greater political ability or political experience—on the contrary, they possess much less —but because political construction, and likewise economic construction, is easier in a new country on the fringes of a civilisation than in the old country at its centre. Evidently, the position in this and in other respects is far more complicated and difficult in Europe; and this itself is a disadvantage from a political point of view. There is, in fact, no easy or right or correct solution of Europe's problems; and that is an additional problem—perhaps the decisive problem. The self-confidence and directness of Rus-

sian policy and American policy, and their clear objectives, are impossible in Europe, because in Europe the objectives are not clear. We may put the European dilemma in a nutshell by saying that, if Europe does not preserve its traditions it will lose the spiritual forces, the belief in itself, the very anchorage, without which no civilisation can hope to survive, while if it maintains its traditions and the diversity and the values which those traditions have created, it will be at a disadvantage—probably at a fatal disadvantage—in a world where large-scale organisation, vast political and economic units, uniformity and standardisation, bring power and the right to have the last word.

In a sense, it might be argued that Europe still remains the centre of the world; but that its position is now reversed. Instead of being a centre from which energy and initiative radiate outwards, Europe has become a centre upon which non-European energy and initiative converge. Instead of the world being a theatre for the play of European activities and rivalries, Europe itself is an arena for the conflicts of extra-European powers. And yet even in this sense the position of Europe is in doubt. For the moment it would seem that the struggle for Europe, because of its great industrial potential, is the dominant theme in the relations of the two surviving great powers, Russia and the United States. But the series of conflicts in Korea, S.E. Asia and Formosa already indicates that the scene may be shifting, and that the sheer demographic weight of Asia—once the process of industrialisation fully activates it and makes its mobilization possible—may become the dominant factor, and in no far distant time leave Europe in a backwash. In any event, the traditional Europe—the Europe of our history books, the Europe of Louis XIV and Napoleon and Bismarck—is dead and beyond resurrection, and we may disabuse our minds of the illusion that there is any special relevance, from the point of view of contemporary affairs, in studying those neolithic figures. If you believe that the study of history has any relevance to current events, then you will gain more, in the present world, by studying the life and times of Alexander the Great, or Caesar and the Roman revolution. And it is perhaps fundamentally important to get this fact firmly in our minds, because there could be no more serious mistake in current policy than to suppose that a return to a Europe similar to that of the nineteenth century can be effected, or to direct political action to the restoration of what is fondly called "the traditional order."

War and Totalitarianism

But if the traditional Europe has passed beyond recall, it does not follow with any rigour or logic of necessity that Europe has no future to look forward to. As Halecki[1] says, the "passing" of Europe does not mean that there will not, in the future, be a European history in the sense in which there was European history in Antiquity, when parts of Europe were joined with Asia Minor and North Africa in the Roman empire. The European community typical of the European age of history—a real unity in all its diversity, clearly distinct from any other part of the world—is disintegrating before our eyes. But individual European countries, or possibly different regions of Europe, will continue to play a role, which need not be inconsiderable, within larger, but not exclusively (or even predominantly) European communities, of which perhaps the so-called "Atlantic Community" is a forerunner.

Furthermore the "passing" of the traditional Europe does not mean that the system of values centring round the worth of human personality and the importance of the human individual, which has been built up in the course of European history, has ceased to count. It is true, I think, that these values are not ultimate, and must not be treated as ultimates. In the course of centuries eastern Christianity built up values with a different but no less real appreciation of the place of the individual in God's universe, and these values—and I say this, of course, without prejudice to the values of the other great religions, Islam, Buddhism, Confucianism—are not to be dismissed as less estimable or less valid than those of the west. Nevertheless western standards will survive, though doubtless shorn of many of the extravagances which marred them in the period of

[1] Oskar Halecki; historian. [Editor's note.]

unbridled liberalism. But we must not expect the same implicit acceptance of those standards as in the past. We can see to-day that the acknowledgement of the system of values built up in the west as an ultimate standard in most parts of the world was, in large part, not a reflection of genuine belief in the validity of those values, but rather a result of the fact that they were the standards of a successful, expanding, forward-thrusting civilisation, and were therefore accepted, on pragmatic grounds, as one of the conditions of success. Now that European civilisation is on the defensive, the attitude of non-European peoples to European standards—as we can see very plainly in the case of India—is far more critical.

Nevertheless we need not fear that the values created and consolidated by European societies in the last 800 or 900 years will perish. They will not perish for two reasons. The first—and the more important—is that they reflect an approach to perennial human problems which is of too universal application to be neglected, a solution which the particular spirit of Europe—and that particular spirit alone—was able to express, but which, once expressed, has become the possession of mankind. And though a far too presumptuous insistence on the superiority of western standards has produced a very natural reaction, particularly against the unbridled individualism of western thought, we may be sure that that reaction in its turn will be followed by a counter-reaction, which will lead to a better appreciation of what is of enduring value in western traditions.

The second reason why European values, though they may be modified and re-assessed, will not perish, is that they are embedded both in Russian and in American civilisation.

RAYMOND ARON

A FRENCH SCHOLAR'S QUALIFIED OPTIMISM

Geoffrey Barraclough has perceptively identified evidence of the decline of Europe and reasons for it. In this selection Raymond Aron points to the potentialities as well as problems of Europe in the mid-1950's. He cautiously explores hopes for a continuation of Europe's "historic vitality."

Aron has combined careers in journalism and in scholarship. During World War II, with General Charles de Gaulle in England, he edited the newspaper *La France Libre*, organ of the French resistance movement that carried on the struggle against Germany after the defeat of France in 1940. After the liberation of France and the end of World War II Aron served as chief news analyst for the distinguished Paris newspaper *Le Figaro* and as a professor in the Institut d'Etudes Politiques. Noted for his penetrating critiques of ideas that many have regarded as sacrosanct, Aron also has shown powers of constructive imagination. Both were displayed in his volume *The Century of Total War*, first published in 1954. The reading that follows is taken from an American edition of that often brilliant analysis.

You will note that Aron was not overly confident in the mid-1950's about Europe's immediate prospects and that he was aware of a number of pressing problems. But you will also note that he was more sanguine about Europe's future than was Barraclough. How sound has Aron's suggestion been to date that "distant perspectives justify optimism"?

Europe, west of the Iron Curtain, in spite of its humiliation is since the last war one of the rare and privileged places where the great majority of people escape the danger of hunger and torture. If we consider the living standard, personal rights, and the limitation of arbitrary interference, she remains almost exemplary compared with the Soviet zone, where police violence strikes at millions of innocent people and compared with immense regions in Asia or Africa, where famine every year carries off millions of helpless victims.

Of course, neither plenty nor formal liberty is the aim or the criterion of civilizations, but the values which Europe realizes less imperfectly than the greater part of mankind are the very ones of which the enemies of the West make empty boast. The Stalinists of France, the rationalists, the progressive Christians denounce economic inequality, the poverty of the masses, the abuses of power. A Soviet regime increases coal or steel production more rapidly than it improves the conditions of existence. It eliminates landowners, capitalists, industrialists, but it replaces them with a hierarchy of prosperous officials and subjects the public to the arbitrary authority of party and police. If the struggle between the two Europes took the form of an examination in morality or in economic efficiency before an impartial tribunal, the verdict would not be in doubt. Unfortunately, that is not the character of historic conflicts. Victory may fall to the more virtuous, but that virtue has nothing in common with a sense of justice or respect for humanity. It is a matter of the stern qualities needed in difficult times — discipline

From Raymond Aron, *The Century of Total War* (1955), pp. 317–318, 320–325. Reprinted by permission of Doubleday and Company and of André Deutsch Ltd.

and devotion on the part of the people, vision and resolution in the rulers. Do Europeans still possess that sort of virtue?

Great Britain has escaped from the political and ideological broils of the twentieth century. The British Fascists were never really taken seriously. The Communists have captured some positions in the trade unions, and they enjoy more sympathy from intellectuals than is generally supposed. But the union leaders remain fiercely hostile to them. The masses of the workers are enlisted in organizations which are faithful to democracy. Reduction of inequalities and the protection of individuals against accidents and excessive poverty have been carried further than anywhere else. The Labour experiment, a sequel to the policy adopted by the National Government during the war is, on its own level, and taking a short view, a success.

One hesitates, however, to be unreservedly optimistic. In Great Britain as well, the contradiction characteristic of our communities is beginning to appear: the disproportion between the tasks which the government undertakes and the authority that it possesses. The discrepancy is not so acute in Britain as in France. The absence of Stalinist agitation moderates the violence of political pretentions, and negotiation in good faith remains the accepted rule and the regular practice. . . .

The crisis, so far as that term may properly be used, is in Great Britain the result of external events rather than of any causes within the nation itself. The same cannot be said of France, Germany, or Italy.

Communism is, in a way, a foreign body within French democracy. But would that democracy work more smoothly if, instead of a Communist Party that separates itself from the community, there were a great Labour Party to deal with, supported by 40 per cent to 45 per cent of the electorate, or even two labor parties, one extreme and the other moderate, competing for the favor of the proletariat? In spite of appearances, the Fourth Republic, in its present form, owes its existence to Stalinism. It is this alone that gives the moderates an influence which would inevitably diminish on the day when the trade unions and the labor parties, freed from Kremlin control, acquired an influence proportional to the number of their adherents and the strength of their organizations.

Modern democracies carry in themselves a seed of corruption, which is at the same time the origin of their merits: the leaders must secure the votes of the citizenry, an obligation that has been rare through the ages and contrary to the traditional order in which the masters make themselves not only obeyed but respected, even worshiped, by their subjects. The minority in power is not united and does not form a permanent hierarchy. Appointments depend on popularity and on competition between individuals, groups, and parties. The angling for votes usually benefits the majority of the people, at least in the short run and as regards the standards of living. Democracies foment discontent, totalitarian regimes organize enthusiasm. The latter have no need to make concessions to the public whose happiness is proclaimed over the loud-speakers every morning. The former try to meet the claims that they encourage. From political equality to equality of income, from the state as protector of the disinherited to the state responsible for the welfare of all, from the state as guarantor of the freedom of individuals and enterprise to the state as director of the economic system, the transition seems almost inevitable, though not equally rapid, in the industrial societies of the West.

This evolution is not, as such, a form of decadence. But the leaders must manage to control its pace. Even the rich democracies are tempted to distribute more purchasing power, in these days, than there are products to consume. The poor democracies, such as that of France, when they are unable to improve really the conditions of existence, are inclined to make countless concessions, the total of which amounts to a proliferation of abuses ruinous to the community.

Historically, parliamentary regimes are a peculiarity of Great Britain that has spread, with more or less success, throughout the world. They have acclimatized themselves with relative ease in countries with a maritime civilization and a bourgeois tradition. In France, with a monarchical past, a centralized administration, but also a powerful bourgeoisie, nearly a century elapsed between the overthrow of the monarchy and the stabilization of a parliamentary republic. The future of the democracies restored after 1945 is still in suspense.

For my own part, I do not feel the slightest temptation to despise formal liberties in the name of the alleged real ones. If one had to choose between the

Fourth Republic on the one hand and Fascism or Communism on the other, no doubt would be possible. The acceptance of decadence would seem less intolerable than the choice of either totalitarianism, that is to say, of abjuration. No one can say definitely that Europe is still capable of finding an original path and reforming the pluralist democracies without the sacrifice of fundamental values. It can only be shown that such a reform is conceivable.

To accomplish the tasks essential to the survival of Europe, the Continental democracies must put into effect part of the program characteristic of the "Right Wing opposition": they must restore to the executive a capacity for decision above the tumult of private and collective interests, restrict the activity of pressure groups, maintain an unpolitical administration, rouse the trade unions to a realization of their duty of educating and disciplining their followers as well as making demands, and advance the promotion of a ruling minority animated by the consciousness of a national mission.

It will be objected that the fate of Europe depends less on Europeans themselves than on events over which they have little control: on the development of the conflict between the United States and the Soviet Union, on the maintenance of the present partition, or, conversely, on the unification of Germany and of the Continent. In a sense, the objection is valid. But, just as the strength of the Communist parties in France and Italy is at least as much the effect as the cause of social decomposition, the Soviet-American conflict is partly the effect, and not entirely the cause, of European impotence. Europe is in danger of being a field of battle, and therefore the victim of the conflict between the big powers. But she is also, through her weakness, one of the causes of the conflict.

Let us leave aside the European Communists and fellow travelers, who detest the United States as the enemy of their real country and hotbed of imperialism. Let us leave aside the intellectuals who, even when they have broken with Communism, continue to abuse capitalism. Let us leave aside the critics of American life, who, mixing true and false, compare the highest successes of Europe with the general level of culture attained by the American masses. In the matter of conditions of living, of productivity, and of social justice, the economic system of the United States, in spite of the term "capitalism," is more progressive than that of the majority of European countries. When Europeans who boast of democratic values denounce the American way of life, they do so at bottom in the name of aristocratic values.

The real ground for the bitterness which so many Europeans display in their references to Americans will not be found in the blunders, the clumsiness, the indecisions of Washington diplomacy in its sudden promotion to a global role. The European nations are themselves, through their wars, responsible for the rise of their transatlantic ally. The political fortune of the United States is inseparable from the humiliation of Europe, and is its symbol. When Europeans deplore the power of the United States, they are unconsciously thinking of their own downfall. They are all the more severe on the shortcomings of American civilization (and shortcomings are not lacking) because they are dependent on the wealth and strength of that distant protector. Even among nations, too great disparity stands in the way of friendship.

When they evoke the past, Europeans vaguely resent America's profit from the disasters of the twentieth century. When they think of the future, they envy America's separation from the potential enemy by thousands of miles of ocean. It is the disparity of risks (real or supposed, for after all, the United States can become the target of atomic attacks) that rouses bitterness. The rest of the argument follows: Neither the people nor the Government of the United States wanted or wants the third world war to attain total violence. Vigorous resistance offers at least as many chances of avoiding the explosion as concessions and signs of weakness. The armaments of the United States are not such as to proclaim to the masters of the Kremlin the nearness and inevitability of hyperbolic war. Someday perhaps, American opinion may tire of limited war, and end by calling for a "showdown" to call a halt to the ordeal before it becomes intolerable. But for the moment there is nothing to justify such accusations.

Certainly an astonishing tumult accompanies the development of foreign policy in the United States. The press and other organs of publicity amplify beyond all measure the voices of journalists, senators, Ministers, and the President, Hollywood stars, or atomic experts. Even when there is basic agreement, a strange cacophony is noticeable, made worse by the alternations of triumphs or disasters casually announced in official or semi-official statements. It is easy for the foreigner to denounce a great power, whose leaders, disagreeing about essentials, publicly evoke possible events tragic to others, such as scorched-earth tactics, the destruction of the Ruhr, or the Breton redoubt. These discussions are the toll levied by democracy: every representative of the American people pretends to form his opinion for himself.

Many Frenchmen, even anti-Communists, like to picture the world as though the Americans had a personal quarrel with the Russians, or the capitalists of Wall Street with the Communists of the Kremlin. Arguing from that viewpoint, the parts are exchanged: Europeans are no longer protected, but victimized. The United States is seeking to recruit mercenaries, not to safeguard national independence. For anyone uninterested in the result of the world struggle, that view may acquire a measure of truth. For those who accept with indifference the ultimate victory of Communism, who fear nothing but war, the American determination not to tolerate the extension of the Russian empire to the Atlantic becomes an obstacle to an integration dreamed of as progressive if not painless.

The gravest reproach which Europeans could address to the United States is seldom formulated: it is the policy followed from 1943 to 1945, the abandonment of Central and Eastern Europe to the Soviet Union. There is no heavier mortgage on the future of the Continent.

Lack of space creates for communities a danger comparable with lack of oxygen for human beings. Western Europe, as long as the Russian Army is established less than 120 miles from the Rhine, will feel herself threatened with suffocation.

She can turn, of course, to the West, and find room for activity there, in the two Americas. The Atlantic would become the center of a civilization, as the Mediterranean formerly was. In Asia, European influence seems to have hastened the ruin of the old societies: perhaps, after the troubled period, it will produce some original syntheses. In any case, whether in promoting economic progress or intellectual exchanges, there is much to be done by Westerners, who, as a privileged minority, dispose of means of production and technical knowledge

considerably superior to those of the majority of mankind.

A civilization must expand in order to live, especially the civilization born in Europe, the most expansive known to history. Driven to fall back on itself in anxious defense, it would be doomed. Thus the Stalinists try to isolate the West by fomenting the peoples of Asia and Africa to revolt against an alleged imperialism. The Europeans have no need of colonial domination or spheres of influence in order to maintain their presence and pursue their historic task. The improvement attained is, in the long run, more useful to the colonizer himself than cruder forms of exploitation. Europe should fear less the collapse of empires than hostility to their former masters from countries that have become independent.

But though these distant perspectives justify optimism, they do not solve the short-term problems posed by the conflict between the Soviet Union and the free world. The resources of Africa or of Asia will not bring Europe the indispensable minimum of security. The evacuation of Central Europe by the Russian Army does not depend only on what Europeans will be or do. Yet their historic vitality will play a part in determining the result of a trial of strength.

We use the expression "historic vitality" without overlooking its equivocal character. Historians and sociologists have not identified all the causes of the greatness and decline of civilizations. We have shown here some of the most obvious and therefore superficial causes of European decadence—the weakness of the parliamentary regimes, the conservatism of the democratic socialisms, the difficulty of balancing possible exports against desired imports, the loss of accumulated wealth, the rupture of ties with other continents, the historical desire to form larger units, and the resistance by the interests and traditions bound up with national states. All these causes are real, but none is decisive. The essential one probably escapes objective grasp. Every social order is one of the possible solutions to a problem that is not scientific but human, the problem of community life. Every civilization is animated by beliefs that transcend reason. Are Europeans still capable of practicing the subtle art required by liberal communities? Have they retained faith in their own system of values?

We ask these questions, to which history alone will reply, merely so as not to be charged with the simplicity of economists or generals who believe blindly in their statistics of steel, divisions, or tanks. Wealth and weapons are not enough to decide the fate of nations.

HANS A. SCHMITT

THE MOVEMENT FOR EUROPEAN UNITY REAWAKENS HOPE

Pointing to Europe's disunity as a "prime cause" of her decline, Barraclough saw great obstacles to unification and worried about the possible cultural consequences of unexpected success in the effort to unify Europe. In his book *The Century of Total War*, Raymond Aron also explored the possibilities and problems of the movement to integrate Europe. In the selection that follows, an American historian provides a concise survey of the major efforts and accomplishments of that important movement in postwar Europe.

The author, Hans A. Schmitt, is Professor of History at Tulane University. Author of several articles on the economic and intellectual history of modern Europe, Schmitt in 1962 published an important book on *The Path to European Union*. The following selection was published as an article by Schmitt in 1963.

What specific accomplishments have been made toward the unification of Europe? Are they likely to be lasting? How much real hope for Europe's future does the integration movement offer? Will it make continued progress? Or, as Schmitt asks, "can Europe progress toward union only under the lash of disaster?"

World War II brought to most of Europe a desolation which the battles of 1914–1918 had wrought only in Eastern France, Poland and European Russia. So vast was the physical and moral damage that an English historian [Barraclough] identified 1945 as the end of European history. For the next five years it seemed as if he had prophesied the obvious. But at mid-century, the nations of Western Europe began to revive economically and politically. They adopted new modes of management and production and showed a willingness to experiment with new political concepts and institutions. Whether the results of these efforts will eventually go down in history as the kind of sudden improvement that often precedes a patient's death or whether they will mark a lasting

revival remains to be seen. To the contemporary, however, the 1950's in Europe were years of heartening, and perhaps unprecedented achievement.

Between 1939 and 1945, years of enforced idleness gave many Europeans the opportunity to ponder ways of avoiding past errors. When the resistance leaders from France, Italy and the Netherlands met at Geneva in the spring of 1944, the most newsworthy result of this soul-searching was a joint declaration for a federated Europe. But the spark generated no conflagration. With the coming of peace on May 8, 1945, the solidarity of suffering gave way to practical concerns of rebuilding cities, villages and neighborhood blocks. Eating was still

From Hans A. Schmitt, "The European Communities," XLV (November, 1963), pp. 257–302. Reprinted by permission of the author and of the editors of *Current History*.

an indispensable habit which men in a highly urbanized society could not indulge unless railroads and highways once again functioned normally. Whatever the attractions of a harmonious Europe, hundreds of thousands of men, women and children in concentration camps, prison enclosures and lonely, broken homes wanted to re-unite their families before giving thought to uniting a continent. It would have been folly at this point to overlook the bruised egos of nations, both large and small, who had for years borne the chains of the invader. In short, reconstruction—from the family homestead to the individual nation—became the order of the day.

A year later, many harassed Europeans had discovered that their economic, social and political reflex actions would not suffice to assure their survival. By the summer of 1947, the economies of France and Britain were closer to collapse than ever; young people from the smaller nations besieged American and Commonwealth consulates for a chance to escape from their hopeless homelands, while starvation still stalked Eastern Europe. From the United States came immediate material help in many forms. But even the most comprehensive legislative commitments, like the European Interim Aid Act of 1947, only confirmed the recipients as hopeless beggar nations.

How long it would ordinarily have taken to replace the hand-out with the build-up, no one can say. Joseph Stalin's gleeful reactions to this continuing crisis quickly impressed upon Secretary of State George C. Marshall the need for joint planning on both sides of the Atlantic to replace unilateral charity. The Marshall Plan offered to aid all of Europe; and Europe, it was hoped, would federate economically to make the most of this opportunity. Reality fell short of these sweeping goals.

Both the Soviet Union and its satellites were invited to participate. As a former State Department official, close to these events, pointed out recently:

It was explicitly recognized that there would be advantages and disadvantages to Russian participation and advantages and disadvantages to Russia's boycotting a cooperative plan involving non-Communist Europe.

But on July 2, 1947, the Soviet Union rejected the profered hand and bade her East European dependencies to act likewise. Thus the Marshall Plan, contrary to the intentions of its originators, began by dividing, instead of unifying Europe.

Nor did the participating nations integrate their national economies. The Organization for European Economic Cooperation, designed to determine the most efficacious uses of aid, operated on the conventional base of the unanimous consent of its 16 members, thereby splitting the recovery effort into a series of national economic problems. Europe was cleft between East and West, and in the West national interest continued to call the tune. Altiero Spinelli, one of the pioneers of European federalism, commented bitterly:

The money which the Americans thought they were giving to help the Europeans to overcome economic nationalism served only to reconstitute old national economies, instead of creating one market and one European economy.

It must be added that the traditional ways of O.E.E.C. did more than offend the survivors of the federalist resistance. American capital raised production, irrespective of demand. Nations strove to reach and surpass the output of 1938 without taking note of what their neighbors were accomplishing in identical industrial sectors. Duplication of effort foreshadowed a repetition of the glut and unemployment that had haunted Europe during the Great Depression. Once again the nations of the continent had chosen well-worn routes of failure, and once again the only predictable outcome was certain disaster.

Happily, the spirit of 1944 was not dead. By the time the O.E.E.C.'s own general report of 1950 discerned the specter of a new depression, powerful voices of protest had formulated alternatives. In May of 1948 there convened in The Hague the first great congress of the movements for European union. In this setting, the summary demand for a European Federation was repeated by men like Paul-Henri Spaak, and supported by the benevolent presence of a host of luminaries, including Konrad Adenauer, Alcide de Gasperi, Winston Churchill, and Leon Blum. The backbone of the gathering was not furnished by career-visionaries but by men who counted in the affairs of their nations.

Something was bound to result; the question was: How much? The meeting proposed that the governments of Western Europe agree to the establishment of a European Parliament. These resolutions lost a good deal in the process of being translated into action, but led to the founding of the Council of Europe.[1] On paper this amounted to little: a council of ministers whose recommendations everyone was free to disregard, and an assembly of parliamentarians, appointed by the national governments in a variety of ways, which might debate matters of common concern as long as it did not trespass into the explosive areas of economics and defense.

The Council became the expected nonentity; the Consultative Assembly, however, disregarded the limitations of its statute. Its members debated at length both the inadequacies of O.E.E.C. and the military implications of the Communist threat. This first regular meeting of European legislators in August, 1949, was a new and stimulating departure. No one can prove that its talks affected the course of history, but in the year that followed Western Europe began to move again.

While the first session of the Consultative Assembly was discussing a number of plans designed to achieve closer economic union among its members, economists of the French *Commissariat du Plan*, under the direction of Jean Monnet, were preparing an ambitious project designed to integrate the heavy industries of France, Germany, and any other Western European country wishing to join such an endeavor. Among the advocates of European union at Strasbourg had been Robert Schuman, France's perpetual foreign minister of those critical years. On May 3, Monnet presented the finished project of his staff's deliberations to Schuman and Premier Georges Bidault.

Schuman rose to the occasion—Bidault apparently failed to grasp the plan's practical and visionary sweep—and turned the proposal into the most exciting stroke of twentieth century French diplomacy. After "selling" the idea to the cabinet, a special emissary was dispatched to Bonn so that West Germany would be informed of this initiative before it was announced. Simultaneously, the United States was briefed and signified warm approval. At four o'clock in the afternoon of May 9, Schuman officially called for the pooling of French and German coal mines and steel mills under a "common high

[1] The original statute was signed by Belgium, Denmark, France, Ireland, Italy, Luxembourg, Netherlands, Norway, Sweden and the United Kingdom, Turkey and Greece later, in 1949, and Iceland in 1950. A year later, the West German Federal Republic became a full-fledged member, and Austria joined in 1956.

authority." He claimed that it would end Franco-German rivalry, integrate two major national economies, and contribute a limited but decisive step toward European union.

The French plan rested on one condition which both Monnet and Schuman defended as holy writ. The new institution would be sovereign and independent from national control. The nations subscribing to the coal and steel pool must surrender those industries to the "common high authority." Germany, Italy, Belgium, Holland and Luxembourg agreed to parley on this basis. (These nations, with France, were known as "the Six," members of Europe's Common Market.) Great Britain refused. Thus on June 20, 1950, the negotiating conference convened at Paris without her.

Since all participants involved were agreed on its purpose, there was little doubt that it would produce results, and much of its efforts were concerned with the resolution of relatively minor details. But as its work began the world scene darkened unexpectedly. A week after the first meeting had been called to order, North Korean troops crossed the Thirty-Eighth Parallel.

Once again, the Consultative Assembly of the Council of Europe picked up the ball. Statutory prohibitions notwithstanding, French Socialist leader Guy Mollet initiated a vigorous debate on military policy. His country recognized that the crisis of the Orient would hasten German rearmament. British representatives joined in the dialogue. Their primary concern was that the Far Eastern war would prompt the United States to withdraw her troops from the continent. With the model of the Schuman Plan to guide him, French Premier René Pleven next drafted an almost identical proposal of military integration, and presented it to the North Atlantic Treaty Organization's Defense Committee on October 28, 1950.

Pleven's scheme ran into more trouble than the Schuman Plan. Britain refused to transfer her forces to a supra-national European command. The United States feared that the drastic reorganization implicit in a merger of national armies would further delay Western rearmament. Many Germans saw the plan merely as an attempt to bloc their nation's military recovery. Some Social Democrats, in particular, viewed Pleven's device as a gross abuse of the European idea. Support for the plan in France was far from unanimous.

War and Totalitarianism

But before the year was out some of this opposition had been converted. Just as the Germans had grasped the supra-nationalism of the Schuman Plan as a means to end allied control and dismemberment of their industries, so they recognized the European army as a means of ending the occupation and recovering their sovereignty. Rearmament in the European context offered the further hope that Germany's second democratic experiment would not again succumb to traditional militarism. Chinese intervention in North Korea forced the United States to reconsider the plan in terms of her own expanding involvements. After France had conceded the interim integration of German combat teams into Nato forces, Washington gave its blessing to the projected European Defense Community.

With 1951 dawned the hope that some European nations at least would soon integrate armies and heavy industries. Negotiations to implement the Pleven Plan opened in February, again with representatives from France, Germany, Italy, Belgium, Holland and Luxembourg around the conference table. On April 18, 1951, these six nations signed the treaty establishing the European Coal and Steel Community, "printed in Louis XIV type with German ink on Dutch velum," and "bound in Belgian parchment . . . adorned with a marker of Italian silk." A year later, in May, 1952, it had been ratified by the national parliaments, while the outlines of a European Defense Community (E.D.C.) emerged in an agreement at Paris. The Coal and Steel Community began to set up house-keeping, to be supplemented soon by the military pact whose ratification was generally taken for granted.

So complete was the certainty of success on all fronts that Chancellor Adenauer urged immediate consideration of the next step: integration of the communities themselves. "The establishment of a six-nation defense community must lead to a unification . . . in the field of foreign policy." The Common Assembly of the European Coal and Steel Community (E.C.S.C.) had hardly organized when the Council of Ministers was asked to design a Political Community. The basis for this request was Article 38 of the E.D.C. treaty, which proposed such an effort but which had not yet been ratified! The Assembly nevertheless accepted the mandate and produced a draft by March 10, 1953. Ten years later it is still a draft and the European Political Community appears no closer to realization than it was then.

The ministers had wanted to build the roof before the walls had been erected. As of March, 1953, none of the signatories had ratified the E.D.C. pact. In four of the six countries a commitment appeared imminent, but Italy procrastinated, waiting for France, and France's governments just waited, hoping perhaps that time would eventually erode the mounting opposition. A succession of shaky cabinets (Pinay, Mayer, Laniel) refused to risk their existence on a controversial issue. Stalin's death removed the sense of urgency which had propelled Western Europe into a succession of impressive experiments. The argument that the Pleven Plan alone would protect France against German rearmament elicited the obvious rebuttal: if German armament was risky, how could the danger be reduced by destroying the freedom of action of the French army? Had Britain joined, the case of the French opposition would have collapsed, but the Eden government refused to reverse British policy.

On the ninth anniversary of VE day (May 8, 1954) France's Asian empire collapsed at Dien Bien Phu. Humiliated in the Far East and facing similar threats in North Africa, the nation was in no mood to surrender her military sovereignty. The commander of Nato ground forces, Marshal Juin, dramatically pronounced against E.D.C. Rene Pleven, Defense Minister in the Laniel Government, was manhandled in the streets of Paris.

E.D.C. died slowly during the long, hot summer of 1954. On June 9 and 18, respectively, the National Assembly's foreign affairs and national defense committees reported against it. Their action coincided with the investiture of Joseph Laniel's spectacular successor, Pierre Mèndes-France. General Pierre Koenig replaced René Pleven as Minister of Defense. Another partisan of the treaty had been replaced by an avowed opponent. Though the new government was chiefly concerned with making the best possible peace in Indo-China, Mendès-France promised action on the European army as well. He attempted to bring together friend and foe of the past to produce a French compromise, but failed. In August he appealed to the other signatories for certain modifications in scope and duration of the treaty, but was turned down. On August 28, debate began in the National Assembly.

Mendès-France refused to commit his government on the outcome. He did not urge the Assembly to ratify, but he presented a candid forecast of the consequences of rejection. The choice he offered was between a European army or German national contingents arranged with Anglo-American support. No amount of scorn and vitriol from disappointed Europeans induced him to go farther. On August 30, the last word was spoken by that paragon of inconsistent opportunism, Edouard Herriot. The aged Radical leader, who had championed a United States of Europe in 1930, now called the supranational idea "monstrous and ridiculous." "For me, for us, the European community spells the end of France," he cried. The E.D.C. treaty itself never even came to a vote.

The breathless progress towards union of the Six had been summarily halted. Perhaps this was as it should be. Painstaking work by trained men had fashioned the Schuman Plan. The Pleven Plan in contrast appeared to be little more than the passing thought of an ambitious imitator. A study of the treaty fails to prove that its army would have been a workable force in nuclear or conventional war. Even less of a case can be made for the still-born European Political Community. It is hard to understand why such a treaty was drafted before its legal basis existed.

The fact that this disaster could have been avoided, if each integrative step had been planned with care and launched with intelligence, cannot alter the fact that it came as a blow to many. These people were not satisfied when E.D.C. was salvaged by the Western European Union (W.E.U.), which subjected the renascent German rearmament to some degree of international control and committed anew the Anglo-American powers to their watch of the continent. New international organizations might well be appropriate palliatives where more ambitious schemes failed, but they were no substitute for a community.

In May, 1955, only weeks after the W.E.U. agreements had gone into effect, Dutch, Belgian and Luxembourg diplomats pressed the foreign ministers of the Six, meeting at Messina, for an effort to resume the European quest. Paul Henri-Spaak of Belgium, Jean Monnet and Franz Etzel of the E.C.S.C. High Authority, aided and abetted by a high ranking civil servant in the German Ministry of Economics, secured the adoption of a document which charted the new course. The memorandum called for a "common European market, free from all customs duties and all quantitative restrictions," and a com-

mon organization to develop nuclear energy for peaceful purposes.

As a first step, the ministers created an intergovernmental commission under Spaak's chairmanship and delegated to it the task of "drafting the relevant treaties." In May of 1956, this work received provisional approval by the same ministers meeting in Venice, and the wheels of progress began to turn once more. Their rate of revolution was accelerated by the Suez war and the Hungarian rebellion. The former complemented Europe's chronic coal shortages with an oil crisis of staggering proportions. The Mediterranean crisis, furthermore, was calmed by the United States and the U.S.S.R.; the Hungarian challenge was strangled by the latter alone. The impotence of Europe, as it was, could not have been more painfully demonstrated.

Following the Venice meeting, therefore, negotiations were continued with renewed vigor, and on March 25, 1957, the treaties establishing a common market for all goods and services among the Six (the European Economic Community or E.E.C.), as well as a European Atomic Energy Authority (Euratom) were signed. They were ratified in record time and went into effect on January 1, 1958. Formally, these new communities provided for less freedom of action for the executive commissions. The advice and consent of the Council of Ministers had to be sought much more often than under the E.C.S.C. treaty. On the other hand, the Council's decisions could only follow Commission requests. The ministers had little policy initiative, and their verdicts did not have to be unanimous. The Commissions could exercise considerable pressure, and have done so. Given the state of West European public opinion, the ministers have neither disregarded nor negated community proposals. The developments within the Common Market reflect this relation. Tariff reductions have progressed far ahead of schedule. In January, 1962, the second stage in the achievement of full economic union, provided by Article 14b of the E.E.C. treaty, was officially entered.

Once more the Six stand where they found themselves in 1953. A major step forward has been taken, but the "more perfect union" lies still ahead, and the question arises: What next?

Political union is the obvious answer. Since 1961, regular discussions on the subject have been held, but they have produced no results. The only well-articulated prospect has been General de Gaulle's *Europe des patries*, lately warmed up as the Fouchet Plan. It rests almost entirely on the superannuated principle of intergovernmental consultation and, if implemented, would result in a proliferation of ministerial, ambassadorial, and secretarial bodies, none of which have or could have any organic relation with the existing communities. The Gaullist plans rehash views propounded for the past 10 years by such major supporters of the General as Michel Debré. There is no likelihood that new solutions will emerge from that quarter. At the same time, neither Germany nor Italy have formulated convincing alternatives. The case for political union has been pleaded most insistently by the small Benelux nations, whose weight has not been sufficient to make a dent in the *status quo*.

Actually, there is room for improvement in the existing communities. E.C.S.C. has been effective, but as the European Economic Community completes its sixth year, a merger ought to be arranged. The integration of European agriculture remains more phantom than substance, to mention just one of the many serious problems besetting the Common Market. Euratom's technological progress has been disappointing. The artificial separation of military and civilian nuclear research becomes increasingly paralyzing as France pursues her *force de frappe*, a policy which in itself raises a whole rat's nest of questions concerning the co-existence of "European" and "Atlantic" policies.

Finally, there remains the question: What is Europe? The existing communities are open; they welcome new members. But except for some treaties of association, the membership has been stagnant. The great coup, the addition of Britain, was foiled early in 1963, again by France. In his explanation of the French position, General de Gaulle underlined his desire to protect the organic homogeneity of the existing communities against ill-advised, hasty, and unnatural expansion. His statement implied two conclusions: 1) That he and his followers have accepted the communities which now exist. That in itself is a concession from a man whose most articulate supporter protested in 1957: "The thesis of integration . . . rests on the political conception of a European nation which is against the nature of things." 2) De Gaulle wants expansion, if any, to proceed slowly. So long as the Six have so much to iron out among themselves this argument does not lack force. Yet if the strains of a growing membership were imposed on E.E.C. would the search for solutions be undertaken with greater energy? And what of the dangers of a prolonged period of inertia? Can Europe become a reality, if its founders have once more become reconciled to prolonged periods of inaction?

Today, as in 1953, the pressures of fear and distress which generated these new European policies have receded. Economic relations with the Eastern bloc have been intensified; luxuriant prosperity is the order of the day at home. Can Europe progress toward union only under the lash of disaster?

WILLIAM H. McNEILL

A CONFIDENT VIEW OF THE FUTURE

The three selections you have read in this section have been largely concerned with the European continent itself and more particularly with Western and Central Europe—"traditional" Europe. The selection that follows takes a broader view. It attempts to assess the future development of world history and the part European Civilization will play in shaping it. The author, William H. McNeill, agrees with other authors that the emergence of the United States and the Soviet Union as global powers has resulted in an "eclipse of Western Europe as undisputed center and arbiter of Western Civilization"; but he is more hopeful about the endurance of

European Civilization than about the future of Western Europe as a political and economic force.

McNeill combines both American and British perspectives. Born in Canada, he obtained almost all of his education in the United States. The author of a number of studies, he is Professor of History at the University of Chicago. His large volume on *The Rise of the West*, published in 1963, was an ambitious analytical survey of the rise and progress of civilization down to the present. Arnold Toynbee called it "the most lucid presentation of world history in narrative form that I know," and a noted American historian described it as "history in the oldest Greek sense of inquiring, investigating." The selection that follows is from the concluding chapter of that volume.

McNeill offers a fitting conclusion to the many readings that have been presented in this collection. In view of all you have read, how sound do you consider his vision of the future to be? What appears most hopeful in his forecast? What seems most disturbing? How reliable is his prophecy of a "world-wide cosmopolitanism" in the future? And if such a vision comes true, do you agree that "no matter how it comes, the cosmopolitanism of the future will surely bear a Western imprint"?

The rise of the United States and the Soviet Union to world pre-eminence since World War II was, indeed, only another instance of a familiar historical phenomenon: the migration of military-political power from more anciently civilized but less effectively organized heartlands to regions nearer the frontier. Machine technology, which within recent memory carried western Europe to the apex of its world domination, seems now, like Zeus of ancient fable, to have turned ruthlessly upon its parent. Since 1917, and more particularly since 1945, the extractive, transport, processing and distribution complexes of modern industrialism no longer fit easily within the narrow frontiers of the old west European nation-states. In 1945, the elbow room of half a continent gave both Russia and the United States a more or less satisfactory basis for military power; yet even this semicontinental scale is sure to become inadequate if any one center of power should succeed in effectively uniting the resources of still greater areas. Modern industrialism and transport, in short, have begun extravagantly to reward mere geographical extent.

A logical terminus to this expansion of political scale would be the creation of a single world sovereignty. Any world war fought in the near future, while only two superpowers are in the ring, would likely lead to such a settlement. Certainly the technical means for asserting effective world sovereignty lie ready at hand. Monopolization of especially powerful "capital" weapons by an organized force obedient to a reliably united central authority would suffice of itself to supersede organized warfare among separate political sovereignties. Such a development seems a distinct possibility, even within the near future.

On the other hand, the shift in political scale from great powers the size of France, Britain, or Germany to superpowers of semicontinental scale may provide a basis for a future balance of power like that of the European Old Regime. A new family of world powers may define itself, in which China and India and perhaps Brazil or some as yet unformed political units of semicontinental scale (e.g., a United Europe or, less plausibly, a United Middle East or a United Africa) would share the leading roles with the two superpowers already on the scene.

The changed scope of politics which has emerged from the two world wars and from the Communist and other totalitarian revolutions of the twentieth century seems as massive and irreversible a feature of the social landscape as is the expanded political scale. What the German General Staff contrived in 1917–18 as an emergency response to the multifold problems of bringing all possible resources to bear upon the tasks of waging war became, in effect, for Russian Communists a norm applicable indifferently to peace and to war. The revolutionary conspirators who came to power in Russia in 1917 took over not merely the traditional apparatus of the state—army, police, and bureaucracy—but extended their control also to banks, factories, farms, and the various media of communication together with labor unions, political parties, and associations of every sort. The revolutionary state even resorted to forced labor when exhortation and wage inducements failed to distribute manpower as desired.

Economics thus dissolved back into politics, which, indeed, became almost coterminal with human life itself, since, at least in principle, art, letters, thought, recreation, and family life were all harnessed to the pursuit of the Communist goal as defined through changing times and circumstances by appropriate and authoritative manipulations of the "party line."

Countries which escaped Communist revolutions did not experience quite so rapid and radical an expansion of the scope of politics, although in most European nations (and in Japan, too), socialist, nationalist, and fascist movements advanced rapidly in this direction during the interwar years. Hitler's Germany lagged only slightly, if at all, behind Stalinist Russia in subordinating all human activity to political ends. During World War II, even the most conservative democracies, where liberal scruple traditionally hedged in the power of the state in time of peace, found it wise to subordinate economic and many other aspects of social activity to the war effort, i.e., to the service of politically defined goals not basically different in kind from those the German Nazis and Russian Communists were simultaneously pursuing by more violent, ruthless and totalitarian means.

Just as the nineteenth-century distinction between politics and economics has collapsed in some countries and is blurring elsewhere, so also the much older distinction between peace and war has everywhere lost its erstwhile clarity. The normal (i.e., peacetime and wartime) practices and organizational patterns developed by the Russian Communists and by the German Nazis strikingly resembled Anglo-American economic-political-military collab-

oration during World War II. Careful strategic and economic planning characterized all three power systems. Human engineering "machined" individuals and groups (the platoon, the division) into interchangeable parts, while industrial engineering turned out tanks and airplanes, proximity fuses and atabrine, trucks and K-rations according to priorities and production schedules keyed to a strategic over-all plan. Finally, an enveloping atmosphere of haste, emergency, and crisis sustained a psychological buoyancy and sense of excited venture among the managers and manipulators of the newly found and furbished springs of power.

Wartime patterns of social organization did not, of course, prevail in the United States after 1945–46, when the machinery of American mobilization was dismantled. Yet the experience of World War II undoubtedly left important traces behind. Notions that would have seemed preposterous a decade before were accepted after the war as perfectly normal. Thus governmental responsibility for maintaining economic prosperity, for subsidizing scientific research, for developing atomic technology, and for assuring an adequate supply of engineers, was taken almost for granted. In each of these cases and in many more, government action inspired by military-political considerations encroached upon or entirely superseded the old sovereignty of the free market postulated by liberal economic theory. An enormous expansion in the size of the United States' armed forces and an extraordinary elaboration of their equipment operated powerfully in the same direction, for with the growth of the armed services, principles of military hierarchy and fiscal bureaucratization have been fastened upon a significant segment of the population and a substantial portion of the economy.

After World War II, when even a conservative country like the United States rapidly extended the scope of political-military jurisdiction over its citizens, the Communist dictatorship of the Soviet Union perceptibly recoiled from the extreme revolutionary effort to regiment the whole variety of Russian thought and action. Autonomy for specialists, each free in his own field from more than lip service to the pieties of Marxism-Leninism, had advanced a long way within the Soviet Union even before Stalin's death in 1953. Since that time, some gestures have also been made toward freeing writers and other artists from the shackles of the official party line. If such developments continue, as might be expected to follow from the growing wealth, complexity, and subtlety of Russian society, the second half of the twentieth century may see a gradual convergence between Russian and American social systems, each of them balancing a bit uneasily between the conflicting demands of welfare and warfare.

Such an evolution would recapitulate the nineteenth-century interplay between the French Revolution and the European Old Regime. A gradual softening of doctrinal rigor must, indeed, be the fate of all successful revolutions; for human variety is always incommensurate over time and in detail with any single idea. But it seems equally certain that the export of successful revolution can only be prevented by those who are ready and able to borrow from the revolutionaries at least some of the practical secrets of their power. This, surely, was the history of nineteenth-century Europe. The pattern of revolutionary challenge and conservative accommodation seems likely to be repeated within the larger circle of the Western world in the twentieth century.

There is a second sense in which the Russian Revolution resembled and, indeed, carried the logic of the French Revolution another step forward. The essence of the French Revolution was the sweeping away of ancient vested interests and corporate obstacles to the concentration of political power in the hands of the People, whose amorphous majesty of necessity delegated the practical exercise of authority, whether to a parliament, cabinet, committee, or dictator. Likewise, the essence of the Russian Revolution, it now appears, was the sweeping away of ancient vested interests and corporate obstacles to the concentration of a much wider range of power—political, economic, moral—into the hands of the same apotheosized abstraction. . . .

. . . Yet in both cases there was room for disagreement as to whether the new conditions of life under revolutionary, rationalized, and arbitrarily created institutions were in fact more satisfying than they had been under the older, more various and idiosyncratic prerevolutionary regimes. In both cases also, old moral dilemmas achieved a poignancy which had been unknown in former times, when the power at human disposal had been smaller and alternatives pressing upon human decision had been correspondingly less drastic. . .

As long as domestic institutions remain in good

working order, masterly inactivity may often serve as a passable substitute for wisdom. But when real crisis looms, then the stalemates and postponements arising from the pulling and hauling of the democratic process of government as developed in the United States and other liberal societies may become truly disastrous. Too little and too late makes a sorry epitaph; yet one may hope all the same that the very slowness and imprecision with which a loosely controlled and directed people responds to the prods of circumstances and of official, semi-official, and unofficial voices may preserve a saving flexibility and versatility in thought and act.

A further dilemma of democratic government in our time arises from the fact that techniques for appealing to subrational and even to subconscious levels of human motivation are still in their infancy when applied to politics. Liberal democratic theory assumed human rationality and discounted the passions; but psychologists and social scientists no longer believe that men are ruled by reason, while advertisers and military men know they are not. The prospects of a royal road to power through clever and unscrupulous exploitation of the non-rational elements of human nature are far too bright to permit a facile optimism as to the future of democracy.

Yet discrepancies between theory and fact, ideal and reality, also afflict Communist regimes, and perhaps in even more acute form. Marx and Lenin assumed that once the revolution had swept away private ownership of the means of production, human rationality and benevolence would take over automatically, after only a brief period of transition. Yet as the Russian Revolution approaches its fiftieth anniversary, the onset of the Communist idyll is not much in evidence. Instead, Communist governments have regularly defied popular wishes, repressed popular movements, and oppressed individual citizens, claiming all the while to know better than the people themselves what was good, right, proper, and necessary. It is perhaps a Communist misfortune that Marxist-Leninist scriptures include rather more than their share of ardent denunciation of oppression, together with magnificently utopian anticipations of a free, leisured, and abundant material future. Given the harsh realities of initial Communist practice—compulsory saving and high rates of investment requiring a ruthless exploitation of the peasantry in order to provide capital for industrial construction—the discrepancies between rosy dream and drab fact, between generous aspiration and

War and Totalitarianism

ugly practice become peculiarly sharp, and difficult to sustain over prolonged periods of time. Clearly, the Russians already feel this strain. An aging and prospering revolution cannot indefinitely justify failures to attain the promised land of communism by pointing to the dangers of capitalist encirclement.

Moral dilemmas such as these are aspects of basic questions of social hierarchy and human purpose which haunt all men in an age when inherited institutions and customary relationships no longer appear natural, inevitable, immutable. Hierarchy and control remain as vital as ever, perhaps even more so; for the complex co-ordination of human effort required by modern industry, government, and warfare make it certain that some few men will have to manage, plan, and attempt to foresee, while a majority must obey, even if retaining some right to criticize or approve the acts of their superiors. But who has the right to manage whom? And toward what ends should human capacities be directed?

The wider the range of human activities that can be brought within the scope of deliberate management, the more fateful these questions become. Or perhaps a really tough-minded critic of twentieth-century society would have to say: The wider the range of human activities brought within the scope of deliberate management, the more irrelevant questions of social hierarchy and managerial goals become. Admittedly, as the managerial elite of any particular country gathers experience and expertise, reduces new areas of human activity to its control, and integrates partial plans into a national (or transnational) whole, the bureaucratic machine exercising such powers becomes increasingly automatic, with goals built into its very structure. The administrative machine, like other specialized instruments, can only do what it was built to do. Scientific personnel classification allows, nay, requires, interchangeability of parts in the bureaucracy; hence individual appointments and dismissals make remarkably little difference so long as they do not achieve too massive a scale or too rapid a rate. The administrative totality, its over-all structure and functioning, and even the general lines of policy remain almost unaffected by changes of elected officials. Even energetic reformers, placed in high office and nominally put in charge of such vast bureaucratic hierarchies, find it all but impossible to do more than slightly deflect the line of march.

A really massive bureaucracy, such as those which now constitute every major modern government, becomes a vested interest greater and more strategically located than any "private" vested interest of the past. Such groupings are characterized by a lively sense of corporate self-interest, expressed through elaborate rules and precedents, and procedures rising toward the semi-sacredness of holy ritual. These buttress a safe conservatism of routine and make modern bureaucracy potentially capable of throttling back even the riotous upthrust of social and technical change nurtured by modern science. Consequently, as the corporate entities of government bureaucracies grow and mesh their activities more and more perfectly one with another, both within and among the various "sovereign" states of our time, use and wont—the way things have "always" been done—may become, bit by bit, an adequate surrogate for social theory. By sustaining an unceasing action, administrative routine may make rational definition of the goals of human striving entirely superfluous.

If and when the possibility of international war ceases to agitate mankind and no longer spurs officialdom within the separate political sovereignties of the earth to ever greater effort, we should expect a heavy weight of bureaucratic routine to fasten itself upon all parts of the globe. Within a comparatively short time, the unutterable but far from impracticable slogan: "Bureaucrats of the world, unite, you have nothing to lose but your jobs," could be counted upon to set powerful brakes upon the dizzy pace of change which gives men vertigo today. The cautious principle: "Whatever is is right—or at least convenient," and the regulation that says: "This action requires a permit, filled out in triplicate on the proper form and can only be issued after a committee at the next higher level has reviewed the proposal," would everywhere come into effect, without requiring formal legislation. Under such a regime, the theoretical dilemmas and moral issues that trouble the mid-twentieth century would fade from men's minds as the Cheshire cat faded from Alice in Wonderland's sight.

Much depends on how soon—if ever—stability through bureaucracy sets in. Perhaps the next step beyond the level of social and human engineering already pioneered by the Russian Revolution will be genetic tinkering with human germ plasm to produce suitably specialized subhuman and superhuman biological varieties. Present-day theoretical knowledge probably would allow this sort of management of human evolution. The potential results in enhanced efficiency and social discipline, thereby further increasing the possibility of concentrating power, seem enormous. Any revolution which made its way by rationalizing and accelerating human evolution might, therefore, like previous revolutions, compel others to imitate at least some of its techniques. If this should ever happen, men of the future may come to differ from those alive today as much as modern domestic animals differ from their wild ancestors; and such a posthuman population might itself become as specialized in function and various in type as the social insects are now.

One may hope that some saving refractoriness of human nature and society—if not of human genetics—may make such a further extension of the realm of deliberate management forever impossible. The fact that even the best laid plans for directing human affairs still often fail may turn out to be humanity's saving grace. Alternatively, the period of grace may prove merely transitional, as human societies pass from their hitherto wild state into a future domesticated condition. Until men have been tamed, we cannot know for sure; for any failure in a first, second—or thousandth—attempt to rearrange human germ plasm according to plan would not prove that the feat was inherently impossible. This sword of Damocles may therefore hang over humanity indefinitely. Like every other important new exercise of power, it raises the old questions Who? Whom? and Wherefore? to a new order of magnitude. After all, "Who tames whom?" differs from the familiar "Who controls whom?" only in the degree of distance assumed between the two parties to the relationship. . . .

More interesting and more promising for the remoter future are the unresolved, and in our time sometimes oppressively confused, problems of aesthetic power. So long as men remain within the human nature known to history, they may be expected to seek beauty in art and in thought. Even in the most efficiently bureaucratized world that a twentieth-century imagination can conceive, there would remain scope, perhaps even abundant scope, for imaginative and intellectual play. Religion, maybe wearing some new guise as yet undreamed, might come into its own again as an agent sustaining personal security and promoting social solidarity. Fine art and belles-lettres might also flourish if a stabilized pattern of life allowed established meanings and symbolisms to unite artists and writers with their

audiences more closely than now seems to be the case. Science too might be expected to continue theoretical elaboration; but a stoutly conservative bureaucratized social order would be most unlikely to rush scientific discoveries into new technology. Technological and perhaps also scientific progress would proceed far more slowly, if only because compelling motives for taking the trouble and provoking the dislocation caused by technological innovation would weaken or disappear.

What such a vision of the future anticipates, in other words, is the eventual establishment of a world-wide cosmopolitanism, which compared with the confusions and haste of our time, would enjoy a vastly greater stability. A suitable political frame for such a society might arise through sudden victory and defeat in war, or piecemeal through a more gradual encapsulation of a particular balance of world power within a growingly effective international bureaucracy. But no matter how it comes, the cosmopolitanism of the future will surely bear a Western imprint. At least in its initial stages, any world state will be an empire of the West. This would be the case even if non-Westerners should happen to hold the supreme controls of world-wide political-military authority, for they could only do so by utilizing such originally Western traits as industrialism, science, and the public palliation of power through advocacy of one or other of the democratic political faiths. Hence "The Rise of the West" may serve as a shorthand description of the upshot of the history of the human community to date. . . .

The burden of present uncertainties and the drastic scope of alternative possibilities that have become apparent in our time oppress the minds of many sensitive people. Yet the unexampled plasticity of human affairs should also be exhilarating. Foresight, cautious resolution, sustained courage never before had such opportunities to shape our lives and those of subsequent generations. . . .

Men some centuries from now will surely look back upon our time as a golden age of unparalleled technical, intellectual, institutional, and perhaps even of artistic creativity. Life in Demosthenes' Athens, in Confucius' China, and in Mohammed's Arabia was violent, risky, and uncertain; hopes struggled with fears; greatness teetered perilously on the brim of disaster. We belong in this high company and should count ourselves fortunate to live in one of the great ages of the world.

War and Totalitarianism

1234567890